On the Road to Freedom

Dietrich Bonhoeffer and Edith Stein, two young Breslauers of the last century – an era that seems, in troubling ways, to be repeating itself – never met, yet walked parallel paths as witnesses to the love of God in Christ and as martyrs under totalitarianism's attempt to erase all meaning beyond the state. Their deaths became the matrix that released their life and work for generations to come.

On the Road to Freedom is a rich reflection on their understanding of freedom and a timely summons to live it anew. It has been my honour to read this work and to recommend it. Professors Burnell, Lorek and Szczerba are to be thanked, and the Evangelical School of Theology and its journal *Theologica Wratislaviensia* applauded, for bringing forth such a contribution in what some fear may be the last days of peace in Europe for a generation.

Guy Christopher Carter, PhD
Worcester, Massachusetts, USA

This collection of studies commemorates two remarkable Christian thinkers of the 20th century, who – despite all their differences – are united by at least three things: Wrocław (Breslau) as their place of birth, a martyr's death during the Nazi regime, and the effort to offer a new, deeper interpretation of the Christian faith. The volume highlights the continuing relevance of their emphasis on freedom and responsibility in our own time, marked by great challenges and grave threats.

Tomáš Halík, PhD
Professor of Sociology,
Charles University, Czechia
President, Czech Christian Academy

In this remarkable volume, Dietrich Bonhoeffer and Edith Stein – two of Wrocław's most courageous voices – speak anew. Written with clarity and conviction, the essays gathered here invite us to rediscover their testimony: that true freedom is found not in power or ideology, but in faithfulness to Christ and love for others. Here lies a gift and a calling for our own time.

Marcel-Valentin Măcelaru, PhD
Professor of Theology,
Head of the Theology Program, Faculty of Humanities and Social Sciences,
Aurel Vlaicu University of Arad, Romania

This is a timely and important collection examining the ongoing influence of two European voices that continue to resonate across different times and places. Bonhoeffer and Stein spoke with courage and clarity in their own contexts. This collection of essays, authored by luminary and emerging scholars, reminds us that their messages and life witnesses continue to have relevance in a world facing its own existential crises.

Dianne Rayson, PhD
Associate Professor of Theology and Ethics,
Pasifika Communities University, Fiji
Secretary, International Bonhoeffer Society-English Language Section

Edith Stein and Dietrich Bonhoeffer: two martyrs, two rigorous and creative intellectuals, two close followers of Jesus Christ, two urgently needed and challenging lights. Their time and our time are disturbingly similar. This important book can help us to relearn what we seem to be increasingly forgetting – the true meaning of freedom.

Miroslav Volf, ThD
Henry B. Wright Professor of Theology, Yale Divinity School,
Founding Director, Yale Center for Faith and Culture,
Connecticut, USA

On the Road to Freedom

Dietrich Bonhoeffer and Edith Stein

Edited by
Joel Burnell and Piotr Lorek

General editor
Wojciech Szczerba

© 2025 Ewangelikalna Wyższa Szkoła Teologiczna

Also published in Poland as *Theologica Wratislaviensia* vol. 17–18 (2022–2023) by Ewangelikalna Wyższa Szkoła Teologiczna, ISBN: 978-83-60567-21-0. ISSN: 1734-4182.

Published 2025 by Langham Global Library
An imprint of Langham Publishing
www.langhampublishing.org

Langham Publishing and its imprints are a ministry of Langham Partnership

Langham Partnership
PO Box 296, Carlisle, Cumbria, CA3 9WZ, UK
www.langham.org

ISBNs:
978-1-78641-210-2 Print
978-1-78641-267-6 ePub
978-1-78641-268-3 PDF

Wojciech Szczerba, Joel Burnell and Piotr Lorek hereby assert their moral right to be identified as the Author of the General Editor's part in the Work in accordance with sections 77 and 78 of the Copyright, Designs and Patents Act 1988.

All rights reserved. No part of this publication may be reproduced, stored in a retrieval system or transmitted, in any form or by any means, electronic, mechanical, photocopying, recording or otherwise, without the prior written permission of the publisher or the Copyright Licensing Agency.

Requests to reuse content from Langham Publishing are processed through PLSclear. Please visit www.plsclear.com to complete your request.

All Scripture quotations, unless otherwise indicated, are taken from the Holy Bible, New International Version®, NIV®. Copyright ©1973, 1978, 1984, 2011 by Biblica, Inc.™ Used by permission of Zondervan.

Scripture quotations marked (ESV) are from The Holy Bible, English Standard Version® (ESV®), copyright © 2001 by Crossway, a publishing ministry of Good News Publishers. Used by permission. All rights reserved.

British Library Cataloguing-in-Publication Data
A catalogue record for this book is available from the British Library

ISBN: 978-1-78641-210-2

Cover & Book Design: projectluz.com

Translators: Monika Szela-Badzińska (articles of Bogdan Ferdek, Leon Miodoński, Piotr Lorek, Janusz Królikowski) and Joel Burnell (article of Marek Prawda)

Langham Partnership actively supports theological dialogue and an author's right to publish but does not necessarily endorse the views and opinions set forth here or in works referenced within this publication, nor can we guarantee technical and grammatical correctness. Langham Partnership does not accept any responsibility or liability to persons or property as a consequence of the reading, use or interpretation of its published content.

Contents

A Few Words on Freedom: Introduction by the General Editor ix

Wrocław Roads to Freedom: A Word from the Editors xiii

Part 1: Dietrich Bonhoeffer and Edith Stein: Two Roads to Freedom

1. Edith Stein and Dietrich Bonhoeffer: An Attempt at a Biographical Comparison 3
   Joanna Giel, PhD

2. Wrocław Roads to Freedom: Edith Stein and Dietrich Bonhoeffer . . . 15
   Bogdan Ferdek, PhD Hab.

3. Beyond Supersessionism: Stein and Bonhoeffer as a Resource for Ecumenical Rapprochement 27
   Samuel Randall, PhD

Part 2: Bonhoeffer and Stein: Freedom as an Idea and a Reality

4. History, Reality, and the Mission of the Church in a World of Abstraction 61
   Joel Lawrence, PhD

5. Between Psychology and Phenomenology: Edith Stein's Philosophical Dilemmas 73
   Leon Miodoński, PhD Hab.

6. *Analogia Liberationis*: Divine and Human Freedom in Bonhoeffer's Theology 91
   Philip G. Ziegler, PhD

7. Absolute Human Freedom in Zen Philosophy (D. T. Suzuki) and Evangelical Theology (D. Bonhoeffer) 103
   Piotr Lorek, PhD Hab.

Part 3: Bonhoeffer and Stein: Freedom in Personal Context

8. Edith Stein and the Jews 119
   Janusz Królikowski, PhD Hab.

9   Bonhoeffer 1941: Peace Aims for the Time after the War in an Ecumenical Perspective: God's Command in a Secular World 135
Gottfried Brezger

10   "Today" Moments in the Troubled Life of Dietrich Bonhoeffer: March 1939 and His Commendation of the Catholic Modernist Friedrich von Hügel as an Example 143
Keith Clements, PhD

Part 4: Dietrich Bonhoeffer: Reception of Freedom in New Contexts

11   The Testimony of the Polish Publicist Anna Morawska about the Theologian Dietrich Bonhoeffer: Consequences for the Present 157
Marek Prawda, PhD

12   Longing for Nature in Confinement: Dietrich Bonhoeffer's Prison Writings 167
Joel Burnell, PhD

13   Freedom and Responsibility in Bonhoeffer's Ethics: A Challenge for our Troubled Times 191
Carlos Caldas, PhD

14   Bonhoeffer's Concept of Freedom, and the Limits as well as the Promises of his Thought in Building a Democratic Community ... 203
András Csepregi, PhD

15   Cheap Grace Abounding: The Barmen Declaration, A Declaration on the "Russian World" (*Russkii Mir*) Teaching, and Protestantism Without Reformation 213
Barry Harvey, PhD

A Few Words on Freedom

Introduction by the General Editor

Dear Reader,
I am very glad that this book on broadly understood freedom in the thoughts of Dietrich Bonhoeffer and Edith Stein has been published in cooperation between Langham Publishing and Evangelical School of Theology in Wroclaw, Poland. I hope it is the start of a close and long-standing collaboration in the exploration of Central European perspectives on theology and spirituality.

As a word of introduction to this volume, I would like to share a few thoughts on freedom from the perspective of philosophical theology, which Bonhoeffer and Stein often referred to in their writings.

The discussion of the concept of freedom in human thought is somehow lost in the mists of time. It is possible to trace its early marks in the ancient Orphic-Pythagorean writings, depicting the human person as a divine particle (*psyche*), embedded in the body (*soma*) as in a grave (*sema*). Its goal is to free itself from the cycles of rebirth and to attain metaphysical salvation. The traces of a discussion on freedom can also be found in the treatises of Sophists of the fifth century BC, diverting from the philosophy of nature (*cosmos*) and focusing on a person as a part of democratic, Athenian society. Such a person, through their free choices and training, can – as, for instance, Protagoras of Abdera teaches – acquire virtue and become a mature citizen of society.

Yet the formal beginning of philosophical reflection on freedom is usually attributed to Plato. A special role in this discourse is played by his famous metaphor of the cave (*Politeia* VII). It can be read simply as a critique of sophists, who, in the disguise of teachers and philosophers, deceive the citizens of Athens and, instead of freeing them from the bondage of their sensual self, make them slaves to mere appearances of reality. It can also be seen as a critique of democratic Athens, which did not recognize the genius of Socrates, accused him of impiety, and sentenced him to death. However, from a strictly existential perspective, the metaphor can be perceived as a depiction of the state of humanity, which in general, remains in the darkness of false appearances and does not see the freeing light of true Being. Humanity is looking – metaphorically speaking – at the moving shades on the wall in the cave and takes them as ultimate reality. Yet these are simply appearances, which keep humans in the darkness, like in the Hades of the Homeric epos. And even though one of the prisoners can be freed from this bondage, gets out of the cave, and experiences reality as it is in the light of the Sun, still, his testimony – when he comes back to the cave – is not accepted by those who are in the dark. The one who experiences the epiphany of true Being is for them merely a madman, who is trying to deprive them of what they have and who they are in the cave. They do not accept the testimony of the one who saw the true light outside of the cave; they do not want to believe that the cave is not the ultimate reality; they simply want to lynch the one who is freely coming back and wants to bring freedom to the prisoners.

The metaphor of the cave read in the context of freedom has found a number of interpretations in the course of centuries. In the twentieth century such thinkers as Isaiah Berlin, Martin Heidegger or Hannah Arendt referred to it. Isaiah Berlin, in his famous essay on two types of liberty, differentiates between *negative* freedom "from" and *positive* freedom "to." The negative liberty, according to him, denotes the freedom from shackles or the possibility of unrestricted choice. The positive liberty signifies the choice of a particular option from an unlimited spectrum of alternatives. And yet, in his liberal approach, Berlin alerts that positive liberty "to," if suggested or imposed from outside, can easily become a new type of oppression, tyranny, or even slavery. It is very risky to impose or even suggest to somebody else their way of life. Perhaps, in the philosophy of Isaiah Berlin can be sensed his fear of Soviet oppression, from which he was freed as a Latvian refugee.

The freedom in its negative depiction "from," was earlier stressed by Martin Heidegger in his famous interpretation of Plato, *The Essence of Truth*. The truth, in his understanding, denotes most of all unveiling (*un-concealment*) of the essence of reality (*a-letheia*), not the technical coherence of definition with reality. A philosopher, in his existential experience – Heidegger writes – perceives being of Being as it is, and based on this experience he is able to free himself from the tyranny of the anonymous, faceless mob. In the light of the existential epiphany, he experiences the truth, which unveils itself before him and leads him to a deep understanding of his own existence. He is free, and as a free person, he is able to return to the cave to share with other prisoners the truth, which reveals reality as it is. Yet was Heidegger really able to get out of his own "brown" cave of the Third Reich?

This is what Hanna Arendt, a former student and a partner of Heidegger, indicates when she criticizes Plato and, in a way, criticizes her former master, in her essay *What is Authority?* She alludes to the positive liberty of Berlin and asks whether the philosopher-prophet of truth, when he returns to the cave and tries to free other prisoners from the shackles, does not paradoxically become a tyrant, who – in the light of *his* lonely existential experience – imposes *his* understanding of freedom on other people. Does he have a right to do it? Is he allowed to discredit the opinions of other people, even if they are mistaken, but nevertheless satisfying for them? Can he forcefully free them? Perhaps, however difficult it is to understand it, not everybody wants to leave their own cave. Perhaps not everybody wants to share the fate of the philosopher-prophet, who is lonely in their experience, but prefers the community and dialogue with others, even if it is happening in the shadowland. Arendt seems to be defending the negative liberty "from." Yet, in the course of her argumentation, does not she incidentally become a prophet of positive liberty "to"? Isn't she trying to impose on the reader her own vision of *eleutheria*-freedom?

How can Dietrich Bonhoeffer and Edith Stein be situated in the above context of the discussion of truth? Those who descend from liberal (von Harnack) and phenomenological (Husserl) traditions of thought paradoxically claim that truth can be found only in God, only in following Christ, or in the mystical experience of Christ. Stein, at the end of her life, asserts that "only those who commit themselves to the love of Christ become truly free" (https://www.vatican.va/content/john-paul-ii/en/homilies/1998/documents/hf_jp-ii_hom_11101998_stein.html). Similarly, Bonhoeffer – advocating "freedom for" – indicates in his *Act and Being* that it is in Christ that a person is liberated from the power of autonomous *ego* and assumes the freedom of a creature *of* and *before* God. And in his *Creation and Fall* Bonhoeffer adds the pragmatic aspect of freedom that "being free means being-free-for-the-other." What does it mean? What kind of freedom do Bonhoeffer and Stein have in mind? What do they understand by freedom in Christ? How far does it coincide with and how far does it oppose the understanding of freedom, which philosophical theology offers and which was so important for them in the context of their existential experiences, conversions? What kind of caves do they leave and in which do they remain? What kind of truth do they convey and is it still actual in 2025? The world of the twenty-first century is quite complex, as characterized by, for instance, sudden climate changes, migration movements, technological revolution, or military conflicts in various parts of the world. Do Bonhoeffer and Stein still have anything to say for today's world?

The following articles refer to these and similar questions in the context of freedom, as it was understood by Dietrich Bonhoeffer and Edith Stein. The volume includes a compelling contribution by Marek Prawda, Undersecretary of State at the Polish Ministry of Foreign Affairs, which formed the foundation of his address at the 2022 Lausitz Kirchentag Evangelical Congress in Görlitz. The speech was subsequently discussed by Michael Kretschmer, the Prime Minister of Saxony, and served as the basis for a broader dialogue addressing contemporary interpretations of Dietrich Bonhoeffer's ideas, particularly in the context of the war in Ukraine and Polish-German relations.

I hope that this essay, along with subsequent articles, will be interesting and inspiring to read. I also hope they will provoke further considerations and discussions on freedom from various perspectives in the uneasy reality of the twenty-first century.

Wojciech Szczerba
Rector/President of Evangelical School of Theology, Wroclaw, Poland
General Editor of *Theologica Wratislaviensia*

Wrocław Roads to Freedom

A Word from the Editors

The first thing a visitor to the Wrocław City Hall sees when they enter is a long hall lined by busts of the town's famous sons and daughters. As befits a place whose motto is "The City of Meeting," the citizens it has chosen to recognize and remember include Poles, Austrians, Germans, Czechs and Jews. The same choice to honour representatives of the various nations, ethnic and religious groups who have played a role in the City's long history is on display on the walls of the University Museum, where pictures of German, Jewish and Polish Nobel Prize winners hang next to each other. In such a historical context and living community, it is only natural that this volume on freedom focuses on two important figures, Dietrich Bonhoeffer and Edith Stein, whose busts stand facing each other between the columns in City Hall.

The articles in this volume were written or presented as speeches in 2022, a time when definitions of freedom were under challenge, and myriad expressions of freedom both treasured and longed for felt threatened. When invitations to participate were sent and accepted, we were in the throes of a worldwide pandemic. Our ability to trust in science and to exercise common sense came into question. Social media was rife with speculation about the hidden agendas of government authorities, the profit margins of pharmaceutical companies, and the power of corporate entities spanning our globe. As contributors wrote their articles, Russia launched the second phase of its war against Ukraine that began with the seizure in 2014 of Crimea and part of the Donbas region. Today, the war in Ukraine continues, along with many armed conflicts around the globe. The polarization of society that was visible then has only deepened since. It often seems that our society as a whole has lost the ability to carry on an honest dialogue about what unites us and what divides us, to seek ways of understanding each other, or to work together to find solutions that benefit all, not only the members of whatever group we represent or identify as our own.

Bonhoeffer and Stein lived in the shadow of two World Wars. Though sooner or later they left their city of birth, they remained true to their family's heritage, and to the values they gained growing up in Wrocław, even as they transcended them. Their life and legacy bears witness to the challenges to freedom they faced under the growing threat of National Socialism, which came to power in 1933 and in the end took their lives, along with over seventy million victims of WWII. As the papers in this volume demonstrate, they continue to speak to us today.

This volume opens with three texts that compare and contrast the life and thought of Bonhoeffer and Stein. Joanna Giel sketches a general biographical comparison of the stages of their lives. Bogdan Ferdek discusses the relation between freedom and truth found in their rich academic writings. Samuel Randall goes on to explore the resources, and potential pitfalls, that the respective legacies of Stein and Bonhoeffer offer for ecumenical dialogue and rapprochement.

The second group of texts explore the meaning of freedom as an idea and a reality. Joel Lawrence approaches this topic by exploring the implications for the church and its mission of Bonhoeffer's argument that anything in the world viewed apart from its relationship to Christ is an abstraction. In the following paper, Leon Miodoński traces the influence of psychology and phenomenology on Edith Stein's philosophical thought and her academic and spiritual journey. Next, Philip Zeigler reflects on divine and human freedom in Bonhoeffer's theology through the lens of Bonhoeffer's own *analogia liberationis*, arguing that our freedom is derived from and determined by the freedom for others of the incarnate Christ, who became "the truly human one." Piotr Lorek rounds out this section by comparing the concept of absolute freedom in Zen philosophy (D. T. Suzuki) and Christian (evangelical) theology (D. Bonhoeffer).

Bonhoeffer and Stein wrote about freedom, not merely as an academic exercise, but on an existential and contextual level, in the context of their own time and their own lives. Janusz Królikowski begins the third group of texts with his consideration of Edith Stein's relationship to her own Jewish heritage, which was deepened by her Catholicism, and was expressed in her conviction of the need to give her life as a kind of expiation for her people. Gottfried Brezger argues that Bonhoeffer found inspiration and strength for his resistance to the evil of his day from his family upbringing, his ecumenical relationships, and his faith in God's reality in the reality of the world. Keith Clements highlights Bonhoeffer's particular response to a "troubled moment" in his life, which came not in the form of an abstract, academic treatise but rather in his commendation of the Catholic Modernist Friedrich von Hügel.

Our final group of texts ask whether Bonhoeffer and Stein have anything to teach us today in our own struggle to understand freedom and to defend it against the attacks on freedom from all sides. Marek Prawda offers an account of the impact of Bonhoeffer's thought, which reached Polish readers through Anna's Morawska's biography of Bonhoeffer and her translations of his "Selected Writings," on Polish-German reconciliation in the 1970s and 80s, and suggests ways Bonhoeffer continues to speak to us today. Joel Burnell takes a look at the impact of freedom lost or denied, through the lens of Bonhoeffer's yearning for nature during his imprisonment. Carlos Caldas and András Csepregi give different answers to the question of whether Bonhoeffer's concept of freedom and responsibility offer a way forward in their own social-political context. Finally, Barry Harvey compares the Barmen Declaration, written by Christians in Nazi Germany against the heresies of the German Christian movement, to the "Declaration on the Russian World (*Russkii Mir*) Teaching," which Orthodox theologians wrote and signed as a response to the support of the Russian Orthodox Church and its Patriarch Cyril for Vladimir Putin's invasion of Ukraine.

Harvey goes on to suggest American Christianity has erred by adopting a domesticated faith, which has failed to struggle for the truth of its confessions, and sees the power of the State, not the Gospel of Christ, as the defender of freedom and religious liberty.

The volume includes both scholarly and general perspectives on freedom by people from different continents, countries, academic, social and religious backgrounds. They are united by the thought and testimony of the lives of Dietrich Bonhoeffer and Edith Stein, to whom they look for inspiration in their own struggle to understand and implement freedom. Let their efforts be an inspiration for you, dear reader, to intellectually, emotionally and practically address the challenges facing you and your environment, in remembering, guarding and nurturing the gift of personal and social freedom. We hope that you will find comfort, hope and strength in the struggle for and defense of freedom in your own religious, social and political contexts.

In the very heart of Wrocław stands the evangelical church of St. Krzysztof, whose origins date back to pre-Reformation times. Behind the altar, rays of sunlight stream through beautifully decorated stained-glass windows. Light penetrates the figures commemorated there, including Dietrich Bonhoeffer and Edith Stein, who sought ways to resist the threat to freedom and human life posed by the forces of Nazi Germany. Their silhouettes, transformed by light, testify to the hardships of human fate, but also to the hope of freedom that transcends this world. What transcends us gives us a sense of freedom, which, although sometimes suppressed, calls us to the courage to act responsibly for ourselves and our neighbours, both near and far.

Joel Burnell and Piotr Lorek

Part 1

Dietrich Bonhoeffer and Edith Stein: Two Roads to Freedom

1

Edith Stein and Dietrich Bonhoeffer

An Attempt at a Biographical Comparison

Joanna Giel, PhD
University of Wrocław
Institute of Philosophy
Centre for the Study of Philosophy History in Silesia
ORCID 0000-0003-0436-7179

About the Author

Joanna Giel received her PhD in literary studies at the Institute of Germanic Philology at the University of Wrocław. Since 2010 she has been employed at the Institute of Philosophy at the University of Wrocław, in the Centre for the Study of Philosophy History in Silesia. Dr. Giel's research focuses on Lutheranism in Silesia, as well as the Silesian-Austrian cultural dialogue. In 2020 she published a source edition of Max Kalbeck's theatre criticism: "Max Kalbeck – Theaterkritiken des Wiener Fin de siècle." Dr. Giel received a monthly scholarship from the Lanckoroński Foundation for a stay in Vienna as part of a project devoted to the reception of Martin Luther's writings in Silesia.

Keywords

Twentieth-century martyrs, Wrocław, imitating Christ, testimony to faith

Abstract

This article offers a biographical comparison of Edith Stein and Dietrich Bonhoeffer, despite the different thought traditions they represented. The analysis is presented according to the following points: 1) The Wrocław context; 2) Stein's and Bonhoeffer's academic path; 3) Two religious cultures, one path following Christ; 4) Martyrs of the twentieth century. The comparison of primarily biographical threads leads to the conclusion that both Stein and Bonhoeffer were guided by the principle "*in obsequio Jesu Christi vivere*" in their choices and decisions. It also allows us to come to the conclusion that faith was a source of strength for both Stein and Bonhoeffer to resist the Nazi regime.

Introduction

Dietrich Bonhoeffer and Edith Stein have been quoted by both Catholics and evangelicals. Various confessional groups cite and respect them as authorities and witnesses to Christian faith. Consequently, as far as the reception of Stein's and Bonhoeffer's works is concerned, the denominational boundaries were blurred a long time ago and have since then remained open for a more ecumenical approach. This is also illustrated by the resonance created by Bonhoeffer's books in recent years – they have been printed in more than half a million copies, and *Nachfolge* (*The Cost of Discipleship*) and *Widerstand und Ergebung* (*Letters and Papers from Prison*) have been translated into numerous languages (Tödt 2015, IX). Edith Stein, on the other hand, was declared by the Holy See a patron saint of Europe in 1999.

The present article attempts to compare Edith Stein and Dietrich Bonhoeffer, primarily from a biographical perspective. The first part – the Wrocław context – presents Stein's and Bonhoeffer's family houses and youth, with emphasis on their upbringing and the early education they received. The second part compares Stein's and Bonhoeffer's academic paths; attention is drawn here to Stein's career difficulties related to her being a woman and a Jew. Part three – two denominational cultures, one way of Christ – indicates Stein's and Bonhoeffer's shared legacy of Christ. Part four presents both of them as twentieth-century martyrs. The analysis of mainly biographical threads will lead to theological conclusions applicable to both authors, despite the different intellectual traditions they represented.

1. The Wrocław context

Edith Stein and Dietrich Bonhoeffer were both born in Wrocław, Stein in 1891, and Bonhoeffer in 1906. Bonhoeffer was therefore fifteen years younger than Stein. They never met in person.

Both Edith Stein and Dietrich Bonhoeffer were raised in well-off bourgeois families. However, already at this point certain biographical differences become apparent – Edith Stein's father died when she was less than two years old, whereas Dietrich Bonhoeffer's father, Karl Bonhoeffer, outlived his son, as he died in 1948. Karl Bonhoeffer, a well-known psychiatry and neurology professor and an acclaimed doctor, was undoubtedly a prominent figure, who played a significant role in his son's life.

Both Edith Stein and Dietrich Bonhoeffer were provided by their parents with a careful upbringing and excellent education in the humanities. When Karl Bonhoeffer became employed at the University of Berlin in 1912, the Bonhoeffer family left Wrocław. Their house in Berlin became the centre for the local university elite, frequented by many scientific authorities of the time. In 1923, Dietrich Bonhoeffer passed his final exams at a gymnasium in Berlin, and, to his parents' surprise, pursued a degree in theology, which he began in Tübingen and continued in Berlin.

Edith Stein passed her final exams in 1911 – merely fifteen years had passed since women in Prussia were allowed to take the Abitur (which occurred in 1896). In 1908, women were fully admitted to higher education. Edith Stein studied philosophy, psychology, German studies and history at Friedrich Wilhelm Silesian University in Wrocław. Two Wrocław university professors who proved most influential for Stein were William Stern (1871–1938) and Richard Hönigswald (1875–1947). William Stern was a famed psychology professor, who offered an alternative to Freud's psychoanalytic methods. In 1904, he founded the Society for Psychology ("Gesellschaft für Psychologie"), and, from 1907, published the psychological journal *Zeitschrift für angewandte Psychologie (Journal of Applied Psychology)*. Through her studies with William Stern, Stein became sensitized to the importance of the category of a person and learned its underlying psychological foundations. The category of a person would later become a significant thread in her phenomenological studies, although it does not occupy an important place in Husserl's philosophy. Hönigswald, on the other hand, is regarded as the founder of the Wrocław school of neo-Kantianism – thanks to him, Stein undertook studies on Kant. In 1913, Stein left Wrocław. Her destination was first the University of Göttingen, where she continued her studies under Edmund Husserl, and then the

University of Freiburg. Stein, in her later years, would occasionally return to Wrocław and her mother's family house.

In Stein's and Bonhoeffer's family houses, religious traditions and practices were cultivated, albeit in quite a liberal way. Bonhoeffer's family house did not nurture the pietistic spirit; rather, it was permeated by the liberal protestant tradition. The reason why he decided to study theology may have been to take a different path than his natural-science-oriented father. It could be said that before Bonhoeffer became a Christian, he was first a theologian.

Edith Stein's family house was also not an orthodox one. Her mother attempted to raise her children in the spirit of Judaism – in Stein's house, Jewish holidays were cherished and celebrated; furthermore, the family regularly attended synagogue services. However, as time went on, Edith Stein's siblings chose atheism. As she confessed in her autobiography, *Life in a Jewish Family / Aus dem Leben einer jüdischen Familie*, Edith Stein, at the age of fifteen, during her nine-month-long visit to Hamburg, consciously and willingly stopped praying; she had been staying with her sister Else and brother-in-law Max, who were avowed atheists (Stein 2000, 109). It was not until her studies in Göttingen that she met religious students from Husserl's circle, which turned her towards faith and, over the years, led her to convert to Catholicism.

Edith Stein's house in Wrocław, in which she lived from 1910, is located at 38 Nowowiejska Street (known earlier as Michaelisstr.). Currently, the house is the headquarters of the Edith Stein Society, which is the centre for research on her person, thoughts and testimony. Dietrich Bonhoeffer, on the other hand, was born and lived in a house located at 7 Bartla Street (known earlier as Am Birkenwäldchen) – there is a commemorative plaque attached to one of the house's walls. Unveiled in 1996, the plaque reads: "In this house, on 4 February 1906, Dietrich Bonhoeffer was born. He was an evangelical theologian, member of the German resistance against national socialism, murdered in Flossenburg concentration camp on 9 April 1945."

2. Stein's and Bonhoeffer's academic paths

Dietrich Bonhoeffer is considered to be one of the most significant evangelical theologians of the twentieth century, whereas Edith Stein was – one could say – a theological outsider. There were two facts – her being, firstly, a Jew, and secondly, a woman – that hindered her academic path, and prevented her from being recognized as a theologian by her contemporaries. In those times, these were obstacles almost impossible to overcome for someone pursuing an academic career.

Stein earned a doctorate in philosophy *summa cum laude* in 1916 in Freiburg, on the basis of her dissertation entitled *Das Einfühlungsproblem in seiner historischen Entwicklung und in phänomenologischer Betrachtung* (*The Problem of Empathy: Its Historical Development and Phenomenological Approach*), written under Edmund Husserl's supervision. It was at that point that she encountered difficulties which ambitious, scientifically-minded women, who pursued an academic career, typically ran into in those times. Stein was Husserl's assistant until 1918. Her relationship with the philosopher was difficult, and it became even more complicated when Husserl did not support her efforts to obtain a habilitation degree (a post-doctoral degree). Edith Stein made, in total, five attempts at earning a habilitation at five different universities, on the basis of two different theses.[1] Her first attempt took place in Göttingen in 1919 under Georg Misch, on the basis of the thesis entitled *Beiträge zur philosophischen Begründung der Psychologie und der Geisteswissenschaften* (*Contributions to the Philosophical Foundation of Psychology and the Human Sciences*)[2] – Stein's application was rejected by the Faculty of Philosophy at the University of Göttingen in June 1919. Almost in parallel with that attempt, Stein undertook efforts to obtain a habilitation under Heinrich Scholz in Kiel, likewise unsuccessfully. Stein's second habilitation project was the dissertation *Potenz und Akt. Studien zu einer Philosophie des Seins* (*Potency and Act: Studies Toward a Philosophy of Being*), which originated in her studies on St. Thomas Aquinas. Initially, Stein endeavoured to earn a habilitation based on this second thesis at the University of Fribourg in 1931; her application was rejected citing "difficult general economic situation," as Stein reported in the letter to Roman Ingarden of 29 November 1931 (Stein 2001, 224–225). According to Stein's other letters, in the same year an informal inquiry was made about the possibility of her obtaining a habilitation at her *alma mater*, Wrocław University, under Professor Koch (Stein 2001, 222–223 and Stein 2000, 177–178); this, however, also did not meet with success. In 1932, Honecker advised Stein to try to earn her habilitation at Münster – however, in the letter of 8 July1932, Stein replied that despite having friendly relationships with Münster philoso-

---

1. The information was taken from the research by Dr Sarah Schmidt from Berlin-Brandenburgische Akademie der Wissenschaften; Dr Schmidt presented the results of research during the conference "Philosophy and theology at Wrocław University. Epistemic perspectives – meaning-influence" (Głuchołazy, 29 September–1 October 2016, organized by the Institute of Philosophy at Wrocław University and Pontifical Faculty of Theology in Wrocław) in the essay entitled "Zum Beispiel Breslau: Edith Steins abgelehnte Habilitationsgesuche."

2. *Beiträge zur philosophischen Begründung der Psychologie und der Geisteswissenschaften* were printed in *Jahrbuch für Philosophie und phänomenologische Forschung* published by Husserl, Bd. 5 (1922), 1–283 (see also: *Edith-Stein-Gesamtausgabe*, Bd. 6).

phers, the habilitation process there would also be problematic for her (Stein 2000, 223–224). This put a definitive end to Stein's habilitation efforts. When analyzing her failed attempts at obtaining a habilitation, one cannot help but notice that her application rejections had never concerned the subject matter of her dissertations. Had her attempts been successful, she would have become the first woman in Germany to earn a habilitation in the field of philosophy.

On the other hand, Dietrich Bonhoeffer pursued as if two seemingly parallel paths – on the one hand, an academic career, on the other, church education (he passed two consecutive theological exams before a church committee and was granted the right to be ordained having reached the canonical age, that is, in 1931). When analyzing Bonhoeffer's academic career, one has to indicate the following fact: in 1927, at the Faculty of Theology of the University of Friedrich Wilhelm in Berlin, he defended his doctorate in theology on the basis of the dissertation *Sanctorum Communio. Eine dogmatische Untersuchung zur Soziologie der Kirche* (*Sanctorum Communio: A Dogmatic Inquiry into the Sociology of the Church*), written under the supervision of Reinhold Seeberg, professor of the history of dogmatics; as the case was with Edith Stein, he graduated *summa cum laude*. The dissertation appeared in print in 1930 in the series published by Reinhold Seeberg entitled *Neue Studien zur Geschichte der Theologie und der Kirche* (*New Studies on the History of Theology and the Church*) (Bonhoeffer 1930). Bonhoeffer obtained his habilitation in the shortest possible time, that is, in 1930, in the field of systematic theology on the basis of the dissertation *Akt und Sein. Transzendentalphilosophie und Ontologie in der systematischen Theologie* (*Act and Being: Transcendental Philosophy and Ontology in Systematic Theology*). After a one-year scholarship in New York at the Union Theological Seminary, in 1931 Bonhoeffer became a docent or associate lecturer at the University of Berlin. However, his academic activity did not last long. In 1936, he was deprived of the *venia legendi* as a Privatdozent in Berlin, due to his and his family's anti-National Socialist involvement.

A question arises: Did Edith Stein and Dietrich Bonhoeffer, who had never met in person, know each other's works? Did they reference each other in any way? Such a reference appears exclusively in Bonhoeffer's dissertation, published in 1930, entitled *Sanctorum Communio*, where the then doctoral student twice cites Stein's treatise *Individuum und Gemeinschaft*, printed in 1922 in Husserl's *Jahrbuch für Philosophie und phänomenologische Forschung* (*Yearbook for Philosophy and Phenomenological Research*). The first reference to Stein's work appears in one of the footnotes in the first chapter entitled "Zur Begriffsbestimmung von Sozialphilosophie und Soziologie" ("On the Definition of Social Philosophy and Sociology") (Bonhoeffer 2015, 17) – Stein appears there as a representative of the phenomenological school. The second reference to Stein's treatise is in the third chapter – "Der Urstand und das Problem der Gemeinschaft" ("The Primal State and the Problem of Community" (Bonhoeffer 2015, 49). The above references demonstrate that Bonhoeffer perceived and quoted Stein as a philosopher rather than a theologian, if even a theologizing one.

3. Two denominational cultures, one way of Christ

In the case of Edith Stein and Dietrich Bonhoeffer, we are dealing with two denominational cultures. However, for both Edith Stein and Dietrich Bonhoeffer, the central category of the New Testament was the defining category of their life choices. What united them was following Christ, which manifested in their life decisions as well as their works.

Before her conversion, Edith Stein was a young Jewish woman who grew up in a liberal atmosphere where Jewish customs were valued but not considered existentially necessary; she sought answers to the question of the meaning of life in psychology and then phenomenological philosophy. A number of factors played a role on the path to her conversion – as mentioned before, Stein was influenced in this regard by students from Husserl's circle, such as Max Scheler and Anna and Pauline Reinach; the former was the wife of Adolf Reinach, who died in 1917, and the latter his sister. Stein was greatly influenced by the autobiography of Carmelite Teresa of Avila, who played a leading role in many other conversion stories. On 1 January 1922, Edith Stein was baptized in a Catholic church in Bergzabern, and a month later she received Holy Communion in the private chapel of Ludwig Sebastian, the bishop of Speyer. Stein later chose to join the Carmelite Order. On 15 October 1933, she was admitted as a novice to the Carmelite Convent in Cologne, took her vows there in 1934, and professed her perpetual vows in 1938.

In 1935, Bonhoeffer took over the leadership of the preaching seminary of the Confessing Church in Finkenwalde, where he founded a monastic fraternity, organizing education in the spirit of *vita communis*. The seminary did not entail "monastic isolation"; rather, the goal was to be inwardly focused in order to minister "outwardly" and to be the church of Christ understood as a community of his word. Bonhoeffer, who allowed private confession and meditation at Finkewalde, saw this as a means of renewal for evangelical pastors. However, this exposed him to charges of non-evangelical rhetoric and promotion of monastic life, which are alien to Luther's teachings. The Reich authorities quickly deemed him a pacifist and enemy of the state – consequently, Bonhoeffer was removed from the University and his Finkenwalde seminary was closed; furthermore, in 1938, the Gestapo banned him from staying in the Reich capital.[3] In 1940, during the war period, Bonhoeffer found peace and quiet at the Benedictine Monastery in Ettal, where he could engage in creative work. To his surprise, the monks in the refectory were reading his book *Gemeinsames Leben* (*Life Together*), published in 1939, in which he had described the idea of *vita communis*, implemented at Finkenwalde from 1935 to 1937.

4. Martyrs of the twentieth century

Edith Stein was murdered with her sister in Auschwitz on 9 August 1942. Dietrich Bonhoeffer was killed in Flossenbürg on 9 April 1945. Edith Stein and Dietrich Bonhoeffer died imitating Christ, and this imitation was at the same time their active participation in the suffering of the world. They died not because of, but despite their confession to Christ. Edith Stein expressed her opposition towards National Socialism through her habitual standing before God and praying for the Jewish people – this was a spiritual, existential resistance. Her entering the Convent in 1933 was not an escape, but a heroic Christian act. Bonhoeffer, on the other hand, opposed National Socialism not only through words, but also active involvement in the conspiracy and contact with Abwehr officers who had been plotting a conspiracy to assassinate Hitler. Initially, the degree of his involvement in the plot was not fully known and therefore he was put in the military prison in Tegel. Bonhoeffer's actual role in the conspiracy was revealed after the failed assassination attempt on Hitler on 20 July 1944, when the Gestapo seized the secret files of a group of conspirators. On 7 February 1945, Bonhoeffer was sent to a concentration camp in Buchenwald, after which, at the age of thirty-nine, he was hanged by summary court.

It is worth pointing out the role of Wrocław in the joint commemoration of Stein's and Bonhoeffer's martyrdom. The stained-glass windows located in Wrocław's Church of St. Christopher bear a special significance to the celebration of martyrs' memory. Placed around the altar of this Lutheran church, the stained-glass windows were consecrated in December 2018 by the Bishop of the Evangelical Church of the Augsburg Confession in Poland, Jerzy Samiec. The idea behind the stained-glass windows was to depict four martyrs of the twentieth century: next to Bonhoeffer and Stein, there are Juliusz Bursche

---

3. He was allowed to privately visit his parents in Berlin (editor's note).

and Maximilian Kolbe; the windows therefore show two evangelicals and two Catholics, two Germans and two Poles. The stained-glass windows in St. Christopher's Church thus constitute an ecumenical commemoration of the martyrs, which, at the same time, transcends national borders.

Conclusions

At the centre of Carmelite spirituality is the rule formulated at the turn of the twelfth and thirteenth centuries by Albert of Vercelli, the Patriarch of Jerusalem, for the Carmelite Order, which was then emerging in Palestine: "*In obsequio Jesu Christi vivere*" ("*To live in the service of Jesus Christ*") – that is, to live following Christ (Kleuting 2004, 25). The idea of "*in obsequio Jesu Christi vivere*" is the connecting element between Edith Stein and Dietrich Bonhoeffer. In his book *Nachfolge*, published in 1937, Bonhoeffer meticulously analyzed the title "following," which is the consequence of meeting the Son of God (Bonhoeffer 1937). For Stein and Bonhoeffer, faith was not just a thought or feeling; it led them to making specific choices which were oriented to Jesus Christ's words and deeds. Even if Stein's and Bonhoeffer's decisions were of a personal nature, their imitation of Christ was never private or internal, but assumed the dimension of concrete and universal solidarity with the other. Edith Stein and Dietrich Bonhoeffer applied not only the rule of "*in obsequio Jesu Christi vivere*," but also "*in obsequio Jesu Christi mori*" ("*To die in the service of Jesus Christ*") (Kleuting 2004, 27–28 and 37).

Despite their different biographies, what was common for Edith Stein and Dietrich Bonhoeffer was such a faith that is the source of strength to resist Christ's enemies, and also gives one the courage to bear responsibility for oneself and others (Fuchs 1986, 26–30). This consists in being a Christian and accepting the consequences of this fact. The courage of Edith Stein and Dietrich Bonhoeffer to make the greatest sacrifice – the sacrifice of their own lives – grew out of the sense of freedom and solidarity gained through their faith. Stein and Bonhoeffer were not the kind of individualists who would live only in the world of inner prayer; quite the opposite – they showed far-reaching solidarity with what was happening in the world and to their fellow human beings. They felt responsible not only for a single person, but also for the entire nation, to mention Edith Stein's words addressed to her sister Rosa as they were going to a certain death: "Come, let us go for our people" (Kleuting 2004, 32). It can be said that Stein and Bonhoeffer maintained a certain balance between the internal and the external.

Analyzing Edith Stein's and Dietrich Bonhoeffer's life events, it is possible to draw common theological conclusions. The first is that both Stein and Bonhoeffer followed Christ in their choices and decisions – their lives were christocentric, oriented towards Christ and the word of God. Whoever worships Jesus Christ as the Son of God and true human being is at the same time making a decision to resist the iniquities of those who seek to be seen as saviours of the nation. The act of faith has a double structure; it consists in accepting the triune God, and at the same time rejecting all manifestations of evil or idols of the world. The second conclusion is related to that; namely, for Stein and Bonhoeffer, faith was the source of strength to resist the regime. Being a witness to faith means being ready to become a martyr – in the case of Edith Stein and Dietrich Bonhoeffer, it was the martyrdom of blood. It is not a coincidence that the Greek equivalent for the words testimony and martyrdom sounds the same: *martyria*. Every martyr bears witness to faith. If one has faith, he or she must be ready to face those who doubt and those who are Christ's enemies. If it was not capable of such active resistance, the Christian faith would be conformist.

Afterword

The response to the increased reception to Dietrich Bonhoeffer's and Edith Stein's works is the topicality of their thoughts and testimonies. Edith Stein combined tradition with modernity through the dialogue between St. Thomas Aquinas's scholasticism and Edmund Husserl's phenomenology. In Dietrich Bonhoeffer's case, on the other hand, one needs to consider how his life events intersected with theology. Bonhoeffer theologically worked through the problems and conflicts he encountered, and did so taking full responsibility for his own life and those of his loved ones. All of his texts show that he consistently followed the path of "imitation" and that he had an extremely sober view of the reality he faced. Edith Stein and Dietrich Bonhoeffer actively resisted evil and cruelty, guided by the power of prayer and Christ's sacrificial love. They put up this resistance until their death. Their martyrdom, like the death of Christ, was a mockery of human dignity. Today, however, it can carry a message of peace for Europe and the rest of the world.

Bibliography

Bonhoeffer, Dietrich. 1930. *Sanctorum Communio: Eine dogmatische Untersuchung zur Soziologie der Kirche* (26. Stück der Neuen Studien zur Geschichte der Theologie und der Kirche. Hg. von Reinhold Seeberg). Berlin-Frankfurt/Oder: Trowitzsch&Sohn.

Bonhoeffer, Dietrich. 1937. *Nachfolge*. München: Chr. Kaiser Verlag.

Bonhoeffer, Dietrich, ed. Martin Kuske, Ilse Tödt. 2015. *Nachfolge* (Dietrich Bonhoeffer Werke. Volume 4). München: Gütersloher Verlagshaus.

Bonhoeffer, Dietrich, edited by Joachim von Soosten. 2015. *Sanctorum Communio: Eine dogmatische Untersuchung zur Soziologie der Kirche* (Dietrich Bonhoeffer Werke. Volume 1). München: Gütersloher Verlagshaus.

Fuchs, Gotthard. 1986. "Die Ökumene der Seliggepriesenen und der Horror Concreti in Theologie und Kirche." In *Glaube als Widerstandskraft: Edith Stein, Alfred Delp, Dietrich Bonhoeffer*, 11–44. Frankfurt am Main: Knecht.

Fuchs, Gotthard, ed. 1986. *Glaube als Widerstandskraft: Edith Stein, Alfred Delp, Dietrich Bonhoeffer*. Frankfurt am Main: Knecht.

Kleuting, Harm. 2004. *Edith Stein und Dietrich Bonhoeffer: Zwei Wege in der Nachfolge Christi*. Leutesdorf: Johannes-Verlag.

Stein, Edith. 2002. *Edith-Stein-Gesamtausgabe. Volume 1: Aus dem Leben einer jüdischen Familie und weitere autobiographische Beiträge*, neu bearbeitet und eingeleitet von Maria Amata Neyer OCD). Hg. im Auftrag des Internationalen Edith-Stein-Instituts Würzburg von Klaus Mass. Freiburg-Basel-Wien: Verlag Herder.

Stein, Edith. 2000. *Edith-Stein-Gesamtausgabe. Volume 2 (Selbstbildnis in Briefen I. 1916–1933)*. Hg. im Auftrag des Internationalen Edith Stein Institutes Würzburg von Michael Linssen. Freiburg-Basel-Wien: Verlag Herder.

Stein, Edith. 2001. *Edith-Stein-Gesamtausgabe. Volume 4 (Selbstbildnis in Briefen. Briefe an Roman Ingarden)*. Hg. im Auftrag des Internationalen Edith Stein Institutes Würzburg von Michael Linssen. Freiburg-Basel-Wien: Verlag Herder.

Stein, Edith. 1922. "Beiträge zur philosophischen Begründung der Psychologie und der Geisteswissenschaften." In *Jahrbuch für Philosophie und phänomenologische Forschung*. 1–283. Volume 5 (1922) (Edith-Stein-Gesamtausgabe. Volume 6).

Tödt, Heinz Eduard. 2015. "Zur Neuausgabe von Dietrich Bonhoeffers Werken." In *Dietrich Bonhoeffer Werke Volume 1* (Sanctorum Communio. Eine dogmatische Untersuchung zur Soziologie der Kirche. Ed. Joachim von Soosten), I–XXI. München: Gütersloher Verlagshaus.

2

Wrocław Roads to Freedom
Edith Stein and Dietrich Bonhoeffer

Bogdan Ferdek, PhD Hab.
Pontifical Faculty of Theology in Wrocław
ORCID: 0000-0001-5787-0523

About the Author

Bogdan Ferdek, professor, lecturer in dogmatic theology at the Pontifical Faculty of Theology in Wrocław, board member of the Polish Section of the International Bonhoeffer Society, most important publications: *Duch Boży nad wodami Renu. Refleksje nad ścieżkami nadreńskiej pneumatologii* [*Spirit of God over the Waters of the Rhine. Reflections on the Paths of the Rhine pneumatology*], Wrocław 2010; *O odpustach 500 lat później. Ekumeniczna lektura 95 tez ks. dr. Marcina Lutra* [*On Indulgences 500 Years Later. An Ecumenical Reading of the 95 Theses of Rev. Dr. Martin Luther*], Wrocław 2017; *Logos nadziei. Camino jako labolatorium nadziei* [*Logos of Hope. Camino as a Laboratory of hope*], Wrocław 2020.

Keywords

Freedom, free will, truth, grace, relativism

Abstract

Both Edith Stein and Dietrich Bonhoeffer left behind a rich scholarly output. We will limit ourselves to the relation between freedom and truth. This combination of freedom and truth poses a challenge. Is truth subordinated to freedom, or is freedom limited by truth? Does freedom liberate truth, or does truth liberate freedom? Stein and Bonhoeffer are adept at solving this problem. Totalitarianism stripped Stein and Bonhoeffer of freedom and life. Both perished in concentration camps: Stein in Auschwitz and Bonhoeffer in Flossenbürg. That is why their theological reflections on freedom appear to be a kind of testimony. They are not merely theology. Stein's and Bonhoeffer's theology of freedom are a commentary on the words of Jesus: "You will know the truth, and the truth will set you free" (John 8:32).

Introduction

The City of Wrocław with its rich history is conducive to reflections on freedom. In 1997, Wrocław hosted the International Eucharistic Congress. The theme was *Eucharist and Freedom*, while the biblical commentary on this theme were the words of the Apostle Paul: "For freedom Christ has set us free" (Gal 5:1 ESV). Concluding this Congress, Pope John Paul II (1997) said:

> Attempts are being made to convince man and whole societies that God is an obstacle on the path to full freedom, that the Church is the enemy of freedom, that she does not understand freedom, that she is afraid of it. In this there is an incredible confusion of ideas! The Church never ceases to be in the world the proclaimer of the gospel of freedom! This is her mission. "For freedom Christ has set us free (Gal 5:1)." For this reason a Christian is not afraid of freedom, nor does he flee from it! He takes it up in a creative and responsible way as the task of his life.

Nor can theology be afraid of freedom or flee from freedom. Freedom was not feared or fled from by the theology of Edith Stein (1891–1942) and Dietrich Bonhoeffer (1906–1945). Both were born in Wrocław (Breslau). This year (2022) marks the one hundredth anniversary of Edith Stein's baptism and confirmation and the eightieth anniversary of her martyrdom in the Auschwitz concentration camp. Last November marked the ninetieth anniversary of Dietrich Bonhoeffer's ordination. Both Stein and Bonhoeffer left behind a rich scholarly output. Stein's *Opera omnia* comprises twenty-eight volumes while Bonhoeffer's – seventeen volumes. It is impossible to present the entire theology of freedom of Stein and Bonhoeffer on the basis of such a rich scholarly output. We will limit ourselves merely to the relation between freedom and truth. This relation of freedom and truth poses a challenge. Is truth subordinate to freedom, or is freedom limited by truth? Does freedom liberate truth, or does truth liberate freedom? Stein and Bonhoeffer were equal to solving this problem. Both lived in a world dominated by Nazi totalitarianism. This totalitarianism – like any other – used the catchword of freedom which was only applicable to its followers. Others were consigned to concentration camps. Totalitarianism stripped Stein and Bonhoeffer of their freedom and their lives. Both died in concentration camps: Stein – in Auschwitz, while Bonhoeffer – in Flossenbürg. Therefore, their theological reflections on freedom form a kind of testimony. They appear to be more than just theology.

1. Edith Stein: freedom as submission to the truth

Stein (2002, 228) believed that: "Every human being is free and is confronted with decisions on a daily and hourly basis." Stein defines freedom as Augustine did as the determination of the will by itself (Stein 2012, 111). The act of freedom thus determined resembles the act of creation *ex nihilo*. Just as the creator creates the world out of nothing, without any prior matter, without any external conditioning, so human beings themselves perform free acts. The created freedom of man is an image of the uncreated freedom of God, who, as it were, delegates something of his freedom to man. God respects the mystery of man's personal freedom. Even in the case of the mystic, God does not wish to possess his soul against his will. For Stein, even the mystic retains freedom. God works in the soul of the mystic only because the mystic gives himself completely to God. This surrender of the mystic to God is the supreme act of his freedom. The mystical nuptials are an expression of the freedom of God and of the human soul. Married to God, the mystic has "so great a power ... that she has not only herself but even God at her service" (Stein 2022, 229). In such a state there is, as it were, a perichoresis of the uncreated freedom of the archetype with the created freedom of the image.

The freedom of the mystic is liberated by truth, which is God himself. Stein uses Aquinas' formulation of truth. St. Thomas believed that truth is *adaequatio rei et intellectus* (*the conformity of the thing and the intellect*), inasmuch as the intellect says that what is is and what is not is not" (Thomas Aquinas 2024). The truth so understood can only be God. For with God there is a complete correspondence of cognition and being because, unlike man, God is not limited by any horizon. He encompasses and permeates everything, and is therefore truth.

United with God, the mystic experiences supreme freedom, for, united with truth, he can embrace all the pros and cons affecting his decisions. However, the situation of the mystic experiencing the liberation of freedom through truth is unique. Stein (2002, 229) is aware of this and therefore asks: "how do matters stand with the large mass of humans who do not arrive at mystical marriage?"

Stein answers as follows: he who seeks the truth, and not merely gathers information, is closer to God than he himself thinks. For God is truth and therefore the search for truth is the same as the search for God (Stein 2022, 229). Touching on the problem of her master's salvation in the philosophy of Edmund Husserl (1859–1938), she wrote: "I am not at all worried about my dear Master. It has always been far from me to think that God's mercy allows itself to be circumscribed by the visible church's boundaries. God is truth. All who seek truth seeks God, whether this is clear to them or not" (Stein 1993, 272). It is not only the search for truth that draws man closer to God, but God himself draws closer to man. For God is the "primary theologian (*Ur-Theologe*)" who creates symbolic theology. This symbolic theology consists of the whole of creation, through which God allows man to know himself (Stein 2003, 41). Ultimately, however, God opens man to himself through his grace: "Enlightened through grace, the eyes of her spirit deserve to see what previously was concealed by her blindness" (Stein 2022, 371). Every human being, therefore, has the opportunity to know God as truth and to experience its liberating power. Stein writes that "Our freedom is submission to the truth" (Stein 2012, 111). In freedom, man delights in something that cannot be taken away from him against his will. This is made possible by truth. For truth can be possessed by all.

Stein is aware of the alienation of freedom. The alienation of freedom is caused by mendacity. "Mendacity means affirming someone or oneself in something other than what one has come to know as the truth" (Stein 1993, 648). Alienated freedom is what Stein calls "arbitrariness," which she equates with "Bolshevik freedom" (Stein 1993, 649). Stein was unlikely to have been familiar with the 1920 propaganda poster from the Polish-Bolshevik War depicting Bolshevik freedom. This poster depicts Lev Trotsky, People's Commissar for Military and Naval Affairs, as a naked red-skinned devil sitting on a pile of skulls. Trotsky holds a bayonet dripping with blood in his right hand and a pistol in his left. A personification of death is hugging Trotsky: a skeleton wrapped in a white cloth. Both are watching Bolshevik soldiers murdering another defenceless victim. In the bottom right corner of the poster, an inscription can be seen which reads (my translation): "The Bolsheviks promised: we will give you peace, we will give you freedom, we will give you land, work and bread. They wickedly deceived: instead of freedom they gave a fist – instead of land – requisitions, instead of work – misery, instead of bread – starvation" (Szczotka 2012, 211). Bolshevik freedom would thus be freedom alienated by lies.

Because of the possibility of alienating freedom, Stein hopes that the fullness of freedom will be a permanent and holy city located in eternity. This city of the future is mentioned in the Letter to the Hebrews (Heb 13:14) (Grzegorszyk 2016, 191–204). It will be the kingdom of freedom. The uncreated freedom of the archetype will not eliminate the created freedom of its image, but will liberate it through the truth. One enters the kingdom of freedom not as a party but through union with God on the model of the union of bridegroom and bride. The summit of this union with God will be man's divinization in eternal life.

> In this new life of union all the appetites and faculties of the soul, all her inclinations and activities are changed and become divine. The soul lives "the life of God" ... The substance (*sustancia*) of the soul is not divine substance, since it cannot undergo a conversion in God substantially (*sustancialmente*), but through the union with God and through being absorbed in him, she is God by participation. Consequently the soul has every right to say: "I live, now not I, but Christ lives in me" (Gal 2:20) ... With this feeling she proclaims like the bride in the *Song of Songs*: "My beloved is mine, and I am his" (Sg 2:16) (Stein 2002, 276–77).

In this union, the truth of God will be the truth of the divinized and therefore the freedom of God will also be the freedom of the divinized creature. This union of the Archetype with the image, which is the divinization, will be the supreme act of freedom, because ontologically, and hence normatively the words will be fulfilled: "you will know the truth and the truth will set you free" (John 8:32). In the permanent and holy city, situated in eternity, truth will liberate freedom and therefore it will be the kingdom of freedom.

2. Dietrich Bonhoeffer: the truth as the brand of freedom

Bonhoeffer's time can be seen as an Orwellian *1984*. In this Orwellian world, there was a "ministry of truth" that fabricated lies. It was thanks to this ministry that many of Bonhoeffer's German contemporaries recognized a lie as truth. Bonhoeffer opposes this almost universal enslavement by lies by preaching the truth. For he is convinced that only the truth makes one free, according to the words of the Gospel by St. John: "you will know the truth, and the truth will set you free" (John 8:32). This statement is considered by Bonhoeffer to be "the most revolutionary passage in the whole New Testament" (Bonhoeffer 2017, 83). The liberating role of truth is illustrated by Bonhoeffer with the example of a child. He is "the knight of truth." For, as Bonhoeffer writes:

> A group of adults is together. In the course of the conversation, a subject that is extremely personally embarrassing to some of those present cannot be avoided. A terribly awkward discussion follows, which is full of lies and fear. A child ... knows something that all the others also know but are shyly keeping hidden. The child is surprised that the others don't seem to know what he knows and now says it right out loud. Shocked dismay goes around the circle ... All at once the talk full of lies and fear has suddenly been cut off, as if by a blow. Suddenly a harsh light falls on lies and fear. They are completely revealed (Bonhoeffer 2017, 53–54).

For the child is liberated by the truth, while adults are enslaved by lies. For Bonhoeffer, the knight of truth was the fool at the courts of princes. At these courts,

> along with the knights, the singers and poets who were the keepers of the tradition and the lies of the court, there was a man whose clothing showed that he did not belong ... He was the fool. He was the only one who was allowed to tell the truth to everyone ... He actually didn't count, but one didn't want to do without him either (Bonhoeffer 2017, 54).

Also the jester was also a man liberated by truth.

For Bonhoeffer, however, the knight of truth is above all the crucified Jesus. He is the man

> beaten and abused, mockingly crowned king with a crown of thorns, stands before his judge and calls himself the king of truth; the one of whom Pilate asks the intelligent but hopelessly worldly question: What is truth? This question, directed to the one who said of himself: I am the truth! (Bonhoeffer 2017, 554)

For Bonhoeffer, truth is not so much something, but it is above all someone, namely Jesus Christ – God incarnate. Truth is personified in Jesus Christ. He is the truth (John 14:6) and therefore everyone who is of the truth listens to his voice (John 18:37). Because Jesus is the truth, he was able to set others free, as the Apostle Paul wrote (Gal 5:1). However, becoming free does not mean becoming great in the world, free in relation to our brother, free in relation to God, but [means] becoming free from oneself, from the lie that I am the only one there, that I am the center of the world, from the hatred with which I scorn God's creation, free from oneself for others. But God's truth alone allows me to see the other . . . Being free means nothing else but being in love. And being in love means nothing else but being in God's truth (Bonhoeffer 2017, 89).

A man liberated by truth is "the most revolutionary human being on earth . . . he is the explosive material in human society; he is the most dangerous human being" (Bonhoeffer 2017, 90). Therefore, such a man "is not the hero people worship and honour, who is without enemies, but is instead the one they reject, whom they want to get rid of . . . whom they kill" (Bonhoeffer 2017, 90). Bonhoeffer himself was such a revolutionary man because he was liberated by truth. He saw Nazism naked, without the costume of humanism and the mask of charity. At the same time, thanks to the truth, which is Christ, he knew that what he was doing was right. Bonhoeffer knew that final liberation through truth would never happen in the present reality, which is marked by the opposition between the *sanctorum communio* and the antichrist (Bonhoeffer 2009, 283). The *sanctorum communio*, or the church – a church that is not perfect and never has been – proclaims liberation through truth. The antichrist, on the other hand, deceives liberation through lies. Liberation through truth will only occur in eschatological reality. Then reality and truth will become the same (Bonhoeffer 2009, 288). For God will be all in all (Bonhoeffer 2009, 289). This will have two effects: all will see the truth and this truth will liberate them to perfect love. The fruit of this liberation will be the freedom of the will of living persons. Through this, all will be one and, at the same time, each will retain his own identity. All will be in God and at the same time each will retain his distinctiveness. All will see the truth and through it will serve each other in love (Bonhoeffer 2009, 288–299). The truth will thus liberate the freedom to love, and consequently the *sanctorum communio* will be a community of free human beings. Truth will be the brand, or, as it were, the identifying mark of these free persons. Everyone will be of the truth and therefore everyone will listen to the voice of the truth. In the *sanctorum communio* the words of Jesus will be ontologically normatively fulfilled: "Everyone who is of the truth listens to my voice" (John 18:37). It is through this listening to the voice of truth, that the *sanctorum communio* will be a church-community of free persons.

3. Liberated freedom

From the theological point of view, there is a conflict continuing from Adam until "the coming of our Lord Jesus Christ" (2 Thess 2:1), behind which stands "the father of lies" (John 8:44), but also "the Spirit of truth" (John 15:26). Stein and Bonhoeffer joined this conflict on the side of the Spirit of truth. They became the losing side of this conflict. Their martyrdom at Auschwitz and Flossenbürg – horrors of hypocritical freedom – was a testimony to the freedom liberated by truth. It was the culmination of their comments on the words of Jesus: "you will know the truth and the truth will set you free" (John 8:32). From these words they derived a theological conception of freedom as a choice dictated by truth. To be free, it is not enough to reject limitations. Freedom has its theological depth, which is truth. It is this that liberates freedom by protecting it from alienation by falsehood. Ultimately, freedom will be liberated by truth in eschatological reality. For with God there is a complete correspondence of knowledge and being, and therefore man, united with God, can embrace all the pros and cons affecting his decisions. With God, reality and truth are one and the same and therefore all the saved will see the truth and this truth will liberate their will.

There is a slight difference between Stein and Bonhoeffer concerning the eschatological liberation of freedom through truth. Bonhoeffer believed that this eschatological liberation of freedom through truth cannot be understood as a mystical fusion of the saved with God. The mystic does not understand the power of love, which, while uniting with God and all the saved, at the same time preserves the individuality of each of the saved. It will be "the most powerful expression of personal life itself" (Bonhoeffer 2009, 288). The concept of mysticism according to Stein, however, is not a fusion of the soul with God. Stein insists that the mystical nuptials are mutual voluntary surrender between God and the soul (Stein 2002, 228). The life of grace is not possible without its free acceptance (Stein 2002, 231). This free acceptance of grace results in man standing before God and making free decisions (Stein 2002, 228). At the core of mysticism is the free acceptance of the grace of union with God, which ensures that the saved will retain their identity each. Bonhoeffer's concern with the mystical fusion of the saved with God is conditioned by Lutheran theological anthropology. Martin Luther (1483–1546) compares God's will to a lightning bolt with which the free will of man is "utterly overthrown" (Luther 2024). Therefore, man remains a passive object in the struggle between God and Satan over him. Man's will is, as it were, a beast between the two. If God sit thereon, it wills and goes where God will . . . If Satan sit thereon, it wills and goes as Satan will. Nor is it in the power of its own will to choose, to which rider it will run, nor which it will seek; but the riders themselves contend, which shall have and hold it (Luther 2024, 51).

Man's free will is therefore unfree, enslaved. Stein, on the other hand, builds on Augustine, according to whom divine grace does not abolish the human will, but transforms it from an evil will into a good will, and helps the good will to persevere in the good (Stein 2012, 125). Grace, therefore, liberates the free will towards the good without, however, destroying the individuality of man. Therefore, the grace of union with God will not be the loss of the distinctiveness of the saved. According to the US Lutheran-Catholic dialogue document *The Hope of Eternal Life* (Almen and Skiba 2011, 44), Catholics and Lutherans believe in the triumph of God's grace that will cause the saved to exist "in harmony with God and with one another in a radically transformed world." The Catholic-Lutheran "divisions do not reach to heaven." Nor do the differences between Stein and Bonhoeffer concerning the mystical fusion of the saved with God, or their mutual distinctiveness, reach heaven.

The theological definition of freedom developed by Stein and Bonhoeffer differs from the political definition of freedom. According to Hannah Arendt (1908–1975), "we can hardly touch a single political issue without, implicitly or explicitly, touching upon an issue of man's liberty" (Arendt 1961, 146). Political freedom is an action realized in the public sphere, "for to *be* free and act are the same" (Arendt 1961, 186). Freedom as an action in the public sphere is doing without constraint or intervention what man wants. A person is not free when he cannot do what he feels like doing. From the political definition of freedom come the ideals embodied in the slogans: "liberation from all constraints," "struggle for freedom," "political freedoms," "rebellion against constraints." All these slogans ultimately translate into one thing: "you can live and act as you please." Freedom thus boils down to the absence of tyranny, which prohibits what is not commanded. Theologically, such freedom follows the path of the first rebel, the biblical tempter, against prohibitions. His lie resulted in the alienation of freedom and consequently Orwellian *1984*.

Orwellian *1984* is not only a year in which Stein and Bonhoeffer lived, but it is a year that continues today. There are still ministries of truth fabricating lies and even creating a system of lies. They can turn reality upside down and replace the force of arguments with arguments of force. As a contemporary example of a system of lies that enslave freedom with the argument of force is not only Putinism, but also student militias preventing the lectures of professors they consider politically incorrect; antifa or Black Lives Matter bands, or leftist militias attacking churches. Freedom without truth ends up with brutal violence and can be fatal. Modern ministries of truth fabricating lies are made easier by relativism. According to Joseph Ratzinger (2024):

> relativism, that is, letting oneself be "tossed here and there, carried about by every wind of doctrine," seems the only attitude that can cope with modern times. We are building a dictatorship of relativism that does not recognize anything as definitive and whose ultimate goal consists solely of one's own ego and desires.

For modern relativism "there is only one truth, namely that no truth exists" (Buttiglione 2005, 481). And since there is no truth, there is also no lie, and therefore "everything is relative except relativity usurping absolute value" (Chyła 2007, 91). Relativism makes talking about truth a politically incorrect topic, to say the least. By talking about truth, one can expose oneself to all those who, like Umberto Eco (1932–2016), claim that: "the only truth lies in learning to free ourselves from insane passion for the truth" (*The Name of the Rose*). Passion for truth could be considered today as the stigma of fundamentalism. Perhaps this is the stigma Stein and Bonhoeffer would receive today. Today Stein and Bonhoeffer would not have an easy life with their vision of freedom liberated by truth either. Their commentary on Jesus's words: "the truth will set you free" (John 8:32) still remains relevant. In the light of the connection between freedom and truth, one could look at the pandemic, where freedom was sacrificed to save lives, and the war in Ukraine, where lives are sacrificed for freedom. Because of the theology that links freedom with truth, confirmed by martyrdom, the Breslau-born Stein and Bonhoeffer prove John Paul II's (1997) words preached in Wrocław:

> For this reason a Christian is not afraid of freedom, nor does he flee from it! He takes it up in a creative and responsible way as the task of his life. Freedom, in fact, is not just a gift of God; it is also given to us as a task!

Stein and Bonhoeffer were not afraid of freedom, but took it up creatively and responsibly as the task of their lives.

Bibliography

Almen, Lowell G., and Richard J. Skiba, eds. 2011. *The Hope of Eternal Life. Common Statement of the Eleventh Round of the U.S. Lutheran-Catholic Dialogue*. Minneapolis: Lutheran University Press.

Arendt, Hannah. 1961. *Between Past and Future. Eight Exercises in Political Thought*. New York: The Viking Press.

Aquinas, Thomas. 1955. *Summa contra gentiles, Book One: God*, translated by Anton C. Pegis. New York: Hanover House. https://isidore.co/aquinas/ContraGentiles1.htm [accessed: 17.04.2024].

Bonhoeffer, Dietrich. 1970. "Prawda was wyzwoli." In *Dietrich Bonhoeffer, Wybór pism*, edited by Anna Morawska, 53–59. Warszawa: Społeczny Instytut Wydawniczy Znak.

Bonhoeffer, Dietrich. 2009. *Sanctorum communio. A Theological Study of the Sociology of the Church*, edited by Clifford J. Green, translated by Joachim von Soosten, Reinhard Kraus, Nancy Lukens. Minneapolis: Fortress Press.

Bonhoeffer, Dietrich. 2017. "Two Messages to Berlin Students (1932) John 8:31–32." In *The Collected Sermons of Dietrich Bonhoeffer Volume 2*, edited by Victoria J. Barnett, translated by Claudia D. Bergmann, Isabel Best, Lisa E. Dahill, Scott A. Moore, Mary C. Nebelsick, Anne Schmidt-Lange, and Douglas W. Stott. Minneapolis: Fortress Press.

Chyła, Janusz. 2007. *Jezus Chrystus Jana Pawła II*. Pelplin: Wydawnictwo Bernardinum.

Grzegorczyk, Anna. 2016. "Nie mamy tu miasta trwałego. Edyta Stein o bycie wiecznym." *Zeszyty Naukowe Centrum Badań im. Edyty Stein – Fenomen wieczności* No. 15: 191–204.

John Paul II. 1997. Homily of John Paul II, 46th International Eucharistic Congress, Poland, 01.06.1997. https://www.vatican.va/content/john-paul-ii/en/homilies/1997/documents/hf_jp-ii_hom_19970601_statio-orbis.html.

Luther, Martin. 2002. *O niewolnej woli*, translated by Wiktor Niemczyk. Świętochłowice: Towarzystwo Upowszechniania Myśli Reformacyjnej Horn.

Luther, Martin. *De Servo Arbitrio "On the Enslaved Will" Or The Bondage of the Will*, translated by Henry Cole. Christian Classics Ethereal Library. https://www.ccel.org/ccel/l/luther/bondage/cache/bondage.pdf [accessed: 19.04.2024].

Ratzinger, Joseph. 2005a. "Mass 'Pro Eligendo Romano Pontifice'." The Holy See. https://www.vatican.va/gpII/documents/homily-pro-eligendo-pontifice_20050418_en.html [accessed: 19.04.2024].

Ratzinger, Joseph. 2005b. "Ku 'dojrzałości' wiary w Chrystusa." *L'Osservatore Romano*, No. 6/2005: 29–31.

Stein, Edith. 1993. Self-Portrait in Letters, 1916–1942, *The Collected Works of Edith Stein Volume 5*, translated by Josephine Koeppel. Washington, DC: ICS Publications.

Stein, Edith. 2002. *The Science of the Cross*, translated by Josephine Koeppel. Washington, DC: ICS Publications.

Stein, Edith. 2003. "Wege der Gotteserkenntnis. Studie zu Dionysius Areopagita und Übersetzung seiner Werke." In *Edith Stein Gesamtausgabe Volume 17*, edited by Beate Beckmann-Zöller, Viki Ranff. Freiburg/Basel/Wien: Herder.

Stein, Edyta. 2012. *Czym jest człowiek? Antropologia teologiczna*, translated by Grzegorz Sowiński. Kraków: Wydawnictwo Karmelitów Bosych.

Szczotka, Sylwia. 2012. "Wizerunek bolszewika w polskich plakatach propagandowych z wojny polsko-rosyjskiej 1919–1920 ze zbiorów Muzeum Niepodległości w Warszawie." Niepodległość i Pamięć, 19/1–4 (2012): 211.

3

Beyond Supersessionism

Stein and Bonhoeffer as a Resource for Ecumenical Rapprochement

Samuel Randall, PhD
Director of Radio Maria, Australia
ORCID: 0000-0001-8107-8157

About the Author

Samuel Randall studied at Cambridge and was ordained as an Anglican priest, serving in many roles including army chaplain during the Gulf War, as a missionary in the West Indies and Bishop's Officer for Church in the World for Bradford responsible for interfaith issues and community relations. He wrote his PhD dissertation at Cambridge on "Vicarious suffering in the church, in Dietrich Bonhoeffer, with particular reference to Edith Stein." He and his wife Maryam were accepted into the Roman Catholic Church in 2016. After serving for a time with Radio Maria England, he became the Founding Director of Radio Maria Australia in 2021.

Keywords

Edith Stein, Dietrich Bonhoeffer, ecumenism, rapprochement

Abstract

"Saints" and those notable Christians of the past who we hold up as examples to emulate and even in some Christian traditions to venerate, are inevitably presented through a particular interpretive lens. Ferdinand Schlingensiepen's critique of recent Bonhoeffer biographies have exposed the ideological slants given to Bonhoeffer's life by Charles Marsh and Eric Metaxas. Susanne Batzdorff and Benjamin Gibbs' correction of aspects of Stein hagiographies provides a similar function. What is needed is not only a hermeneutic of suspicion when reading the biographies of notable Christians but also, when possible, a return to original texts and context. Gollwitzer, in a written response to Bonhoeffer's essay "On the Question of Church Communion" (1936) criticized those who sought to interpret Bonhoeffer through a selective reading. Gollwitzer writes: "how rare is the art of reading properly and of understanding things in context." What is required is close attention to the complete available corpus of the literature of those discussed, even if the evidence of their writings appears contradictory or ambiguous. It is also essential that careful appreciation is given to the broader social, religious, linguistic and cultural context. In the light of this approach, this paper considers whether Bonhoeffer and Stein offer any guidance or encouragement to ecumenical rapprochement.

Introduction

"Saints" and those notable Christians of the past who we hold up as examples to emulate and even in some Christian traditions to venerate, are inevitably presented through a particular interpretive lens. Ferdinand Schlingensiepen's critique of recent biographies of Dietrich Bonhoeffer (Schlingensiepen 2023) has exposed the ideological distortion given to Bonhoeffer's life by Charles Marsh (2014) and Eric Metaxas (2010). Susanne Batzdorff (2003) and Benjamin Gibbs (2012) "correction" of aspects of hagiographies of Edith Stein provides a similar function. What is needed is not only a hermeneutic of suspicion when reading the biographies of notable Christians but also, when possible, a return to the original texts of those discussed even if the evidence of their writings appears "unorthodox," contradictory, or ambiguous.

It is not generally the intention of biographers or interpreters to distort or obfuscate but unless close attention is given to the context and the writing of those discussed this can be an unavoidable consequence. Peter Collins begins his paper on Stein "Footsteps to Truth" (2019) with a quotation from Stein: "Whoever seeks the truth is seeking God." Collins is not unique as a Catholic writer in suggesting that the Jewish Stein's search for "truth" led her inevitably into the Catholic Church (Sullivan 2004, 37), however the question remains as to whether religious "truth" and personal experience represents an objective reality or whether it suggests only a personal conviction? Unfortunately, in his essay Collins fails to reference Stein's statement but when it is contextualized its ecumenical significance is apparent.

Stein's beloved former professor Edmund Husserl had been baptized into the Lutheran Church in 1886 when he was twenty-seven years old but his conversion from a secularized Judaism was of a formal nature. In 1936 rumours regarding Husserl's conversion from his nominal Protestant faith to Catholicism had been circulating. In a letter to her friend Hedwig Conrad-Maritus, Stein denies these rumours and stated that if Husserl were thinking of making such a move Stein believed that she would be the first to know (Stein 2000/2006, 216). When asked in March 1938 by Sr. Adelgundis Jaegerschmid about the dying Husserl's "eternal fate," Stein (2000/2006, 285) wrote,

> I am not worried about my dear Master. It has always been very far from my mind to think that God's mercy is limited to the limits of the visible Church. God is the truth. Whoever seeks the truth seeks God, whether he realizes it or not.

In order to appreciate and assess the ecumenical significance, or otherwise of those individuals who are considered notable such as Stein and Bonhoeffer, their writings are of primary significance, but of secondary importance are contemporary witnesses. For Bonhoeffer, Eberhard Bethge functions in this capacity. Bethge was a close friend and colleague and married into the Bonhoeffer family. For Stein, this would include Stein's niece Susanne Batzdorff, and Stein's friend "Hatti" (Hedwig Conrad-Martius). Batzdorff provides credible biographical information that can be useful in correcting the effusive and sometimes controversial biographies and hagiographies, particularly when these are presented as part of a supersessionist narrative.

It is also essential that careful appreciation is given to the broader social, religious, linguistic and cultural context of the "saints" discussed. Helmut Gollwitzer, in a written response to Bonhoeffer's (2013, 679) 1936 essay on church communion, criticized those who sought to interpret Bonhoeffer through a selective reading. Gollwitzer writes, "how rare is the art of reading properly and of understanding things in context" (Bonhoeffer 2013). In the light of this approach, this paper considers whether the Lutheran theologian Bonhoeffer and the Jewish convert and Carmelite Edith Stein offer any guidance or encouragement to a more generous ecumenical rapprochement.

Breslau

Both Bonhoeffer and Stein both spent periods of their lives in Breslau which, in the early twentieth century was a small provincial city in the German Empire's eastern Prussian Province of Silesia. Breslau was known for its Jewish and Polish communities and this was the home city for the Bonhoeffer family before they moved to Berlin when Dietrich, one of the youngest in the family, was six years old. The Steins first moved to Breslau in 1890 living in a small, rented apartment before moving in 1910 into a nineteenth-century neo-classical villa which remained the Stein family home until 1939 when it was seized under the Nazi arianisation laws. The official German census of 1905 listed 470,904 residents of Breslau which included 20,536 Jews, 6,020 Poles and 3,752 "others." Two-thirds of the non-Jewish community were listed as Protestant and one third Catholic and it was the Protestant community that dominated.

Faith traditions, whether Jewish, Catholic or Protestant are not necessarily homogenous, monolithic, uniform traditions. Rather they are not only historically conditioned and particular, they are also differentiated, diverse and complex. The Protestant church in Breslau, as in the rest of Germany, was dominated by the *Evangelische Kirche*, organized as *Landeskirchen*.[1] The Bonhoeffers identified as Lutheran and were members of the State *Evangelische Kirche*. In addition the Protestant community included other church denominations, including the *Altlutheraner* (Old Lutherans).[2] Controversy between the *Alt Lutherans* and the *Evangelische Kirche* was a feature of Protestant church relations in Breslau throughout the nineteenth century.[3] Other smaller Protestant denominations existed which were known collectively as "pietists" (Railton 1998, 9 and 13).[4] The Protestant "context" was complex and this complexity was compounded after the Nazis came to power in 1933 and the creation of the *Bekennende Kirche* and those Protestants who refused to accept the reorganization of the Protestant churches by the Nazi government

---

1. The *Evangelische Kirche* had been formed in 1817 following the State-sponsored union between the Reformed (*evangelisch-reformiert*) and Lutheran (*evangelisch-lutherisch*) churches.

2. *Alt Lutherans* had been established in 1834 and included those Lutheran churches who refused to join the *Evangelische Kirche*.

3. Some *Alt Lutherans* emigrated to America to escape persecution but relations improved and by 1883 a seminary for the *Alt Lutherans* had been established in Breslau. By 1905 Breslau had seventy-five pastors and fifty-two thousand *Alt Lutherans* members.

4. Pietism was diverse but included the Moravians and the followers of Count Zinzendorf, the traditional Free Churches such as Baptists and Methodists, but it also included the members of *Landeskirchen* who had been influenced by the eighteenth-century Protestant *Erweckungsbewegung* (revival) and those influenced by the late nineteenth century American "holiness movement."

and its policy of *Gleichschaltung* (forcing into line). Of the eighteen thousand Protestant ministers in Germany fewer than one-third were supporters of the *Deutsche Christen* movement (Bergen 1996, 178), a further third remained neutral. The *Bekennende Kirche* had approximately five thousand members (Helmreich 1979, 156). In October 1943 the twelfth *Bekenntnissynode* of the *Evangelische Kirche der altpreußischen* Union met in Breslau and issued a condemnation of the anti-Semitic actions of the state. This statement declared:

> The destruction of people simply because they are relatives of a criminal who are elderly, insane or of a different race, is not the wielding of the sword given by God to government (Gutteridge 1976, 248).

1938 and the events of Kristallnacht was described by Bethge as "the low point of the church Struggle" (Bethge 2000, 596), and it was then that Bonhoeffer "began to distance himself from the rear-guard actions of the [*Bekennende Kirche*] defeated remnants" (Bethge 2000, 607). Bonhoeffer, writing in the early twentieth century and from his own context believed that the concept of "church" was not being grasped fully by the nationalistic and provincial attitude of the German Protestant churches (Bethge 2000, 61). In a sermon for Ascension Day, 1933 in the Kaiser Wilhelm *Gedächtnis Kirche*, Bonhoeffer compared the "poor Protestant church," which didn't offer much "earthly joy," with the "Catholic" experience of "inexpressible joy" at the Lord's presence in the sacrament of Holy Communion (Bonhoeffer 2009, 468–471). Bonhoeffer in this sermon suggested that this should become the experience of all Christians because it was actually "archetypically Christian" (Bonhoeffer 2009, 470).

Breslau had the third-largest Jewish community in Germany and before 1933 it was a confident, vibrant and politically assimilated community, with many social, charitable, cultural and educational organizations. Breslau became a model for other German cities and the first Jewish students' fraternity in the German Empire, the Viadrina, was created in 1886 in Breslau. Edith's mother Auguste was a successful businesswoman, although not unique in this role (Rahden 2008, 31)[5] and it is a mistake to assume that the Jewish community in Breslau was comprised of mainly professional or business members who belonged either to the *Kleinbürgertum* (petite bourgeoisie) or the *Bürgertum* (bonne bourgeoise). Although the Jewish community of Breslau was the third largest in Germany and one of the most affluent, many traditional civil ser-

---

5. At the turn of the century 36 percent of single Jewish women in Breslau, whether unmarried, divorced or widowed were economically active.

vice bourgeois occupations including university professorships and secondary school teaching positions excluded Jews and many in the community struggled to survive. The Jewish community, as with other communities, was composed of both the wealthy and the very poor (Rahden 2008, 52). The Steins might be described as *Kleinbürgertum*.

In the nineteenth century the religious Jewish community in Germany experienced a period of rapid change and growth and it was the Jewish community at Breslau which set the precedent for the division in Germany of the "liberal and traditional factions" (Meyer 1988, 111). This included the introduction into some synagogues of new and revised prayerbooks and liturgies. In addition, many Jews in Germany during this period abandoned their "orthodox belief and practice" (Meyer 1988, 119). The reformed movement was established in Breslau by Abraham Geiger and, although controversy and opposition from members of the Orthodox community initially prevented his appointment, Geiger was finally appointed as Breslau's rabbi in 1840 and he remained in Breslau until 1863. However, the relations in the congregation remained very contentious and in 1849 two separate congregations were constituted – the Orthodox and the Reformed. In 1872 the construction of the liberal Storch Synagogue or "Neue Synagogue" was completed. The Neue Synagogue was built to serve the non-Orthodox religious community – it was the largest synagogue in Breslau and one of the largest in the German Empire and survived until 9–10 November when it was destroyed on Kristallnacht. The Stein family were members of the Neue Synagogue which Stein's mother attended although the children only attended on High Holy Days.[6]

Breslau's rabbi Geiger, along with Samuel Holdheim, Israel Jacobson and Leopold Zunz, were the founders of Reformed Judaism, although Geiger is considered the most significant (*New World Encyclopaedia of Judaism*, 2022). Geiger, disillusioned with Jewish traditionalism, taught that Judaism was an evolving and changing religion and he sought to remove from the Jewish Faith any nationalistic emphasis, including an understanding of the Jews as "chosen" and that the Torah and the Talmud should be studied critically and historically. Geiger believed that Judaism, Christianity and Islam were three branches of the same monotheistic faith and that Jesus was a liberal Pharisaic reformer. Geiger was a prolific writer, publishing studies on the Mishnah, on the history of Jewish exegesis, apologetics and philosophy and biographies of Maimonides

---

6. In Breslau the White Stork Synagogue was the home for the Orthodox Jewish community.

and Judah Halevi.⁷ Geiger's "liberal" legacy was continued in Breslau by Manuel Joël, who was appointed the rabbi for the Reformed Jewish community in 1863. Joël made important contributions to the study of the mediaeval period,⁸ and in *Beiträge zur Geschichte der Philosophie* (1876) he produced important studies on the relations between Jewish philosophy and medieval scholasticism.⁹ Joël also wrote on the early period of the development of Christianity (Joël 1880). Joël was followed in 1890 by Jacob Guttman, who served until 1919 and was the rabbi during Stein's childhood and the period prior to her conversion. Among Guttman's publications was a study on the influence of scholasticism (Guttman 1902), Duns Scotus (Guttman 1893, 26–39) and Aquinas on Judaism (Guttman 2010). There is no evidence that Stein read either the writings of Joël or Guttman, but their writings and academic interest demonstrate that, at least in the academic world, mutual inter-change and interest existed which is notable given Stein's later interest in both the writings of Aquinas and Scotus. Guttman was succeeded in 1920 by Hermann Vogelstein, who left on 4 November 1938, a few days before the synagogue was destroyed. Reinhold Lewin was the last rabbi for the community. Lewin along with his wife Evie and two children were deported to the Auschwitz concentration camp in 1943 where they were murdered.

Stein's Jewish identity

The concept of *Stamm* – "tribe" or of *Stammesbewußtsein* – "tribal consciousness" was used by Jewish commentators during this period as a term of self-definition. These terms were used by the Jewish Breslau paper, the *Allgemeine Zeitung des Judentums* (1870), the *Israelitische Wochenzeitschrift* (Lazarus 1887), and the *Jüdisches Lexikon* (Joseph 1930 cited by Rahden 2008, 96). *Stamm* emphasizes a common descent and history but not a religious affiliation or belief. The concept of *Stamm* was not unique to the Jewish community but was used by the historian Theodor Mommsen, an important classicist of the nineteenth century, to defend Jews against anti-Semitic attacks (Rahden 2008, 10). Stein was not "religiously" Jewish but belonged to the Jewish *Stamm*, an

---

7. Geiger's most influential writing during this period was *Urschrift und Uebersetzungen der Bibel* where he considered the controversies during the Second Temple period between the Sadducees and the Pharisees and the Samaritans and the Jews.

8. Joël's writings include a study on the history of Jewish philosophy, the school of Aqiba, on Ibn Gabirol and on Maimonides.

9. In *Beiträge zur Geschichte der Philosophie* Joël attempted to show that Albert the Great derived some of his ideas from Maimonides and how Spinoza was indebted to the same writer.

identity important to Stein. The philosopher Daniel Feuling was present with Stein when they met with Stein's friend, the philosopher Alexandre Koyré at Neuberg Abbey. Feuling's description of this encounter and conversation provides an insight into Stein's fundamental Jewish consciousness. According to Feuling it was important to Stein and Koyré that they identified different philosophers as Jewish and he writes that "He is another of ours" was a constantly recurring phrase in their conversation. "Ours" was not a reference to religious observance but ethnicity and Feuling states that he was amused the way his companions would say "we" when speaking of Jews and Jewish matters (Feuling 1998). When the twelve-year-old Batzdorff asked Stein why she had decided to enter Carmel, Stein replied, "What I am doing does not mean that I want to leave my people and my family" (Batzdorff 2003, 37). Stein's conversion was not a repudiation or rejection of her Jewish heritage. Scott Spector (1988, 39; see Brenner 1994, 258) writes:

> Stein's turn to Christianity was never described by herself in terms of disavowal; to the contrary, she insisted upon the close kinship of her Catholic spirituality and her Jewishness.

Given Stein's Jewish consciousness, the comments following her arrest on Sunday 2 August 1942 at the Carmelite monastery at Echt are understandable. In some biographies Stein is reputed to have said to her sister Rosa, "Come, let us go for *our* people" (Oben 2001; 1987, 28; Herbstrith 1985, 180). The statement is absent from the Posselt and Koeppel biographies.

Edith Stein and the "subversion of memory"

Among the Steinian biographies that Batzdorff critiques in her book, *Aunt Edith. The Jewish Heritage of a Catholic Saint*, is that by Sr. Teresia Renata Posselt (Posselt 2005). Although Posselt knew Stein as the Novice Director and then Prioress of the Cologne Carmel, her niece Batzdorff was very familiar with her aunt's character but more significantly the religious practices of the family home.[10] Batzdorff provides a useful guide to Stein's pre-Carmelite life and has identified a number of the embellishments, elaborations and distortions that are a feature of Posselt's popular biography (Batzdorff 2003, 101). Regrettably Posselt seemed intent on exaggerating and misrepresenting Stein's

---

10. Batzdorff has identified problems that have arisen because of mistakes in the 1965 abridged version of Stein's autobiography *Aus dem Leben einer jüdischen Familie* (*Life in a Jewish Family*).

Jewish religious background for polemical reasons (Batzdorff 2003, 95–96). Posselt is not alone in misrepresenting Stein's religious upbringing. Spector (1998, 33) states "Stein was raised in a ritually observant family." However, the Stein family were racially Jewish but *not* religiously Orthodox. Stein, in correspondence to Gertrude von le Fort, suggests that her mother may have had "qualms of conscience" because her mother Auguste had failed to raise her daughter as a practising Jew (Stein 1993, 160). Stein was *not* raised as an Orthodox Jew and all that can be said was that Stein's experience of her Jewish faith was limited and, as Batzdorff states, Stein "might have followed a different path, had she been given a thorough grounding in her Jewish heritage" (Batzdorff 2003, 197). Stein made a conscious decision to become Catholic and not to explore further her own Jewish heritage or, unlike many of her friends, to become Protestant, and it cannot be known whether her decisions would have been different if she had known a richer form of her Jewish heritage or a more attractive experience of the Protestant Church.

It is possible, although unlikely, that the Stein family remained orthodox in their religious practices while attending the progressive Neue Synagogue. However, according to Batzdorff, the family religious observance was minimal and she refutes the suggestion that the Stein household was Jewish Orthodox:

> In her eagerness to picture my grandmother's home life as devoutly Jewish, Sister Teresia . . . states that "grace was said in Hebrew and every appropriate ceremonial prescription of the Talmud was precisely carried out" . . . My mother (Erna Stein), upon reading this, consistently and vehemently denied that Hebrew prayers were spoken at mealtime; in fact she would remark that her mother was "much too busy" to find time for prayers, before or after meals. As for the laws of the Talmud, Grandmother would have had no knowledge of these (Batzdorff 2003, 95–96).

The narrative about Stein's "Orthodox" Jewish faith and background permeates the literature (Herbstrith 1985, 127; Neyer 1972, 20).[11] Sr. Teresia de Spititu Sancto's biography not only references Stein's "Jewish home" she says that it was like "the house of a devout Rabbi" (Spiritu Sancto 1952, 3) and in his analysis of conversions, Karl F. Morrison describes Stein as "observant" and traditionalist (Morrison 1992, 87). It is an inconvenient truth to those seeking for religious absolutes that Stein not only attended infrequently Bre-

---

11. Sr. Electa, in a report held at Carmel in Cologne describes Stein's mother as "Orthodox." Edith-Stein-Archiv, Karmel Köln.

slau's Reformed synagogue, she also attended one of Breslau's State Elementary schools (*Viktoriaschule*) and a state High School (*Mädchenschule*) and not Breslau's "Jewish" school. Furthermore, it is evident from her autobiography and correspondence that Stein thought of herself as an assimilated German-Jew, conscious of her Jewish racial identity but that her academic and social milieu was entirely secular and German. Benjamin Gibbs (2012, 6) writes that Edith and her friends,

> regarded themselves as fully "assimilated" Jewish Germans ... [with] little or no allegiance to the traditions and values of Judaism. Their intellectual and social culture, their assumptions and interests, their tastes in literature, art and music, their social attitudes, were entirely German and almost entirely secular.

Stein – A Jewish "atheist"?

Unlike many "saints," Edith Stein has provided an autobiography for her early years: *Aus dem Leben einer jüdischen Familie*, most of which was begun in 1933 following the Nazi seizure of power and written as a response to the "horrendous caricature" (Stein 1986, 23) of the antisemitic propaganda of the National Socialists. In her autobiography Stein states that when she was fifteen years old she "deliberately and consciously" gave up praying (Stein 1986, 148). Batzdorf states that "several biographers and commentators have deduced that Edith Stein became an atheist" (Batzdorff 2003, 67). Included among those who make this assumption is Eugene Fisher, who provides the introduction to Batzdorff's (2003) book. Batzdorff suggests that this gives too much weight to Stein's "one brief remark," and states "we do not know what sort of prayers she had been accustomed to until then" (Batzdorff 2003, 67). Gibbs considers that Stein's experience is common for many young people, including Catholics, who can "lose interest in the faith and give up practising it, without actively rejecting it or declaring their conversion to atheism" (Gibbs 2012, 5). Teresa of Ávila, who was to become significant to Stein, describes in her biography her own struggles with prayer as a professed religious Carmelite (Teresa of Ávila 1957, 45).

One of her biographers, Waltraud Herbstrith, in the first chapter of her biography: "Childhood and Loss of Faith" states that "from thirteen to twenty-one [Stein] could not believe in the existence of a personal God" (Herbstrith

1985, 26; Koeppel 1990, 38).¹² Perhaps, inadvertently Herbstrith has indicated something analogous to Stein's experience – it was not belief in the existence of God that was the issue for Stein but the nature of God to whom she believed she had formerly prayed. Was God understood in a "personal," intimate way? Or perhaps this was an early example of her philosophical inclinations and her desire for "truth." If God is "God" then why bother praying, particularly if "prayer" is only understood as an act of intercession or petition rather than an expression of a relationship. Furthermore, Stein describes herself as growing up with "rationalistic prejudices" (Stein 1986, 260–261).

After Aquinas' "mystical" experience on 6 December 1273, when he suggested that his previous work seemed like "straw" in comparison to the revelations he had then received, it is commonly assumed that Aquinas ceased to write or dictate. However, Aquinas writes one final letter to his friend the abbot of Monte Cassino Bernhard of Ayglier. Some of the Bernhard's community had decided that intercessory prayer was unnecessary and meaningless because God, "already knows what he ordains and ordains what he knows" (Schenk 2013, 65). The point about this historical digression and to Aquinas who was to prove important to the Catholic Stein, is to suggest that "giving up prayer" might seem reasonable for someone like Stein, who was naturally quizzical and philosophical, but it does not necessarily presuppose atheism. It also does not indicate either the general inadequacy of their familial religious tradition or the superiority of the faith community that Stein was subsequently to embrace. The evidence from Stein's biography and writings would seem to suggest that in her pre-conversion period, Stein was agnostic about faith but not atheistic.

Gaining a new soul

Throughout her academic, professional and religious life Stein was interested in the nature of the human person and with community. For her undergraduate degree at the University of Breslau Stein chose to study psychology, philosophy, history and German philology (1911–1913). It was at Breslau that she first discovered Edmund Husserl's phenomenology and consequently transferred to Göttingen University where Husserl was teaching. Following the outbreak of war in 1914, Stein left university to train as a Red Cross nurse at the *Allerheiligenhospital*. Stein was then sent to a lazaretto (*Seuchenlazarett*), a large isolation hospital in Mährisch-Weisskirchen, Moravia, for soldiers who had

---

12. Josephine Koeppel writes that Edith gave up prayer because "she no longer believed in God."

been wounded and those suffering from contagious diseases. The hospital was "a place of great suffering" (Palmisano 2012, 64). Stein served there for six months for which she was awarded a medal for bravery. The wounded and staff at the hospital came from many different nationalities and social classes from the Austro-Hungarian Empire and beyond. To facilitate communication at the *Seuchenlazarett* Stein relied on a manual in nine languages (MacIntyre 2006, 71).[13] The intense experience of death and suffering at the hospital was to influence Stein's later philosophical development (Calcagno 2007, 122–123; Brenner 1994, 80), but she also demonstrated her considerable linguistic competence.

Stein later not only taught German language and literature at St. Magdalena, a Dominican High School and teacher training institute, she also translated for publication Newman's letters and journals from English (1928). In 1931 Stein translated into German two volumes of Aquinas' (1932) *Questiones disputatae de veritate*.[14] Stein's translation was one of the first attempts to make Aquinas' writings available in the German vernacular (Koeppel 1990). Stein was also able to present complex philosophical concepts in French. Stein was invited by the French scholastic philosopher Jacques Maritain to attend a conference in September 1932 for a meeting of the Societé Thomiste at Juvisy near Paris (La Phénoménologie, 1932). Stein "dominated entirely" the discussion concerning the connection between the scholasticism of Thomas Aquinas and the phenomenology of Edmund Husserl. Stein, "developed her thoughts with such clarity, in French, when necessary, that she made an extraordinarily strong impression on this learned company of scholars" (Golay 2009, 158).

In 1263 Aquinas published a short "opusculum': *Contra errores Graecorum, ad Urbanum IV Pontificem Maximum*, where he sets out the principle of "benevolent interpretation" and the impossibility of intelligibly translating a concept or idea between two languages by simply translating "word for word" from the host language to the target language (Pieper 1991, 90–91).[15] This illustrates the challenge of translation, but Stein's linguistic competence also indicates her innate ability to transcend cultural and religious identities that

---

13. The nationalities at the Mährisch-Weisskirchen hospital included Russians, Turks, Germans, Austrians, Hungarians, Slovaks, Slovenians, Italians, Poles, Ruthenians, Czechs and Roma gypsies.

14. For this achievement Stein received from Eugenio Pacelli, the future Pius XII, an apostolic blessing.

15. *Against the Errors of the Greeks, to Pope Urban IV*. Aquinas considered translation as "something altogether impossible, that the many-faceted idea is expressed differently and yet equally rightly and truly, in each language after its own fashion . . . the wording must be altered if the sense is really to be carried over into the other language."

are necessarily embedded and transmitted by language. This has relevance to her conversion and religious choices because faith, culture and language are intimately connected.[16] The Spanish poet Juan Rámon Jiménez wrote: *Quien aprende una nueva lengua adquiere una nueva alma* – who acquires a new language acquires a new soul (Jiménez 2016).[17] Stein's linguistic abilities and polyglot personality enabled her to transcend language and cultural barriers to successfully explore alternative concepts and to provide a "benevolent interpretation."

Stein's linguistic interest and competence also indicates an empathic personality that is able to transcend religious and cultural boundaries and this relates, not only to her commitment and interest in the concept of *Einfühlung*, but also the ability to hold in tension conflicting identities.

An empathic personality

Stein returned to the university and completed her doctoral studies in August 1916 at the University of Freiburg. Her PhD thesis, *Zum Problem der Einfühlung*, for which she was awarded *summa cum laude*, was published in 1917. The term *Einfühlung* is believed to have been conceived by the German philosopher Theodore Lipps, from the Greek *empatheia*, meaning "feeling into." *Einfühlung* refers to the phenomenon of feeling (or thinking) one's way, "into the experimental life of another" (Palmisiano 2012, 160) and in her thesis Stein argues for the importance of dynamic interpersonal relationships (MacIntyre 2006, 136–137). The term *Einfühlen* (empathy/feeling into) is linked to the related term *Mitfühlen* (sympathy) and these terms share the etymological root *fühlen* (feel/sense) but differ in the prepositional prefixes of *ein* (in/into) and *mit* (with). *Mitgefühl* can suggest emotional distance and possible dissonance whereas *Einfühlung* suggests an entering "into the experimental life of another" (Palmisiano 2012, 160; Häring 1978, 90; Nolan 1993, 37). This is a good description of the experience of conversion.

If Posselt's hagiographic narrative is correct, Stein completed her doctoral studies before she "discovered" faith. However, although Stein's thesis is about empathic relations, in her dissertation God, who possesses complete knowledge, receives the repentant sinner and is present in the life of the believer. Stein in *Einfühlung* describes the experience of God (Stein 1989, 11, 50, 93 and 117).

---

16. For an exploration of the significance of language to cultural and religious identity see: Chomsky 1972.

17. *Mit jeder neu gelernten Sprache, erwirbt man eine neue Seele.*

The Speyer years and the Bergzabern Circle (1923–31)

According to Joachim Felders Stein's involvement with the Bergzabern Circle has been almost completely ignored by her biographers, which is notable given that this period follows her baptism on 1 January 1922 and was prior to her entry into the Carmel in October 1933 (Feldes 2015, 125–138; 2016, 239–252). Stein, who had a life-long academic interest in the nature and importance of community, was also concerned to experience this as a reality and one of the significant communities for Stein was the group of friends who met regularly at Baergzabern, in the home of Theodor Conrad and Hedwig.[18] In addition to Stein, Theodor Conrad and Hedwig, those regularly attending included Jean Hering, Hans Lipps, Alexandre Koyré and Alfred von Sybel. It was Stein's response to Reinach's death in the winter of 1917/18 that gave the group its initial momentum. The intention was to establish a phenomenological institute at Bergzabern, which was to be known as the *Phänomenologenheim* (home of/refuge for the phenomenologists), and the focus of their shared philosophical interests were religious and political issues (Feldes 2015, 4). Stein was the only Catholic in the group, but it also included the Jewish Koyré. All the other members were Protestant who had renewed their faith or who, like Hedwig and Conrad, had experienced a conversion. Von Sybel writes that he was seeking for "the 'Living' behind the church's tradition [and] the 'Real' which seized the first Christians and changed them" (Sybel 1923, 2, 4, 8–9; Feldes 2016, 246). He wrote that through the influence of Theodor Conrad, Hedwig and Stein he had experienced a renewal and as a consequence of this he began studying Theology at Tübingen (Feldes 2015, 7). Koyré's 1923 dissertation was *L'idée de Dieu dans la philosophie de St. Anselme* and he considered conversion, but whether this was to Catholicism or Protestantism is uncertain. However, like Franz Rosenzweig (1953), who did much to renew Judaism during this period, Koyré chose to remain Jewish (Glatzer 1978, 27).[19] This was an ecumenical group united in a belief that religious faith was the basis for phenomenology and in their rejection of Heidegger's "atheistic" philosophy.

---

18. Other significant communities for Stein were her family, her Jewish *Stamm*, the Carmelite communities she joined at Cologne and Echt and the groups associated with the Phenomenological Movement.

19. Rosenzweig, in a letter to his mother wrote, "that connection of the innermost heart with God which the [non-Jew] can only reach through Jesus is something the Jew already possess . . . he possesses it by nature, through having been born one of the Chosen People."

A Carmelite vocation

According to Josephine Koeppel, Stein's decision to become a Catholic "coincided" with her desire to become a Carmelite (Koeppel 1990, 82). Stein described her baptism "as a preparation for entrance into that Order" (Posselt 1963, 100) and her conversion was not just to Catholicism but to a particular form of Catholicism that she believed fulfilled her emotional and intellectual needs. Her close Protestant friend Hatti described Stein's personality as "almost exclusively religious" (Conrad-Martius 1959,[20] 163) and Stein says in a letter to Hatti that there is a calling to the cloistered life and a calling for those outside (Stein 1993, 163–164). It also needs to be acknowledged that Stein's decision and choices were informed, not only by particular encounters and experiences of the different faith traditions but also, as Alasdair MacIntyre indicates in his study of Stein, by her personality and philosophical studies which includes her "empathetic perception and understanding to which she had devoted so much philosophical attention" (MacIntyre 2006, 172 and 180; see Gibbs 2012). In October 1933 Stein entered the Carmel at Cologne and that month wrote to her friend Fritz Kaufmann that she was finally going to the place which she had "long considered" was hers (Stein 1993, 161). It might reasonably be suggested that Stein's conversion was not from Judaism to Catholicism but from a secularized, assimilated Jewish life to a religious, cloistered, Carmelite vocation. This is not to suggest that Stein's Jewishness was of no consequence, but that her experience was of a particular secular Jewishness and certainly not Orthodox. This also does not suggest that the broader Catholicism she encountered as a faith tradition was unattractive to Stein, as is evidenced from her writings (Stein 1986, 399, 401).

Biographies and hagiographies are not always nuanced and can resort to polemics and absolutes. Gibbs states that Posselt's biography went through four editions before she received a letter from Fr. Johannes Hirschmann who had known and spoken with Stein in Holland. Hirschmann's letter describes the significance to Stein of her visit to Anne Reinach following the news of the death of Anne's husband Adolf. Adolf, who had been Stein's friend and academic mentor at Göttingen, had a mystical experience on the battlefield and the Reinachs were subsequently baptized as Lutherans in 1917, which brought them, as Anne states, into "communion with Christ" (Oesterreicher 1998, 117). Hirschmann states that in Stein's encounter with her bereaved friend she "experienced a proof of the truth of the Christian religion and became

---

20. The text was originally written on the occasion of a conference given at the Society for Cooperation between Christians and Jews and published in Hochland (October 1958).

open to it" (Gibbs 2012, 21). It should be acknowledged that this was with a Lutheran and Anne's subsequent spiritual journey and her later entry into the Catholic Church does not invalidate that significant encounter. Posselt adds this encounter to future editions of her biography and she does this as a first-person narrative in which Stein is reputed to have said:

> It was the moment in which my unbelief was shattered, Judaism paled and Christ radiated before me: Christ in the mystery of the Cross (Posselt 1963, 59–60).

Gibbs states that Posselt has turned Hirschmann's words "into a putative direct quotation of Edith's own words, couched in effusive, theatrical terms, with inventive additions" (Gibbs 2012, 21). Not only is this statement, which Posselt included in subsequent biographies, a distortion, it is inconsistent with Stein's appreciation for her Jewish mother's faith and prayers. Stein in letters to her Protestant friends Theodor Conrad (June 1933) and to his wife Hatti (31 October 1933) describes her mother's "firm belief in God, which has guided her throughout her long and difficult life" (Stein 1993, 148). In a letter to Gertrud von le Fort Stein describes her mother's "very strong and genuine love for God" (Stein 1993, 160) and in a letter to Conrad's wife Hatti, Stein describes her mother's faith and inner strength (Stein 1993, 163). Nowhere in her correspondence does Stein suggest that her mother's Jewish faith is insufficient or inadequate. Stein, as Ann Astell indicates, was a Jew who never disavowed her Judaism (Astell 2018, 6; Batzdorff 2003, 188).

On 14 September 1936 Stein came to renew her Carmelite vows along with other members of her community and on the same day, her mother, Auguste died (Posselt 2005, 167).[21] In her letter to Sr. Adelgundis in which Stein mentions these events she writes that she does not have confidence in her prayers or merits but that she is convinced that her mother was called by God and that, *Er verschwenderisch an Liebesbeweisen ist, wenn Er eine Seele annimmt* (And that he is extravagant in demonstrating his love when he accepts a soul) (Stein 2000b, 272). There was no doubt in Stein's mind that her mother had been welcomed into the love of God (Stein 2000b, 199).

According to a previous letter there had been rumours that Stein's mother, Auguste had converted which Stein, not only rejects, she affirms the validity of her mother's prayers and Jewish faith (my translation):

---

21. Posselt states that as Stein renewed her vows she felt the presence of her mother "quite distinctly." This is not confirmed in the letters that are referenced.

> The news of her conversion was a completely unfounded rumour. I don't know who brought it up. My mother held to her faith to the end. Her faith and firm trust in God from childhood has supported her into her 87th year and through her recent suffering. I have confidence that she has found a most merciful judge and that she is now my most faithful helper so that I too can reach my goal (Stein 2000, 200).

Stein states that it was the writings of Teresa which provided the inspiration for her conversion (Stein 2000b, 5). According to Posselt, this encounter took place through Stein's discovery of Teresa's *Das Leben der Heiligen Teresa von Jesus: Von ihr selbst geschrieben* (1868), by "chance" in the library of her friends Theodor Conrad and Hedwig Conrad-Martius in the summer of 1920. Teresa's autobiography is known in English as *The Book of Her Life* (Stein 1950, 58; Teresa of Ávila 1985) and Posselt writes that, after reading *Life* all night, Stein closed the book and said, "That is the truth." The narrative of the radical effect of discovering Teresa's *Life* is a feature of many subsequent biographies (Herbstrith 1985, 64–66; Koeppel 1990, 55) but is described by Gibbs as a "travesty" of the truth (Gibbs 2012, 27). There are several difficulties with Posselt's narrative. According to her friend, Gertrud Koebner, Stein encountered the writings of Teresa in 1920, which was the second year of their friendship and a year before Posselt's narrative of the "discovery" of Teresa's *Life* (Gibbs 2012, 64–65). Furthermore, although Stein may have read other Teresian books and not *Life*, Hedwig stated that their library never held a copy of Teresa's book (Dobhan 2009, 80; ref. Gibbs 2012, 27). Conrad-Martius' statement was confirmed in the Beatification procedures when Pauline Reinach testified that Stein had been gifted a copy of Teresa's *Life* at the Reinach home. These details do not invalidate the significance of Teresa's writings to Stein, but they do call into question Posselt's effusive narrative (Batzdorff 2003, 83).

Although Stein's decision to become a Catholic was understandably devastating to her Jewish family and incomprehensible to her mother it wasn't sudden or dramatic. The process of Stein's conversion began in Göttingen in April 1913 and it was in Göttingen in March 1921 that she confronted what she believed was the "most important decision" of her life (Stein 1986, 239). As Gibbs (2012, 28) writes, "Edith never disclosed to anyone exactly how, when and why she was finally converted to the Catholic faith."

Stein's personal encounters with the Protestant church were not satisfying (Stein 1986, 316). This only indicates that her limited experience of the Protestant church was unsatisfying, including, according to Koebner, her reading at that time of Sören Kierkegaard's *Einübung in Christentum* (Herbstrith 1982, 64; Kierkegaard 1924).[22] Bonhoeffer's siblings, whose initial encounter and experience of the Protestant church had also been in Breslau, described the church as *ein kleinbürgerliches, langweiliges und schwächliches Gebilde* (a petty-bourgeois, boring and feeble institution) (Bethge 2000, 61).

Stein was baptized as a Catholic on 1 January 1922, in the church of St. Martin, Bergzabern, by Fr. Eugen Breitling and was resolved on a Carmelite vocation (Stein 2000a, 350; cf. Dobhan 2009, 80; cf. "Pauline Reinach's testimony" in *Beatificationis et Canonizationis* 183, 437; Posselt 2005, 63). In attendance at her baptism and as her godmother was her friend the Lutheran Hedwig Conrad-Martius. The choice of a Protestant godmother, for which she sought and was granted special permission, is not only understandable, given Conrad-Martius' friendship with Stein it was presumably unusual, ecumenical, but consistent with Stein's generous orthodoxy. Stein chose for her baptism name "Teresa Hedwig" – a Catholic-Protestant synergy. Hedwig described herself as a "kindred spirit" of Stein (Sullivan 2020).

Secretum meum mihi

Hedwig and Stein discussed their different faith choices and the "divine summons" which, she writes, took them in different directions (Stein 1960, 65 and 72). Hedwig describes Stein as exhibiting *eine außergewöhnlich verschlossene, in sich versiegelte Natur* (an extraordinarily private nature) (Stein 1960, 61). In a 1959 article in *Archives de Philosophie*, Conrad-Martius made the following observation:

> It is not an easy task to speak about Edith Stein. Primarily since ultimately it is impossible to make an adequate expression about a specific religious person. The internal life of such a person lies in the mysteries of God. Thereafter Edith Stein, later St. Teresia Benedicta of the Cross, was of a type extraordinarily sealed in itself. The expression *Secretum meum mihi*, my secret is mine, that she once told me, in truth exists in all her biography (Conrad-Martius 1959, 163).

Stein's response, *secretum meum mihi* (My secret is for myself, or That's my secret), is the Latin Vulgate rendering of Isaiah 24:16:

---

22. This has also been translated as *Practice in Christianity*.

From the ends of the earth we have heard praises, the glory of the just one. And I said: My secret to myself, my secret to myself, woe is me: the prevaricators have prevaricated and with the prevarication of transgressors they have prevaricated (Douay-Rheims translation).

Ken Casey (2016, 262), in an article on Stein's use of the phrase writes,

> Stein's whole philosophical endeavour is also an attempt to justify why explanations has some clear limits, why theological explanations at their deepest level must remain mysteries.

Religious experiences can be too sensitive, too private, or too mysterious to be easily described and they are by their very nature deeply personal. John of the Cross also used *secretum meum mihi* to describe the secrecy of a private supernatural communication and he advocated that people should demonstrate reticence when speaking about the interior life and its motivations: "Be silent concerning what God may have given you and recall the saying of the bride "My secret for myself" (John of the Cross 1991, 96; Newman 1890, 2).[23]

The use by Stein of the phrase *secretum meum mihi* to her Protestant friend Hatti indicates, perhaps, not only her reluctance to describe the various incidents and encounters she experienced or the different thoughts and emotions that had led her to her religious convictions, but also to engage in any religious polemics. Stein, according to Conrad-Martius, demonstrates a private nature. Batzdorff (2003, 116–117) states that her aunt "tended to keep her private thoughts private all her life . . . and her family characterized Edith as "a book sealed with seven seals." Ultimately, as Hedwig said regarding Stein's decision, "The Internal life of such a person lies in the mysteries of God" (Stein 1960, 61; cf. Conrad-Martius 1959, 163).

---

23. John Henry Newman felt compelled to respond when his own decision to become Catholic was criticized by Charles Kingsley even though he wished his conversion to remain a private matter. Newman became a Catholic in 1845 and he responded to his critics nine years later in 1864 in his *Apologia Pro Vita Sua*: "It may easily be conceived how great a trial it is to me to write the following history of myself; but I must not shrink from the task. The words, *Secretum meum mihi*, keep ringing in my ears; but as men draw towards their end, they care less for disclosures."

The Teresian Stein

Stein's religious writings contain frequent references to Teresa[24] and Stein's religious aspirations have been described as fundamentally "Teresian" (Stein 1935, 122–123; cited by Herbstrith 1985, 71; cf. Graef 1955, 33), which she understood as "a powerful empathic givenness for the world" (Palmisano 2012, 84; Teresa of Ávila 1985a, V.2; 1985c, 3:2, 3:8, 3.11; 2012, 7.5–6). Stein shared with Teresa the potentially vicarious interpretation of suffering that is a feature of the Carmelite vocation (Green 1989, 145; cf. Teresa of Ávila 1985c, VII, 4.15; VI, 7.13–14; 2012, 1.2; Williams 2004, 38). The religious life was understood by Teresa as an apostolic calling – to suffer vicariously for others with and for Christ (Teresa of Ávila 2012, 26.4–6; 32.6–7; 32.7; Williams 2004, 134) as a service for the world (Burton 2004, 48).[25]

It is possible that Stein, in her Carmelite vocation was, like her Spanish sixteenth-century Jewish predecessor, seeking affirmation of finding value "inwards rather than outwards" (Williams 2004, 38) and a refuge from a society that was anti-Semitic and oppressive. The religious life offered to both Teresa and Stein were a sanctuary and the kind of alternative society that took seriously the demands of discipleship and social engagement. When a society restricts liberty and erects social barriers, a life of prayer can liberate and equalize. As Rowan Williams describes it, "the interior affirmation of dignity, being spoken to freely by God and speaking freely to God, compensates for the injustice and irrationality of the external order of things" (Williams 2004, 35). However, in her correspondence and religious writings Stein repeatedly returns to the theme of vicarious suffering. In 1930 in a letter to Sr. Adelgundis Jaegerschmid, Stein described her own life as a sacrifice or offering for others (Stein 2005, 109–110; 1993, 59–60), and she uses the term "*holocaustum*" (Stein 1976, 110). In her use of this evocative term Stein was emulating the words of another Carmelite, Thérèse of Lisieux, who became an important influence on Stein (1993, 137; 2000, 29; 1992, 6).

Koebner describes the effect reading Teresa of Ávila had on the pre-Catholic Stein:

---

24. Her writings include biographical essays on Teresa of Ávila (Stein 1987a); St. Elizabeth of the Trinity, St. Teresa Margaret of the Sacred Heart, Sr. Marie-Aimée de Jésus (Stein 1992, 19–90; Stein 1987b) and Elisabeth von Thüringen (Stein 1990, 126–138); her essay, *Kreuzesliebe: Einige Gedanken zum Fest des heiliger Vaters Johannes vom Kreuz* (Stein 1992, 91–93; Stein 1987b, 110–113); and her study on St. John of the Cross (Stein 1950) and her correspondence (Stein 1993; 2002; 2014; 1950; 1976; 1977; 1991).

25. The *Trésor du Carmel* describes the Carmelite vocation.

> You could see that it absorbed her utterly, that this was truly "home" for her. Yet she never distanced herself from her family or lost any of her immense affection for them. Even after she had fully decided on her future course and was only working out her method of procedure, she never let anything interfere with her love for her [family] (Dobhan 2006, 80; ref. Herbstrith 1985, 71).

It is evident from her writings and from the testimony of friends that Stein refused to describe her decision in terms of the superiority of Catholicism, to express the necessity for conversion to Catholicism, or to engage in any explicit missional activity. Although a memoir from the Cologne Carmel states that Stein "hoped to influence religiously" her family (Kölner 1962; cited by Batzdorff 2003, 129), one of the last relatives to visit her before she left for Holland was her niece Lotte Sachs who received from Stein a novella by Bjornssen. Batzdorff (2003, 128) writes:

> [Stein's] choice of a farewell gift to her young niece also throws light on her disinclination to make any sort of missionary attempts towards members of her own family.

The avoidance by Stein of proselytism is not only evident with members of her family, but also with her friends and associates. Koebner states that Stein "scrupulously avoided any attempt" to draw her away from her Jewish faith (Dobhan 2006, 73).

In a final observation on "conversion" – it is not a static but an ongoing process. Stein formally entered the Catholic Church, but this was not the end of her spiritual journey but a new beginning. On 12 February 1928 Stein (1993, 54) wrote to Sr. Callista Kopf:

> Immediately before and for a good while after my conversion, I was of the opinion that to lead a religious life one had to give up all that was secular and to live totally immersed in thoughts of the Divine. But gradually I realized that something else is asked of us in this world and that, even in the contemplative life, one may not sever the connection with the world. I even believe that the deeper one is drawn into God, the more one must "go out of oneself"; that is, one must go to the world in order to carry the divine life into it . . . one is to consider oneself totally as an instrument, especially with regard to the abilities one uses . . . We are to see them as something used, not by us, but God in us.

During her period at the Cologne Carmel, Stein produced a number of short meditations and among these is her "Mystery of Christmas." In this meditation is a section entitled "the Mystical Body of Christ." Here Stein (2002) describes the universal call to union with God and that those united to God in love are simultaneously joined in a common bond to all who have given their assent, whatever their faith traditions, because, as Stein writes, there are no strangers.

The ecumenical Bonhoeffer

Bonhoeffer is invoked by a plethora of different (and sometimes conflictual)[26] theologies and among these, as I have previously indicated, is Charles Marsh. Keith Clements has ably demonstrated Bonhoeffer's ecumenical commitments (Clements 2015), but in the concluding section of this paper I want to take issue with Marsh's (2014, 58) description of Bonhoeffer's Catholic sympathies as "a young man's infatuation with the Holy See."

Bethge describes Bonhoeffer's attitude towards Catholicism as "critical affection and affectionate criticism" (Bethge 2000, 62) and although there is no indication that Bonhoeffer was attracted to the Catholic Church as an institution, he was certainly interested in Catholic spirituality and liturgy and contrary to Marsh, Catholic Rome became a permanent influence on Bonhoeffer (Green 1999, 143 n. 81). He told an acquaintance in Barcelona in 1928 that Catholic Rome had been "a real temptation" (Green 1999, 143 n. 81; Bethge 2000, 64). This is notable given that his Spanish experience included encountering an uncultured clergy and an educated populace often vehemently opposed to the church (Schlingensiepen 2003, 50–54). In Barcelona, Bonhoef-

---

26. Theologies which have looked to Bonhoeffer for inspiration include: secular, postmodernist and liberation theologies. Stephen R. Haynes (2004) suggests that there are those who see Bonhoeffer as a seer (a radical); a prophet (a liberal); an apostle (a conservative evangelical); a bridge (a universal humanist); and a saint. Clifford Green (1994) sought to identify Bonhoeffer with the principals of liberation theology. Green has identified four methods used in analyzing and utilizing Bonhoeffer's theology: his own "historical" approach (Green 1999); thematic approaches such as Larry L. Rasmussen's (2005) *Reality and Resistance*; comparative studies such as *Bonhoeffer and King: Speaking Truth to Power*, by J. Deotis Roberts (2004); and those which demonstrate a teleological bias such as John A. Phillips' (1967) *Christ for us in the Theology of Dietrich Bonhoeffer*. Bonhoeffer did not limit his theological insights to the pressure of immediate circumstances, but retained a large space of freedom for his theological reflection.

fer encouraged the congregation to rediscover the meaning of a word which for Protestants was,

> infinitely banal ... indifferent and superfluous and associated with "boredom." That word was "church." "Church" for Catholics evoked "tremendous feelings of love and bliss," stirred "the most profound depths of religious feeling" and engendered "gratitude, reverence and self-surrendering love" (Bonhoeffer 2008a, 505).

Bonhoeffer's "Catholic" ecclesiology

Heinrich Ott (1972, 62), William Kuhns (1969), Brendan Leahy (2008, 32–59), Hans Urs von Balthasar (1975, 41–42 and 48–49) and Ernst Feil (1991, 142–152) are among those who believe that notable similarities exist between aspects of Bonhoeffer's theology and contemporaneous Catholicism or that Catholic theology represents an important source of inspiration. Feil's hypothesis is that Bonhoeffer assimilated various insights from the Catholic tradition and that, because of this creative contact, he gained "at the beginning of his theological development a fundamental impression through his experience with the Catholic Church, which he [then] formulated ecclesiologically in his *Sanctorum Communio*" (Feil 1991, 144).

There are indications throughout Bonhoeffer's writings of his ecumenical interests and Catholic sympathies including the writings of Karl Adam and Romano Guardini. Bonhoeffer considered that the contributions of the Catholic Church to European culture could not be overestimated, that Catholicism had developed an unparalleled spiritual power and that it was a church of "infinite diversity," which had succeeded in preserving unity in all its multiplicity. His "affectionate criticism" towards the end of his life is shown in a letter to his parents (15 May 1943) when he mentions his sympathies for the *via contemplative* describing his prison experience as "a time of enforced silence" (Bonhoeffer 2010, 81).

Social and political changes and challenges

Although Stein and Bonhoeffer lived during a period of unprecedented religious, economic, social and political changes and challenges, these years were also "culturally and intellectually perhaps the most vivid years of recent German history – full of tensions, ruptures and contradictions" (Zaborowski 2019, 44). This was the extraordinarily rich intellectual and social context in which Stein lived and worked. What is notable for any consideration of Bonhoeffer's theology and Stein's faith choices and philosophical interests was that this was a period when the inner-ecclesial reform movements of the Catholic Church had rediscovered "the reality of the body of Christ" (Kasper 2015, 130); when there was a new ecumenical discovery of the significance of holy Scripture; and when Thomistic studies were being re-imagined by philosophers including those known to both Bonhoeffer and Stein including Jacques Maritain and Erich Przywara. Stein participated in this resurgence and it influenced, not only the Catholic Church but also attentive Protestant theologians such as Bonhoeffer, as well as Emil Brunner and Karl Barth.

The end is their beginning

On Sunday 2 August 1942, two S. S. officers entered the Carmelite monastery at Echt, and Edith Stein and her sister Rosa were arrested and taken to the prison camp at Amersfoort where they joined hundreds of other Jewish prisoners, including some other Jewish-Catholic Religious. On the night of 3 August Edith and Rosa along with twelve hundred other Jews were forced onto a train and taken to Westerbork, the central detention camp for the north of Holland. From here, on 6 August, they were transported to Auschwitz where many of them were immediately murdered. Some of the eyewitness testimonies to Stein's presence and reports of conversation during this transitional period between Echt and her death at Auschwitz on 9 August have been collected and published. One of these appeared in a Dutch-language Catholic daily newspaper *De Tijd* in 1952. The author of the article, Mr Wielek (cited by Herbstrith 1985, 186–187) writes:

> From the moment I met her in the camp at Westerbork... I knew: here is someone truly great. For a couple of days she lived in that hellhole, walking, talking and praying... like a saint... During one conversation she told me, "For now, the world consists in opposites... But in the end, none of those contrasts will remain. There will only be the fullness of love. How could it be otherwise?"

This comment, indicating Stein's generous orthodoxy, is entirely consistent with her writings.

Bonhoeffer's final liturgical act was ecumenical. On 8 April 1945 Bonhoeffer was held prisoner in a former school house in Schönberg. With Bonhoeffer and other mostly Catholic Germans were two British officers, Payne Best and Hugh Falconer, and the nephew of the Soviet Foreign Minister, the Russian

Vasily Kokorina. The prisoners, including Kokorina, asked Bonhoeffer to lead them in a prayer service. Bonhoeffer reluctantly agreed and led a meditation on Isaiah 53:5: "With his wounds we are healed." Bonhoeffer prayed for the group and then led them in singing Luther's hymn *Ein feste Burg ist unser Gott* (A Mighty Fortress is Our God). Shortly after this Bonhoeffer was taken by the Gestapo. Before he left his congregation he said to Best: "This is the end – for me the beginning of life" and he then asked Bell to give a message to the Anglican Bishop George Bell. Bonhoeffer asked Best to tell Bell that, "With him I believe in the principle of our universal Christian brotherhood which rises above all national interests and that our victory is certain" (Payne 1950, 200; Bethge 2000, 926ff). Bonhoeffer was hanged the next day.

On 9 August Stein was murdered by the Nazis and her final communication, written as she was being transported to her death at Auschwitz-Birkenau, was *Grüße von Schwester Teresia Benedicta a Cruce. Unterwegs ad orientem* (Wulf 2017, 240). The use by Stein of the Latin *ad orientem* (to the East) suggests, not only that this was the geographic direction of her transport but also of Stein's faith and hope in a God who welcomes all.

Conclusion

This paper suggests that the conceptual and religious absolutes or "opposites" that too often provide the interpretive lens in presenting and assessing the lives and witness of "saints" such as Bonhoeffer or Stein are not only unhelpful to the broader ecumenical vision that they present, but they are also inconsistent with the generous ecumenical vision that both demonstrate in their decisions, their writings and in their submission to the divine will. Stein wrote "that the deeper one is drawn into God, the more one must 'go out of oneself'; that is, one must go to the world in order to carry the divine life into it" (Stein 1993, 54). Although expressed as a personal commitment and vision it resonates with Bonhoeffer's (1998, 560) ecclesial motif: *Die Kirche ist nur Kirche, wenn sie für andere da ist* (the church is only the church when it exists for others). It is in this broader concern for the οἰκουμένη – the whole earth – that the Jewish, Carmelite, philosopher Stein and the Lutheran theologian connect beyond ecclesial identities and supersessionism to a vision of God who embraces all.

Bibliography

"Abraham Geiger." *New World Encyclopaedia of Judaism*. https://www.newworldencyclopedia.org/entry/Abraham_Geiger [accessed: 14.12.2022].

Aquino, Thomas von. 1932. *Untersuchungen über die Wahrheit (Questiones disputatae de veritate)*, 2 Vols. Breslau: Verlag von Otto Borgmeyer.

Astell, Ann. 2018. "Carmel in Cologne, Echt and Auschwitz: Edith Stein's Last Journeys and the Meaning of Place in Exile." In *Listening to Edith Stein. Wisdom for a New Century*, edited by Kathleen Haney. Washington, DC: ICS Publications.

Balthasar, Hans Urs von. 1975. *Katholisch, Aspekte des Mysteriums*. Einsiedeln: Johannes.

Batzdorff, Susanne. 2003. *Aunt Edith. The Jewish Heritage of a Catholic Saint*. Springfield: Templegate Publishers.

Beatificationis et Canonizationis Servae Dei Edith Stein. Summarium super dubio: An eius Causa, introducenda si Vol. 3. 1983. Rome.

Bergen, Doris. 1996. *Twisted Cross: The German Christian Movement in the Third Reich*. Chapel Hill: University of North Carolina.

Best, Payne S. 1950. *The Venlo Incident*. London: Hutchinson & Co.

Bethge, Eberhard. 2000. *Dietrich Bonhoeffer: A Biography*. Minneapolis: Fortress Press.

Bonhoeffer, Dietrich. 1998. *Widerstand und Ergebung. Briefe und Aufzeichnungen aus der Haft. Dietrich Bonhoeffer Werke Volume 8*, edited by Christian Gremmels, Eberhard Bethge, Renate Bethge, Ilse Tödt. Gütersloh: Gütersloher Verlagshaus.

Bonhoeffer, Dietrich. 2008. *Barcelona, Berlin, New York: 1928–1931. Dietrich Bonhoeffer Works Volume 10*, edited by Clifford J. Green, translated by Douglas W. Stott. Minneapolis: Fortress Press.

Bonhoeffer, Dietrich. 2009. *Berlin 1932–1933. Dietrich Bonhoeffer Works Volume 12*, edited by Larry L. Rasmussen, translated by Isabel Best and David Higgins. Minneapolis: Fortress Press.

Bonhoeffer, Dietrich. 2010. *Letters and Papers from Prison. Dietrich Bonhoeffer Works Volume 8*, edited by John W. de Gruchy, translated by Isabel Best, Lisa E. Dahill, Reinhard Krauss and Nancy Lukens. Minneapolis: Fortress Press.

Bonhoeffer, Dietrich. 2013. "Third Session: Evangelization [Volksmission] and Chamby Conference April 15–August 23, 1936." *Theological Education at Finkenwalde: 1935–1937: Dietrich Bonhoeffer Works Volume 14*, edited by H. Gaylon Barker and Mark S. Brocker, translated by Douglas W. Stott, 605–717. Minneapolis: Fortress Press.

Brenner, Rachel Feldhay. 1994. "Ethical Convergence in Religious Conversion." In *The Unnecessary Problem of Edith Stein. Studies in the Shoah Volume IV*, edited by Harry James Cargas. Lanham, New York/London: University Press of America, 1994.

Burton, Richard D. E. 2004. *Holy Tears, Holy Blood: Women, Catholicism, and the Culture of Suffering in France, 1840–1970*. New York: Cornell University Press.

Calcagno, Antonio. 2007. *The Philosophy of Edith Stein*. Pittsburgh: Duquesne University Press.

Casey, Ken. 2016. "Edith Stein and 'Secretum meum mihi': Are Religious Conversions Necessarily Private?" In *Edith Stein: Women, Social-Political Philosophy, Theol-*

ogy, Metaphysics and Public History. New Approaches and Applications, edited by Antonio Calcagno, 253–266. Cham: Springer.

Chomsky, Noam. 1972. *Language and Mind*. New York: Harcourt Brace Jovanovich Inc.

Clements, Keith. 2015. *Dietrich Bonhoeffer's Ecumenical Quest*. Geneva: World Council of Churches.

Collins, Peter M. 2019. "Saint Edith Stein, Footsteps to Truth." *Homiletic and Pastoral Review*. https://www.hprweb.com/2019/09/saint-edith-stein.

Conrad-Martius, Hedwig. 1959. "Edith Stein." *Archives de Philosophie* 22.2, Avril-Juni: 163–174.

Dobhan, Ulrich. 2006. "Edith Stein – die Karmelitin." *Edith Stein Jahrbuch 2006* 12:75–123.

Dobhan, Ulrich. 2009. "Vom 'radikalen Unglauben' zum 'wahren Glauben,'" *Edith Stein Jahrbuch 2009* 15:53–84.

Feil, Ernst. 1991. "Bonhoeffer's Ecumenical Ethics in View of Restorative and Revolutionary Tendencies." In *Bonhoeffer's Ethics, Old Europe and New Frontiers*, edited by Guy Carter, René van Eyden, Hans-Dirk van Hoogstraten, and Jurjen Wiersma, 142–152. Kampen: Kok Pharos.

Feldes, Joachim. 2015. "A Yet Hidden Story: Edith Stein and the Bergzabern Circle." In *Intersubjectivity, Humanity, Being – Edith Stein's Phenomenology and Christian Philosophy*, edited by Mette Lebech and John Haydn, 125–138. Oxford: Peter Lang Verlag.

Feldes, Joachim. 2016. "The Bergzabern Circle: Towards a More Comprehensive View of Edith Stein," In *Edith Stein: Women, Social-Political Philosophy, Theology, Metaphysics and Public History. New Approaches and Applications*, edited by Antonio Calcagno, 239–252. Cham: Springer.

Feuling, Daniel. 1998. "Short Biographical Sketch of Edith Stein." In *Never Forget, Christian and Jewish Perspectives on Edith Stein*, edited by Waltraud Herbstrith, translated by Susanne M. Batzdorf, 260–263. Washington, DC: ICS Publications.

Fisher, Eugene J. 2003. "Introduction." In *Aunt Edith. The Jewish Heritage of a Catholic Saint* by Susanne Batzdorff. Springfield: Templegate Publishers.

Gibbs, Benjamin. 2012. "My Long Search for the True Faith. The Conversion of Edith Stein." 21. *Mount Carmel*, 60.3 (July–September 2012).

Glatzer, Nahum N. 1978. "Franz Rosenzweig: The Story of a Conversion." In *Essays in Jewish Thought. Introduction to Rosenzweig's Little Book of Common Sense and Sick Reason*. Tuscaloosa: University of Alabama Press.

Golay, Didier-Marie. 2009. *Edith Stein in Devant Dieu pour tous*. Paris: Editions du CERF.

Graef, Hilda. 1955. *The Scholar and the Cross*. London: Longmans, 1955.

Green, Clifford J. 1994. "Bonhoeffer, Modernity and Liberation Theology." In *Theology and the Practice of Responsibility: Essays on Dietrich Bonhoeffer*, edited by Wayne W. Floyd and Charles Marsh. Valley Forge: Trinity Press International.

Green, Clifford J. 1999. *Bonhoeffer: A Theology of Sociality*. Grand Rapids: Eerdmans.

Green, Deirdre. 1989. *Gold in the Crucible – Teresa of Avila and the Western Mystical Tradition*. Shaftesbury: Element Books.
Gutteridge, Richard. 1976. *Open Thy Mouth for the Dumb!: The German Evangelical Church and the Jews, 1879–1950*. New York: Barnes & Noble Books.
Guttman, Jacob. 1893. "Die Beziehungen des Johannes Duns Scotus zum Judenthum" *Monatsschrift für Geschichte und Wissenschaft des Judentums* 38.1 (1893): 26–39.
Guttman, Jacob. 1902. *Die Scholastik des 13. Jahrhunderts in ihren Beziehungen zum Judentum und zur jüdischen Literatur*. Breslau: M. & H. Marcus.
Guttman, Jacob. 2010. *Das Verhältnis des Thomas von Aquino zum Judentum und zur jüdischen Literatur (1891)*. Whitefish: Kessinger Publishing.
Häring, Bernard. 1978. *Free and Faithful in Christ Volume 1*. Slough: St. Paul.
Haynes, Stephen R. 2004. *The Bonhoeffer Phenomenon – Portraits of a Protestant Saint*. London: SCM.
Helmreich, Ernst. 1979. *The German Churches under Hitler: Background Struggle and Epilogue*. Detroit: Wayne State University.
Herbstrith, Waltraud. 1985. *Edith Stein: A Biography*, translated by Bernard Bonowitz. San Francisco: Ignatius.
Jiménez, Juan Rámon. 2016. *Ideolojía, The book of aphorisms, volume IV of Metamórfosis*. https://yolainebodin.com/the-language-nook/quotes/he-who-learns-a-new-language-acquires-a-new-soul.
Joël, Manuel. 1880. *Blicke in die Religionsgeschichte zu Anfang des zweiten christlichen Jahrhunderts*. Breslau: Druck und Verlag von S. Schottlaender.
John of the Cross. "The Sayings of Light and Love 153." In *The Collected Works of Saint John of the Cross*, translated by Kieran Kavanaugh and Ottila Rodriguez, 96. Washington, DC: ICS Publication.
Joseph, Max. 1930. "Stammesgemeinschaft." In *Jüdisches Lexikon*, 4, 628–629. Berlin: Jüdischer Verlag.
Kasper, Walter. 2015. *The Catholic Church. Nature, Reality and Mission*, edited by R. David Nelson, translated by Thomas Hoebel. London and New York: Bloomsbury T&T Clark.
Kierkegaard, Søren. 1924. *Einübung in Christentum. Gesammelte Werke Volume 9*, edited by Christoph Schrempf. Jena: Diederichs.
Koeppel, Josephine. 1990. *Edith Stein. Philosopher and Mystic. The Way of the Christian Mystics Volume 12*. Collegeville: Michael Glazier Books.
Kölner Selig - und Heiligsprechungsprozess der Dienerin Gottes Sr. Teresia Benedicta a Cruce (Edith Stein). 1962. Cologne: Kloster der Karmelitinnen.
Kuhns, William. 1969. *In Pursuit of Dietrich Bonhoeffer*. Colorado Springs: Image Books.
La Phénoménologie, Juivsy, 12 septembre 1932. 1932. Juvisy: Editions du Cerf.
Lazarus, Moritz. 1887. *Israelitische Wochenzeitschrift*. Berlin: Cronbach.
Leahy, Brendan, "'Christ Existing as Community': Dietrich Bonhoeffer's Notion of the Church." *Irish Theological Quarterly* 73 (2008): 32–59.
MacIntyre, Alasdair. 2006. *Edith Stein: A Philosophical Prologue*. London: Continuum.

Maria A. 1972. *Edith Stein. A Saint for our Times*, translated by Lucia Wiedenhöver. Cologne: Carmel.
Marsh, Charles. 2014. *Strange Glory: A Life of Dietrich Bonhoeffer*. New York: Alfred A. Knopf, 2014.
Metaxas, Eric. 2010. *Bonhoeffer – Pastor, Martyr, Prophet, Spy – A Righteous Gentile vs. The Third Reich*. Nashville: Thomas Nelson.
Meyer, Michael A. 1988. *Response to Modernity. A History of the Reformed Movement in Judaism*. Detroit: Wayne State University Press.
Morrison, Karl F. *Understanding Conversion*. Charlottesville and London: University Press of Virginia.
Newman, John H. 1890. *Apologia Pro Vita Sua. Being a History of His Religious Opinions*. London: Longmans, Green, and Co. https://www.gutenberg.org/files/22088/22088-h/22088-h.htm#chapter_i.
Newman, John H. 1928. *Briefe und Tagebücher 1801–1845*. Munich: Theatiner Verlag.
Nolan, Ann Michele. 1993. "Edith Stein: A Study in Twentieth-Century Mysticism." Master thesis, Massey University. https://mro.massey.ac.nz/server/api/core/bitstreams/1ad238c5-7403-4c2a-9d34-d64412a709f0/content.
Oben, Freda M. 1987. "Edith Stein the Woman." In *Edith Stein Symposium. Teresian Culture*, edited by John Sullivan, 3–33. Washington, DC: ICS Publications, 1987.
Oben, Freda M. 2001. *The Life and Thought of Edith Stein*. New York: Alba House/St. Paul's.
Oesterreicher, John. 1998. *Never Forget: Christian and Jewish Perspectives On Edith Stein*, edited by Waltraud Herbstrith. Washington, DC: ICS Publications.
Ott, Heinrich. 1972. *Reality and Faith*. Philadelphia: Fortress Press.
Palmisano, Joseph R. 2012. *Beyond the Walls – Abraham Joshua Heschel and Edith Stein on the Significance of Empathy for Jewish-Christian Dialogue*. Oxford: Oxford University Press.
Phillips. John A. 1967. *Christ for us in the Theology of Dietrich Bonhoeffer*. New York: Harper & Row.
Posselt, Teresia R. 1963. *Edith Stein. Eine Grosse Frau unseres Jahrhunderts*. Freiburg-Basel-Vienna: Herder.
Posselt, Teresia R. 2005. *Edith Stein, The Life of Philosopher and Carmelite*. Washington, DC: ICS.
Rahden, Till van. 2008. *Jews and Other Germans: Civil Society, Religious Diversity and Urban Politics in Breslau, 1860–1925*, translated by Marcus Brainard. Madison: University of Wisconsin Press.
Railton, Nicholas. 1998. *The German Evangelical Alliance and the Third Reich. An Analysis of the "Evangelisches Allianzblatt."* Bern: Peter Lang.
Rasmussen, Larry L. 2005. *Bonhoeffer: Reality and Resistance*. Louisville: Westminster John Knox Press.
"Die Reichen." 1870. *Allgemeine Zeitung des Judentums* 34 (1870): 569–572.

Roberts, James D. 2004. *Bonhoeffer and King: Speaking Truth to Power*. Louisville: Westminster John Knox Press.

Rosenzweig, Franz. 1953. *On Jewish Learning*, edited by Nahum N. Glatzer. Madison: The University of Wisconsin Press.

Schenk, Richard. 2013. "Theology, Metaphysics and Discipleship." In *Thomas Aquinas and Karl Barth. An Unofficial Catholic-Protestant Dialogue*, edited by Bruce L. McCormack and Thomas Joseph White. Grand Rapids: Eerdmans.

Schlingensiepen, Ferdinand. 2009. *Dietrich Bonhoeffer 1906–1945: Martyr, Thinker, Man of Resistance*. London: T&T Clark.

Schlingensiepen, Ferdinand. 2023. "Schlingensiepen on Metaxas and Marsh Biographies." *The Bonhoeffer Center*. https://web.archive.org/web/20210613084558/https://www.thebonhoeffercenter.org/index.php?option=com_content&view=article&id=37%3Aschlingensiepen-on-metaxas-and-marsh&catid=21&Itemid=263 [archived 06.13.2021].

Spector, Scott. 1998. "Edith Stein's Passing Gestures: Intimate Histories, Empathic Portraits." *New German Critique*, Autumn 1998, 7: 28–56.

Stein, Edith. 1917. *Zum Problem der Einfühlung*. Halle: Buchdrucheri des Waisenhauses.

Stein, Edith. 1935. "Eine Meisterin der Erziehungs-und Bildungsarbeit: Teresia von Jesus." *Katholische Frauenbildung im deutschen Volk*, 48 (February 1935): 122–123.

Stein, Edith. 1950. *Endliches und ewiges Sein: Versuch eines Aufstiegs zum Sinn des Seins. Edith Steins Werke Volume 2*, edited by Leuven Romaeus, Gelber Lucy. Louvain: Nauwelaerts.

Stein, Edith. 1960. *Briefe an Hedwig Conrad-Martius*. Munich: Kösel.

Stein, Edith. 1976. *Selbstbildnis in Briefen. Erster Teil 1916–1934. Edith Steins Werke Volume 8*, edited by Leuven Romaeus, Gelber Lucy. Druten: De Maas & Waler.

Stein, Edith. 1977. *Selbstbildnis in Briefen. Zweiter Teil 1934–1942. Edith Steins Werke Volume 9*, edited by Leuven Romaeus, Gelber Lucy. Druten: De Maas & Waler.

Stein, Edith. 1986. *Life in a Jewish Family: An Autobiography, 1891–1916. The Collected Works of Edith Stein Volume 1*, translated by Josephine Koeppel. Washington, DC: ICS Publications.

Stein, Edith. 1987a. "Die 'Seelenburg' der Teresa von Ávila." *Zeitwende* 58 (1987): 210–231.

Stein, Edith. 1987b. *Verborgenes Leben: hagiographische Essays, Meditationen, geistliche Texte. Edith Steins Werke Volume 11*, edited by Lucy Gelber, Michael Linssen. Druten: De Maas & Waler.

Stein, Edith. 1989. *On the Problem of Empathy*, translated by Waltraut Stein. Washington, DC: ICS Publications.

Stein, Edith. 1989. *On the Problem of Empathy*, translated by Waltraut Stein. Washington, DC: ICS Publications.

Stein, Edith. 1992. *The Hidden Life: Hagiographic Essays, Meditations, Spiritual Texts. The Collected Works of Edith Stein Volume 4*, translated by Waltraut Stein. Washington, DC: ICS Publications.

Stein, Edith. 1993. *Self-Portrait in Letters, 1916–1942. The Collected Works of Edith Stein Volume 5*, translated by Josephine Koeppel. Washington, DC: ICS Publications.
Stein, Edith. 2000a. *Aus dem Leben einer jüdischen Familie. Edith Stein Gesamtausgabe Volume 1*, edited by Maria A. Neyer. Freiburg: Herder.
Stein, Edith. 2000b. *Selbstbildnis in Briefen II (1933–1942). Edith Stein Gesamtausgabe Volume 3*, edited by Maria A. Neyer. Freiburg: Herder.
Stein, Edith. 2001. *Selbstbildnis in Briefen III: Briefe an Roman Ingarden. Edith Stein Gesamtausgabe Volume 4*, edited by Maria A. Neyer. Freiburg: Herder.
Stein, Edith. 2002. *The Science of the Cross. The Collected Works of Edith Stein Volume 6*, translated by Josephine Koeppel, Washington, DC: ICS Publications.
Stein, Edith. 2005. *Selbstbildnis in Briefen I (1916–1933). Edith Stein Gesamtausgabe Volume 2*, edited by Maria A. Neyer. Freiburg: Herder.
Stein, Edith. 2014. *Letters to Roman Ingarden. The Collected Works of Edith Stein Volume 12*, translated by Hugh C. Hunt. Washington, DC: ICS Publications.
Stein, Edith. 2022. "The Mystery of Christmas." *Plough*. https://www.plough.com/en/topics/culture/holidays/christmas-readings/the-mystery-of-christmas [accessed: 23.05.2023].
Sullivan, John. 2004. *Edith Stein: Essential Writing*. Maryknoll: Orbis Books.
Sullivan, John. 2020. *Sartorial Sharing: St. Edith Stein and her Godmother Hedwig Conrad-Martius*. https://www.discalcedcarmel.org/blog/sartorial-sharing-st-edith-stein-and-her-godmother-hedwig-conrad-martius [accessed: 23.05.2023].
Sybel, Alfred von. 1923. *Abschriften von Briefen 1922–1923*.
Teresa of Ávila. 1957. *The Complete Works of St. Teresa*, translated by Edgar Allison Peers. London: Sheed & Ward.
Teresa of Ávila. 1985a. *The Book of her Foundations*, edited and translated by Kieran Kavanaugh and Otilio Rodriguez. Washington, DC: ICS Publications.
Teresa of Ávila. 1985b. *The Book of Her Life*, edited and translated by Kieran Kavanaugh and Otilio Rodriguez. Washington, DC: ICS Publications.
Teresa of Ávila. 1985c. *The Interior Castle*, edited and translated by Kieran Kavanaugh and Otilio Rodriguez. Washington, DC: ICS Publications.
Teresa of Ávila. 2012. *The Way of Perfection*, edited and translated by Kieran Kavanaugh and Otilio Rodriguez. Washington, DC: ICS Publications.
Teresa von Jesus. 1868. *Das Leben der Heiligen Teresa von Jesus: Von ihr selbst geschrieben*, translated by Ida von Hahn-Hahn. Mainz: Kirchheim.
Teresia de Spiritu Sancto. 1952. *Edith Stein*, translated by Cecily Hastings and Donald Nichols. London and New York: Sheed and Ward.
Williams, Rowan. 2004. *Teresa of Avila*. London: Continuum, 2003.
Wulf, Claudia Mariéle. 2017. "Sacrifice – Action within a Relationship: A Phenomenology of Sacrifice." In *Sacrifice in Modernity: Community, Ritual, Identity. From Nationalism and Nonviolence to Health Care and Harry Potter*, edited by Joachim Duyndam, Anne-Marie Korte, and Marcel Poorthuis, 230–240. Leiden: Brill.

Zaborowski, Holger. 2019. "Contradiction, Liturgy and Freedom: Romano Guardini's Search for Meaning after the Cataclysm of World War I." *Modern Theology* 35(1): 43–54.

Part 2

Bonhoeffer and Stein: Freedom as an Idea and a Reality

4

History, Reality, and the Mission of the Church in a World of Abstraction

Joel Lawrence, PhD
Executive Director, Center for Pastor Theologians

About the Author

Joel Lawrence (PhD, Cambridge University) is the President of the Center for Pastor Theologians. Prior to this role, Joel served as the Senior Pastor of Central Baptist Church in St. Paul, MN, Teaching Pastor at Calvary Church in White Bear, MN, and as Associate Professor of Systematic Theology and Ethics at Bethel Seminary in St. Paul, Minnesota. Joel holds degrees from Texas A&M University (BA), Dallas Theological Seminary (ThM), and Cambridge University (MPhil and PhD). He is the author of *Bonhoeffer: A Guide for the Perplexed* (T&T Clark, 2010) and co-editor of *Confronting Racial Injustice: Theory and Praxis for the Church* (Cascade, 2022) and *Reconstructing Evangelicalism* (Cascade, 2023). In addition, Joel has an active ministry speaking in churches, seminaries, and conferences worldwide. Joel and his wife Myndi live in St. Paul, MN, and have four children: Bethany, Anna, Katherine, and Micah.

Keywords

Bonhoeffer, reality and abstraction, Christology, the church's mission and history

Abstract

In this presentation, we will explore how Dietrich Bonhoeffer's theological anthropology, as developed in *Creation and Fall* and the Christology lectures, shapes his understanding of history. For Bonhoeffer, humanity, created to live in the reality of God, has rejected that life and turned away from reality and toward abstraction. This turn means that history east of Eden, that is, history produced by the heart turned in on itself, is marred by the conflict that arises when humanity lives in self-referential idealizing abstraction. We will then reflect on how Bonhoeffer's vision of the church calls us to live for reality by living against the abstractions of history. The presentation will conclude with the encouragement for all who confess Jesus to faithfully witness to Christ in our time of deep historical volatility by living in the hidden reality of Christ.

1. The abstractions of history

We are living in a time of great historical instability. The list of challenges facing the world is long and varied: the lingering effects of the global coronavirus pandemic, the economic uncertainty driven by surging inflation, and the volatility of political regimes across the world. In my homeland, the USA, the ongoing lies of President Trump have created convulsions that have weakened political institutions and brought a division that will inevitably grow worse; there is gun violence that is a scourge on American society; and racial tensions are heightened by a rising tide of white nationalism.

And of course: war in Europe. Russia's unprovoked and unjust invasion of Ukraine has brought unimaginable suffering to the people of Ukraine and has deeply impacted the people of Poland. The war has brought global economic turmoil through rising energy prices, the prospect of growing food instability, a rise in tensions among the great military and economic powers of our age, and a return of the menace of nuclear war. In America, we have watched with horror at the devastation, as well as awe at the resilience of both the Ukrainian people, who have suffered so much, and of the Polish people who so eagerly stepped up to aid refugees fleeing the destruction.

Of course, this is not the first time the world has faced the ravages of history; the past is filled with countless eras noted for their instability and uncertainty. So, as we navigate our difficult times, we are comforted by two things: 1) The Lord is in his holy temple, and 2) others have gone before us who have faced similar times of historical instability, people whose witness to Jesus in times of deep uncertainty give us comfort as we face the difficulties of our day.

History, Reality, and the Mission of the Church in a World of Abstraction

We are gathered to reflect on two children of Wrocław who confessed that Jesus is Lord during another deeply unstable era of history, a time of another European war. These two, Dietrich Bonhoeffer and Edith Stein, were followers of Jesus in word and deed, even unto death. We turn to them seeking wisdom and insight from their witness as we pursue God's guidance in living out our common confession of Christ as the Lord.

Ours is an ecumenical gathering; by nature, that means that there are many things on which we don't agree. As those who come from different ecclesial traditions, we hold different confessional convictions and have distinct theological understandings of the church, humanity, God's work in salvation, the nature of the state and the church's relation to the politics of the state. Had Bonhoeffer and Stein met and talked theology, one a Lutheran Protestant pastor and the other a Roman Catholic nun, there would have been many things they didn't agree on. But they did agree on the one person who united them, the same who unites us: Jesus the Messiah. This means that we share a core confession with Bonhoeffer, Stein, and with each other: Jesus Christ is the Lord.

This puts before us a fundamental question: How do we, followers of Jesus, gathered from varied traditions, together confess Jesus as Lord in these unstable times? How can we encourage each other in our varied vocations? My prayer is that our gathering would be an encouragement to our weary souls, souls seeking footing as we walk the unstable ground of our era. As we take these steps, as we look for our footing, may we hold onto each other as we hold onto our shared confession of Jesus.

I want to begin our time reflecting on our shared confession of Christ as Lord, and how we are to live out that confession in these uncertain times, by investigating a cluster of themes from Dietrich Bonhoeffer's theology. These themes are history, reality, and the mission of the church. To do this, I will explore how Dietrich Bonhoeffer's theological anthropology, as developed in *Creation and Fall* (1932–33) and the Christology (1933) lectures, shapes his understanding of history. As I will demonstrate, for Bonhoeffer, humanity was created to live in the reality of God but has rejected God and so turned away from reality and toward abstraction. This turn means that history east of Eden, that is, history produced by the heart turned in on itself, is marred by the conflict that arises when humanity lives in self-referential idealizing abstraction. I will then conclude with a reflection on how Bonhoeffer's vision of the church in *Life Together* (1938) calls us to live for reality by living against the abstractions of history, and will conclude with a call to us, as followers of Jesus, to be the church that lives in reality, against, and so for, humanity in its abstraction.

2. Theological anthropology and history

In 1932–1933, Bonhoeffer was a lecturer at the University of Berlin. During this time, Germany was beginning its descent into the chaos of Nazi power. In January of 1933, just one kilometer from the lecture theater where Bonhoeffer was teaching, Adolph Hitler became the Reich Chancellor and, over the next few months, enacted laws giving him greater and greater authority. During this time, two lecture series taught by Bonhoeffer explored the foundational account of God's creation of the heavens and the earth, of humanity made in the divine likeness, of the rebellion of humanity against God, and the promise of the Messiah who one day would trample the head of the serpent, through this developing a theological anthropology that contains a vision of history.

A. Creation and Fall

In *Creation and Fall*, Bonhoeffer speaks of the creature of dust made human through the breath of life. Humans are earthly beings, created a little lower than the angels; Bonhoeffer is insistent that humans are material beings, created by God through the combination of dirt and breath, created to be God's image with earthen feet connected to the ground. As material beings, we were created to eat the fruit of the earth, to steward its providentially given resources, and to dwell in loving fellowship with God and neighbour in the goodness of the creation.

In this material life, Adam and Eve were called to live outward from the self, toward God and neighbour in a life of self-giving that reflects the triune God, whose eternal divine reality is in God's being for the other. However, in Genesis 3, humanity turns from this calling by taking the fruit of the tree of the knowledge of good and evil. For Bonhoeffer, this story, rooted in the mists of time, reveals the condition of the heart in rebellion against God. By taking the fruit, humanity rejected God's blessing, rejected God's gift of life in relation to him, our neighbour, and the providential earth, which Bonhoeffer calls our "mother" (Bonhoeffer 1997, 57).

In doing this, humanity storms the center, taking the place where God was to dwell, taking to ourselves that which belongs to God. Now, rather than living outward toward God and neighbour, we live as the *cor curvum in se*, the heart turned in on itself. As those weighed down by the inward curve, humans live in self-reference, according to our knowledge of good and evil. Told by the serpent that this would be a blessing, humanity finds out too late that it is, in fact, the curse; being our own reference point, our own gods, unleashes death into the world. On this, Bonhoeffer writes, "Fallen Adam lives on his way to death . . . Why? Because by eating the fruit of the tree of knowledge, Adam as a human-being-*sicut-deus* has ingested death into himself. *Adam is dead before he dies*" (Bonhoeffer 1997, 135). This is the death of human separation from God. In that separation, humans move from living in reality to living in abstraction.

To understand Bonhoeffer's vision of history as it is rooted in his theological anthropology, we must understand what he means by abstraction. Abstraction is an important theme in Bonhoeffer's theology and is rooted in the heart turned in on itself. No longer living toward God at the center, humanity now becomes the center of our own reality, which is, in fact, a life of abstraction. For Bonhoeffer, to live in abstraction is to live according to principles, rules, laws, and ideals that are produced by the heart turned in on itself, generated from our own will and out of our own resources. Living according to the knowledge of good and evil, living a life of autonomy, humanity-in-Adam now lives from our own self-generated ideals. These ideals are abstractions because they are disconnected from true reality, God. They are rooted in human self-reference rather than in divine reality, and so take on the form of ideologies. Ideologies act as interpretive frameworks of the heart turned in on itself, creating a vision of the world that is false because it isn't a vision of the world's relationship to God, but to humanity. Creating ideals, the human heart generates a self-referential vision of how the world ought to be, and then pursues its own plans for how to make that vision reality.

But it's not reality, at least not God's reality. History east of Eden, the history of political power and military conquest, the history of human suffering and achievement, the phenomena of the seen, is abstraction. The great powers, the colossuses who stride the face of the earth, from Caesar to Putin, are abstracters. Because of this, those who believe they are making history are in fact creating ideologies; history becomes the clash of the abstract ideals of hearts turned in on themselves. Created to live in the reality of God's presence, humanity now lives in abstraction, creating the phenomena of history that exist as the abstractions of human ideals that shape the world around the heart turned in on itself.

As I mentioned above, Bonhoeffer delivered his lectures on Genesis 1–3 in the winter semester of 1932–1933. Having explored the foundational texts of God's creation of the heavens and the earth, Bonhoeffer then turns his attention to the coming of the Jewish Messiah, the one who in himself is reality. In his lectures on Christology, given during the summer of 1933, Bonhoeffer continued to develop his theological anthropology, and the vision of history that arises from the human rejection of God's reality.

B. The lectures on Christology

At the beginning of the lectures, Bonhoeffer engages the question of history by starting his lectures with the Christ who is present today. This was an unusual move in German Protestant theology, which normally began christological reflection with the historical Jesus, looking to establish the historicity of Jesus of Nazareth's earthly life, determining the relation between the Jesus of history and the Christ of faith. This methodological approach privileged history, establishing historical research as the means for evaluating what could be known about Jesus's life, and through this establishing the reliability of the Scriptures. For the German liberal tradition, the Jesus of history, by which was meant the Jesus whose life could be reconstructed through the methods of historical research according to the criteria of *Wissenschaft*, is the only Jesus we have access to; any other is the "Christ of faith," a later invention of Paul and the early church.

Bonhoeffer takes a different approach. By starting with the present Christ, Bonhoeffer resists the German liberal methodological approach to Christology. In doing this, he doesn't eliminate history or its critical importance for creaturely life, doesn't make Christianity a purely transcendent religion and the church an ahistorical community. But he does adopt a methodology that places history under Christology because, as we have seen in our review of *Creation and Fall*, Bonhoeffer is keenly aware of the abstractions of the human heart. Rather than approaching Christology from history to the present, which assumes that history is the method for establishing knowledge of Christ, Bonhoeffer believes that the Christ who is present today is the historical Christ (Bonhoeffer 2009, 310). In other words, we have access to the historical Jesus through the present Christ, not vice versa. It's the present Christ who testifies to his own historical reality through the word and sacraments (Bonhoeffer 2009, 315–322).

Following on from *Creation and Fall*, in the Christology lectures, Bonhoeffer declares the centrality of God over against the human pretense to occupy the center of life, the center of history, the center of reality. He does this through the contrasting characters of the opening pages of his lectures: the logos and the counter logos. For Bonhoeffer, the logos is "the immanent logos of human beings" (Bonhoeffer 2009, 302), while the counter logos is the incarnate Christ, who confronts the human logos in its self-assured mastery of the world. The logos, separated from God and bent to the self, assumes its own autonomy and priority. It claims and consolidates the center through what Bonhoeffer calls the "questions of classification," which is the action of the human logos to assign all phenomena a place in the schema of reality. The two classifying questions that the human logos asks are "First, what is the cause of X? Second, what is the meaning of X?" (Bonhoeffer 2009, 301). Through the classification questions, the logos seeks to "understand a classification of relationships; how does this object X fit into the classification that I already have at hand?" (Bonhoeffer 2009, 301).

In saying this, Bonhoeffer does not denigrate the pursuit of knowledge itself, as this is inherent to our creaturely life. However, when the logos assumes its autonomous centrality, and approaches the world through its immanent frame without the proper reference to God that we were created to enjoy, the logos assumes that reality is what accords with our own assessment and our own projects. If we can describe and discover the truths of the world around us through the human logos, then that makes us lords over reality. As those who define and assign, we also master. And this is how we engage Christ, treating him as a classifiable phenomenon of the immanent. In this, we treat Jesus as the "idealistic founder of a religion," rather than approaching him as the Son of God (Bonhoeffer 2009, 315). In making this move, humanity assigns Jesus his place as an idealist in the classification schema of the logos, viewing him in terms of the relationships of meaning available to the human logos.

But, Bonhoeffer asks, "What happens if it is claimed that the human logos is dead, condemned, superseded?" (Bonhoeffer 2009, 302). In other words, what happens if one appears who claims lordship over the logos? When this happens, the self-referential mastery of the logos is confronted and "the logos sees that its autonomy is being threatened from outside" (Bonhoeffer 2009, 302). In response, the logos moves to shore up its position of mastery by continuing to ask the classification questions of him: "What are you?" "How can you be both God and human?" By asking questions of classification, the logos continues to assert its lordship by operating out of its assumption to be the autonomous determiner of reality.

But the counter logos refuses all efforts of classification and turns the question back on the human logos. Confronted by the counter logos, now, "Human beings are those who must die . . . Here it is no longer possible to fit the Word made flesh into the logos classification system. Here all that remains is the question: 'Who are you?'" (Bonhoeffer 2009, 302). For Bonhoeffer, "Who are you?" is the proper christological question because it is the question that recognizes that Jesus is Lord, and so reveals the human logos in its abstraction, in its centering the world on itself. As Bonhoeffer says, "This is the question asked by a horrified, dethroned human reason, and also the question of faith: Who are you? Are you God's very self?" (Bonhoeffer 2009, 302). When this question is asked, "Every possibility of classification falls short, because the existence of the Logos means the end of my logos. He *is* the Logos. He *is* the counter Word." (Bonhoeffer 2009, 302, italics in original).

In this schema of logos and counter logos, Bonhoeffer asserts the lordship of Christ over against the self-proclaimed lordship of humanity turned in on itself. This confrontation not only redefines humanity, but also redefines history. For Bonhoeffer, the counter logos makes it clear that history properly understood is Christocentric, as Christ is the center of history. This means that we can't understand the true meaning and nature of history through the resources of the human logos, nor through the visible phenomena of historical events. History, in its essence, is not what Guido de Graaf calls "a chaotic flux of arbitrary phenomena" (de Graaf, Kirkpatrick 2016, 125) but is, instead, in Bonhoeffer's words, "the work of God that links promise and fulfillment" (Bonhoeffer 2009, 325). Expounding on this idea, Bonhoeffer says that

> Christ is at the center of history by being both its boundary and its center, that is, history lives between promise and fulfillment. History carries a promise for us, that of becoming God's people, and also the promise of the Messiah . . . The meaning of history is nothing other than the promise of the Messiah (Bonhoeffer 2009, 325).

This history, Christ as the center of history, is hidden history. The phenomena that we see are real, but don't accord with reality. It is abstract because it is divorced from the reality of Christ, the center of history. For Bonhoeffer, abstract history "is struggling [toward] the impossible fulfillment of a degenerate promise. History knows about its messianic destiny, but is defeated by it" (Bonhoeffer 2009, 325). In other words, the logos turned in on itself pursues the fulfillment of history, asserts its own messianic projects, but is a history that cannot achieve its desired ends; history as the abstraction of the logos turned in on itself always ends in defeat.

Christ is the hidden center of history because Christ is not an ideal, not an abstraction, not a vision birthed out of the classifying, mastering human soul. Christ is not a projection of the heart turned in on itself that then must be actualized through the resources of the logos. Instead, Christ is reality, the gift of God's grace to be with and for humanity, even in our abstracting rejection of God. God has embraced the world in Christ, reconciling humanity to himself and so establishing the essence of history. History finds its meaning in Christ, the Messiah of Israel, because in him God's promise is fulfilled. Bonhoeffer writes, "In Christ, the messianic expectation of history is crushed as well as fulfilled. It is crushed because its fulfillment is hidden. It is fulfilled because the Messiah has truly come. The meaning of history is swallowed up in an event that takes place in the deepest desolation of human life, on the cross. History finds its meaning in the humiliation of Christ" (Bonhoeffer 2009, 325).

The reality of history is found at the cross. The cross is no ideal; the cross is no abstraction. The cross is where the messianic projects of the logos turned in on the self are crushed, because the cross is where Adam-in-sin is crushed in the crucified body of the Messiah. Here history, as God's promise and fulfillment, is accomplished. Here reality, though hidden, is revealed. Here history as abstraction is swallowed up so that history can be made real.

3. The church's mission and history

Bonhoeffer's vision of history, idealism, and abstraction are deeply consequential for understanding the church's mission in history. As we move toward our conclusion, I want to draw out how Bonhoeffer's vision of history and abstraction connects with his vision of the church's mission in history.

In the lectures on Christology, Bonhoeffer writes, "The church should be seen as the center of history" (Bonhoeffer 2009, 326). In saying this, Bonhoeffer points to the church's participation in the reality of Christ, who, as we have seen, is the hidden center of history. As the church participates in the reality of Christ becoming real in the world, the church lives as the community at the center of history. This means that dwelling at the center of history is essential to the church's mission, that living at the center must define our vision of the church's vocation of presence in the world.

However, in saying that the church is the center of history, we must be very clear about what this means. We must remember that Christ as the center of history is hidden; Christ doesn't take the places of power, doesn't strive for the visible positions that the world believes are the center of history. To do so would mean that Christ has become an abstracter, an ideologue. Christ's centrality is not visible, because Christ is not an ideal. Christ is the center of true history, of God's hidden messianic history, not of the world's visible ideological history.

If this is what it means for Christ to be the center of history, then it must also be what it means for the church to be the center of history. Too often, this is not how the church has understood her mission in the world. Rather than taking our place at the hidden center of history, the church has sought to occupy the place of those who drive visible history. When the church does this, she becomes the chief of abstracters. The church today is filled with abstraction. So how might Bonhoeffer's theological anthropology and his vision of history help the church better understand our mission in this unstable time, and help us to resist falling into abstraction? To answer this, let's turn to *Life Together* to find there Bonhoeffer's reflections on the church and abstraction.

In *Life Together*, Bonhoeffer writes, "Christian community is not an ideal, but a divine reality" (Bonhoeffer 1996, 35). This sentence places before us the clear contrast of the ideal vs the divine, which is the contrast we have seen in *Creation and Fall* and the Christology lectures. *Life Together* is an exploration of the nature of community and the dangers that threaten Christian community; one of the greatest dangers to the church is the idealization of the church, which makes the community that is called to live according to the reality in Christ itself an abstraction.

People come to church with all kinds of ideals in mind, all kinds of visions of what the church is to be, all kinds of expectations of what church will do for them. The danger with these ideals is that we have no guarantee that they will be in alignment with divine reality. Bonhoeffer writes, "Those who want more than what Christ has established between us do not want Christian community. They are looking for some extraordinary experiences of community that were denied them elsewhere. Such people are bringing confused and tainted desires into the Christian community" (Bonhoeffer 1996, 36). As we have seen, these tainted desires, these self-produced ideals, are the ideals of the logos turned in on the self that separate us from the divine reality. The result, Bonhoeffer writes, is that "On innumerable occasions, a whole Christian community has been shattered because it has lived on the basis of a wishful image" (Bonhoeffer 1996, 35). When the wishful image drives the community, when human ideals shape the church, rather than divine reality, the inevitable result is the destruction of the community.

Idealism and abstraction are clear threats to the life of the church. But I want to suggest that it is also a threat to the church's mission in the world. This is because we too often base our life in the world on our own ideal, failing to live according to the divine reality. We have too often believed that the mission of God necessitates the church exerting power that can shape history toward the ends we believe are from God, but all too often are, in fact, our own ideals. We have confused the church at the center with ecclesial strength. But as we have seen, Christ as the center of reality is hidden. Christ at the center of reality is exemplified in his humiliation on the cross. True history, God's history of promise and fulfillment, swallows up the messianic visions of the logos through the weakness of Christ on the cross, in whom, as Bonhoeffer says in the prison letters, God is pushed out of the world. This doesn't mean that logos history defeats God; rather, it means that God's history is not the abstraction of logos history, and so God doesn't compete with humanity for power over abstraction. Rather, God enacts reality.

This means that church is called to bear "the cross of reality," to borrow a phrase from Gaylon Barker (Barker 2015). We are not the center of logos history; we are the center of Christ's history, the hidden history of God's promise and fulfillment. This doesn't mean that the church is ahistorical, nor that the church is to be disengaged from the world. But it does mean that the church must be clear about our calling to be the center of history. We are to be with the world, we are to be for the world, as those who are against the abstraction of logos idealism. We are to love the world from the center, not competing with the logos on the field of abstract ideals, but loving proclaiming to the world its reconciliation to God that is the essence of history.

4. Conclusion

This essay begins by asking the question, "how can we confess our common faith in Christ in our unstable times?" Bonhoeffer's vision of history and abstraction call us to take our place on the cross of reality, to understand our calling to live at the center of hidden history. Rather than seek the places of power that appear to steer history, we are called instead to serve history, to serve the world, as those who repent of the abstraction of the human logos, turn to reality, and entrust ourselves to the God who is hidden at the cross. In this, I pray that we might follow Dietrich Bonhoeffer, and Edith Stein, in being true witnesses of Christ's Lordship in our time.

Bibliography

Barker, Gaylon. 2015. *The Cross of Reality*. Minneapolis: Fortress Press.

Bonhoeffer, Dietrich. 1996. *Life Together and Psalms: Prayerbook of the Bible. Dietrich Bonhoeffer Works Volume 5*, edited by Geffrey B. Kelly, translated by Daniel W. Bloesch and James H. Burtness. Minneapolis: Fortress Press.

Bonhoeffer, Dietrich. 1997. *Creation and Fall. Dietrich Bonhoeffer Works Volume 3*, edited by John W. de Gruchy, translated by Stephen Bax. Minneapolis: Fortress Press.

Bonhoeffer, Dietrich. 2009. "Lectures in Christology." In *Berlin 1932–1933. Dietrich Bonhoeffer Works Volume 12*, edited by Larry L. Rasmussen, translated by Isabel Best and David Higgins, 299–360. Minneapolis: Fortress Press.

de Graaf, Guido. 2016. "Overcoming Ethical Abstraction: Peaceableness, Responsibility, and the Rejection of Foundationalism in Bonhoeffer and Hauerwas." In *Engaging Bonhoeffer: The Impact and Influence of Bonhoeffer's Life and Thought*, edited by Matthew D. Kirkpatrick, 115–138. Minneapolis: Fortress Press.

5

Between Psychology and Phenomenology

Edith Stein's Philosophical Dilemmas

Leon Miodoński, PhD Hab.
Professor of the University of Wrocław
ORCID: 0000-0001-8525-3813

About the Author

Leon Miodoński – since 2002 Professor of Philosophy at the University of Wrocław, Head of the Department of German Philosophy and Head of the Research on the History of Philosophy in Silesia. Research interests: holistic thinking, German idealism, philosophy in Silesia, reception of German thought in Poland. Publications: over ninety publications; author of four books, editor of five books.

Keywords

Edith Stein, William Stern, person, experimental psychology, phenomenology

Abstract

The essay deals with the first phase of Edith Stein's scientific life: the intellectual conditions in which she grew up and studied in Wrocław. The central issue concerns her attitude towards experimental psychology, as represented by William Stern. In spite of her critique of psychology, Edith Stein takes up the key concept created by Stern, the notion of "person," gives this notion a phenomenological sense and creates an anthropological concept. The essay consists of four parts: "The Jewish context," "Studies at the University of Wrocław," "The problem with experimental psychology," "Subject or person?," and the conclusion.

Introductory remarks

Specialist literature typically distinguishes three periods that characterize Edith Stein's thought: phenomenological, Thomistic and mystical (Chojnacki 2015, 30), with phenomenology laying down the foundations of her philosophizing in general. Researchers, however, have directed little attention to her time as a student at the University of Breslau (present-day Wrocław) (1911–1913). This raises the legitimate question of whether these studies left a significant mark on her thinking and work. Or was this time completely lost? It is worth noting here that Edith Stein studied under the guidance of two eminent professors, William Stern and Richard Hönigswald, both of whom held a prominent place in German philosophy at the time. Hönigswald developed the autonomous current of Neo-Kantianism, while Stern was a world-renowned psychologist.

Another important question arises here: namely, why, despite her earlier enthusiasm for broad humanistic studies, including Germanic studies, history, philosophy, psychology, and pedagogy, Stein nevertheless abandoned Breslau and chose a completely new field of philosophical interest – phenomenology.

The main thesis of this article is then formulated against the backdrop of these two questions: crucial philosophical issues addressed in Edith Stein's later works, including the phenomenological and Thomistic writings, had their origins in the studies in Breslau, with the phenomenological and psychological notion of the "person" and the methodologically grounded approach to the analysis of philosophical issues coming to the fore.

The article consists of four parts. The first part, "The Jewish context," deals with Edith Stein's youthful intellectual search, fascination with German culture, science in general, including philosophy. Part two, "Studies at the University of Breslau," considers the research tendencies – psychology and neo-Kantianism – that characterized Breslau philosophy. Part three, "The problem with experimental psychology," takes a look at her studies under William Stern and Edith Stein's distancing from experimental psychology. In contrast, the fourth part, "Subject or Person?," can be considered crucial on the grounds that the concept of "person," taken from William Stern constitutes the central category of the dissertation, as well as the writings in philosophical anthropology and theological anthropology.

The Jewish context

Contemporary research on Edith Stein's thought emphasizes – and not without reason – the importance of the cultural-religious anchoring of the values and patterns that the future saint brought from her family home, in particular the role of her mother, her efforts to pass on Jewish traditions and to shape in her children an honest and ethical attitude to life. It would be worthwhile at this point to make a comment that perhaps allows us to better understand the mechanism that may have influenced Edith Stein's subsequent life decisions.

As it is, the fundamental problem that Jews have had to confront for centuries is the tragic choice between the need to preserve tradition and at the same time the desire (or necessity) to participate in the life of the region in which they lived. In this respect, Breslau, and the time in which Edith Stein's youthful years fell, was the success of a certain socio-cultural experiment called the Jewish Theological Seminary (Jüdisch-Theologisches Seminar. Fränkelsche Stiftung). It made it possible, within the realities of the social policy of the Prussian State and later of the German Empire, to find a balanced parity between the unifying power of Prussian law and the preservation of the cultural identity of the Jews. As the first institution of its kind in the world, the seminary gave its graduates a comprehensive knowledge of Jewish culture and religion, as well as knowledge of contemporary science and philosophy. Its essential modernizing role was that it made it possible to break out of the previous confessional confinement and cultural self-closure, to educate Jewish intelligentsia and rabbis, and to participate vividly in normal social life (Seidel 2013, 70–80).

The Stein family lived precisely in this cultural space, which the Jewish Theological Seminary had been co-creating since 1854. Edith Stein's mother intuitively found the right balance between her own culture and the real world in which she lived. In the case of her children, on the other hand, things went even further in terms of their acceptance of German culture: Edith Stein's crisis of faith is derived from this process. German culture, including great literature and poetry, monumental philosophy, law and social order were all intellectually attractive factors for any intelligent and eager person.

In Edith Stein's First World War correspondence, especially with Roman Ingarden, one can find more than one place with a strong declaration of cultural identity: "You see, I can no more be in love with Germany than with myself for, after all, I am myself it, that is, a part of it" (Stein 1993, 40); "today my individual life has ceased and all that I am belongs to the state" (Stein 1993, 41).

Studies at the University of Breslau

The very fact that Edith Stein undertook her studies at the University of Breslau is an exemplification of the modernist tendencies outlined above in the milieu of the Breslau Jews. Furthermore, it was evidence of her deep need for education and intellectual development and – what seems important from the point of view of cultural identity – a definite turn towards German culture, a full affirmation of it. Nota bene, in 1911 only exceptional women had the courage and strength to undertake academic studies. And this fact should also be taken into account. Her all too extensive range of interests – German studies, history, philosophy, psychology, pedagogy – also stemmed from her fascination with German culture (Stein 2020, 258–261).

Breslau philosophy – in the time in which Edith Stein studied – inherited two important traditions. On the one hand, Dilthey's hermeneutics (understanding method) and modern worldview research (*Weltanschauung*). Dilthey moved away from an idealist interpretation of the philosophy of history, for which the key meaning was not so much facts as ideas and ordering concepts like perfection or purposiveness, and instead turned towards Burckhard's historical enlightenment. In general, this meant contrasting Hegelian historiosophical speculation with a self-reflexive attitude towards history (Alechnowicz-Skrzypek 2013, 236–239). On the other hand, a prominent place was occupied by the current of experimental psychology, which was initiated by Benno Erdmann and continued by Hermann Ebbinghaus, author of the well-known and highly regarded work *Über das Gedächtnis* (1885). Before taking up his post as professor of philosophy in Breslau, he founded the first laboratory for experimental psychology in Berlin. Berlin was also the scene of a famous dispute with Dilthey over the method of psychology – understanding or experimental (Rodi 2003, 173–183). Ebbinghaus's intellectual experience eloquently illustrates the path taken by many German philosophers of that era – from distancing themselves from speculative concepts to affirming an empirical-scientific interpretation of philosophy (Lück 2009, 51). Through Ebbinghaus's efforts, Breslau was at the forefront of several German universities developing experimental psychology.

Edith Stein found herself at the centre of the dynamic process of the formation of modern philosophy. She had direct contact with two prominent representatives of Breslau academia: with William Stern and Richard Hönigswald.

William Stern was active in two directions. Firstly, he was involved in pioneering research into the developmental psychology of children. In doing so, he was able to improve on the not very precise method of determining children's intellectual performance proposed at the beginning of the century by the French researchers Alfred Binet and Theodore Simon. The method is still used today and is called an intelligence quotient (IQ) (William Stern, *Die psychologischen Methoden der Intelligenzprüfung und deren Anwendung an Schulkindern*, 1912).

Secondly, and most importantly, Stern's idea of "differential psychology" from the beginning of his stay in Breslau – in modern language, this means: personalistically oriented psychology – referring to the person and the specificity of his formation. The concept was formulated as the antithesis of the deterministic view that resulted from the state of naturalistic research at the end of the 19th century (*Die Differentielle Psychologie in ihren methodischen Grundlagen*, 1900). Individual differences can be identified in three areas: the differentiation of the individual as such, the differentiation of the conditions, and what the differentiations reveal (Stern 1921, 4). Further research, observation and analysis led to the mature concept first articulated in the first volume *Person und Sache* (1906), one of the most important sources of modern personalism.

Richard Hönigswald, on the other hand, represented the neo-Kantian current, with his interest in an exceptionally broad spectrum of philosophical issues: theory of cognition, psychology of thought, pedagogy, philosophy of politics, philosophy of language, and systematics of philosophy. It was his intention that the above-mentioned areas should not form a whole as elements of one large philosophical system, as was the case in the German tradition, but that they should complement each other on a correlative basis. Owing to the lack of a crucial concept that would systemize the considerations, the problems and the search for appropriate interpretative spaces came to the fore (Zeidler 1995, 75–138). In this sense, the question of the meaning of cognition, the transcendental point of reference, could not be reduced to classical neo-Kantian approaches, since for Hönigswald the psychological and empirical perspective was equally important. While referring to Kant, he no longer focused on contemporary neo-Kantianism, rather produced his own Breslau version of neo-Kantianism (Kapferer 2001, 21). At the same time – once Edith Stein had left Breslau – Hönigswald strongly distanced himself from phenomenology (Orth 1996, 133–146).

Influenced by such intellectual tendencies, the then twenty-year-old Edith Stein began her studies (Oost 2004, 203–228). In her diaries we find much information that allows us to better understand the intellectual atmosphere of the time. We can see it in the way she participated in student self-education groups (the Pedagogical Group), in the books she read, and in the dilemmas she had about student life. Among various pieces of information, there is also one on psychology. Of interest for us is a brief comment of hers: "This might have been a portent since the four semesters I studied in Breslau found me occupied principally with psychology" (Stein 1986, 186). At the same time, the evaluation of the psychology course taught by Stern, i.e. experimental psychology, was challenging: "Stern's presentation was elementary and easily understood; I sat there as though attending a pleasant social gathering and was somewhat disappointed" (Stein 1986, 186). Stein recognized the fundamental weaknesses of this new field of knowledge – psychology did not yet have a fully developed research method or a structure of adequate concepts. "All my study of psychology had persuaded me that this science was still in its infancy; it still lacked clear basic concepts; furthermore, there was no one who could establish such an essential foundation" (Stein 186, 222).

At the same time, she studied philosophy under Hönigswald and had the opportunity to compare the two fields of knowledge:

> Hönigswald's class was then all the more demanding. His penetrating insight and his rigorous thought process fascinated me. Avowedly, his was the critical philosophy of Kant; indeed, he is today one of the few who have remained loyal to this approach. One had to be familiar with the conceptual thinking apparatus of Kantianism to follow his presentation. The young persons in his seminars were enticed into engaging in dialectical skirmishes against such finely-honed weapons. Anyone who tried to introduce the fruit of an idea which had not ripened on Hönigswald's acre was reduced to silence by his superior dialectic and biting irony, but, at heart, was rarely vanquished ... Nevertheless, he afforded us excellent training in logical thinking; and at the time that sufficed to make me happy (Stein 1986, 186).

Edith Stein intuitively sensed the essential difference between the descriptive character of psychology and the conceptual character of philosophy. Yet, in no way was she attracted to the way of philosophizing represented by Hönigswald. Arguably, Stein needed a philosophy that was more connected to life, to the direct experience of human beings – a philosophy that would not be pure speculation, but would offer the hope of discovering the truth. By chance, she decided that when preparing a paper for Stern's seminar on the psychology of thought, she noticed that many of the studies she was using referred to Husserl's *Logische Untersuchungen*. By coincidence, she was also in close contact with Dr Georg Moskiewicz, a co-participant in the Pedagogical Group, who was preparing his habilitation in experimental psychology and had a semester of study under Husserl at Göttingen. Moskiewicz suggested to Stein that she read the second volume of Husserl's *Logische Untersuchungen*. "'Leave all that stuff aside,' he said, 'and just read this; after all, it's where all the others got their ideas.' He handed me a thick book" (Stein 1986, 218). From this moment onwards, one can speak of a re-evaluation of Edith Stein's philosophical aspirations. Nothing had value but phenomenology; she was convinced that "Husserl was *the* philosopher of our age" (Stein 1986, 219). Her fascination with phenomenology was the primary reason for suspending her psychology studies and leaving Breslau.

> [W]hat I had learned about phenomenology, so far, fascinated me tremendously because it consisted precisely of such a labor of clarification and because, here, one forged one's own mental tools for the task at hand (Stein 1986, 222).

The problem with experimental psychology

The opinion on psychology and on her studies in Breslau, quoted above, dates from the early 1930s, when Edith Stein was preparing her autobiographical volume, *Life in a Jewish Family*, completed in 1933. Her attitude to psychology was retrospective and could not contain the emotional charge that had accompanied the young student twenty years earlier. Rather, the reflections contained in the autobiographical volume should be seen in the perspective of the life path she had undergone – an intellectual transformation from an atheistic attitude to an affirmation of religion and a deep theological study of Christian thought in general and the thought of St. Thomas Aquinas in particular. In this configuration, the question of what is important, what is the essence of life and what constitutes the path to truth, looks very different from the point of view of a beginner student just seeking her place in the world.

The prospect of writing a dissertation under William Stern should be considered a normal course of action. The bulk of her time was occupied by psychological issues – lectures, exercises, seminars, self-education circles – while she should have consistently pursued a PhD. This is in fact what happened. Stern turned out to be a very understanding professor, and tried to meet the student's interests while at the same time situating the dissertation in an area that he himself had dealt with with great success. Therefore, he proposed the topic Stein was working on, preparing a paper on the psychology of thought for the seminar. Two points are worth noting. Firstly, some inspiration to take up the psychology of thought was probably provided by Hönigswald's lectures on exactly the same topic (Stein 1986, 219). It can be inferred that she was significantly influenced by her professors. Secondly, the work on this paper allowed her to become acquainted with the extensive phenomenological literature in the psychology of thought (Stein 1986, 217–218). By then it was already clear that she was attracted to the phenomenological approach more than to the psychological one. Nevertheless, Stern proposed the topic for her doctoral dissertation: "the development of the thought process in children . . . based on . . . experimental interrogation," and Stein accepted it without enthusiasm (Stein 1986, 221).

Even at that time, in 1913, the vision of a doctoral dissertation in developmental psychology aroused a kind of resistance, which was probably fuelled by conversations with more scientifically advanced friends, such as Georg Moskiewicz (Stein 1986, 218). That is probably why Husserl's planned one-semester stay at the University of Göttingen offered Stein the hope of resolving this dilemma. The fact that the question of a doctorate in psychology was still open was mentioned by Edith Stein in her autobiographical notes (Stein 1986, 268–269). Indeed, in Göttingen, in addition to her studies with Husserl, she came into contact with the Institute of Psychology, where both experimental method in an anti-phenomenological spirit (Georg Elias Müller) and the practice of psychology on a phenomenological basis (David Katz) were relied upon (Stein 1986, 265). In addition – and this may be puzzling – there were close contacts with Leonard Nelson representing a strand of philosophy – ambivalent to Husserl – that referred to neo-Kantianism and the thought of Fries. Nelson dealt with, among other things, what was troubling Edith Stein at the time, namely the theory of cognition. In this respect, he represented a position critical of the dominant currents (Noras 2012, 377–392). All these activities testify to Stein's permanent search for a path of further intellectual development.

After a semester in Göttingen, Edith Stein returned to Breslau, and wrote "a report of this semester's developments," which she handed over to Stern (Stein 1986, 268). Stern, in turn, invited her to "the most intimate circle of his students" and even involved her in the organization of "an important pedagogic conference and a psychological exhibition" (Stein 1986, 272). But her stay in Göttingen in no way brought her closer to the realization of her previously planned doctorate in psychology. It would probably have been a largely descriptive dissertation, if it had been written, concerning a research area and method not suited to her creative personality.

On the other hand, the phenomenological method she mastered through her studies with Husserl gave her the sense of being a true philosopher, and gave her the courage to face difficult problems. The subject she chose, and which Husserl accepted, was particularly ambitious, since it was about how the objective world is known in intersubjective experience. Husserl – with reference to Theodor Lipps – referred to this as the problem of "empathy" (*Einfühlung*), but failed to explain the details. Stein recognized this research "lacuna" and decided to take up the challenge (Stein 1986, 269). The problem of empathy combined two perspectives she valued: the phenomenological and the psychological, together creating a new cognitive quality (see Chojnacki 2015, 21–25; Zyzak 2015, 167–170).

Psychology at the beginning of the twentieth century developed in a multifaceted way. The academic status was assigned to experimental psychology, headed by Wilhelm Wundt, the creator of the first psychological laboratory (Lück 2009, 58–65). Psychology developed as one of the methods of interpretation in humanistic research. The psychological interpretation of history and the concept of "understanding psychology" was developed by Wilhelm Dilthey (Eckardt 2010, 91–97). Theodor Lipps, one of the main representatives of psychologism, combined the traditions of German idealism with psychologically informed inner experience. Max Dessoir focused on psychological aesthetics (Eckardt 2010, 32). Psychology was alluded to by phenomenologists. Max Scheller, for example, developed the transcendental and psychological method in parallel. This whole context forms the basis of Stein's doctoral dissertation *On the Problem of Empathy*.

Gradually, Edith Stein's attitude towards William Stern's psychology had somewhat changed, if seen in a broader perspective – as a question about the adequacy of psychological description and the heuristic character of psychology on the way to the knowledge of the truth about human beings. It is worth noting the lecture series "*Der Aufbau der menschlichen Person. Vorlesung zum philosophischen Anthropologie*" ("*The Structure of the Human Person: Lectures on Philosophical Anthropology*"), which was written in the winter semester of 1932/1933, at the same time as the autobiography was completed. One important place was found there to find the right balance between Stern's psychology and Stein's phenomenology. The problem lies in the possibility of conceptually defining individuality, the "individual human being" (a concept inspired by Thomistic thought). According to Edith Stein, cognition as the grasping of objects in a notion and the generality of notions lead to a situation in which only an approximate definition of individuality will be possible. And at this point there is a direct reference to Stern: "This concept underlies the psychographic schema that was developed in the school of William Stern" (Stein 2015, 74).

Stein drew attention to an important fact, namely that a disharmony arises between the laws that govern the material world and the methods of studying these laws and the spiritual world, the "individual human being," which cannot be reduced to purely quantitative factors. Identifying as many of the characteristics of the individual under study as possible enables only a rough characterization, but does not enable a full understanding of the individual in a complex psycho-physical structure (Stein 2015, 74–75). There is no doubt that experimental psychology is a science. Such a term appears in Stein's writings many times (e.g. Stein 2015, 64). But with a formal-naturalistic and descriptive approach, it is impossible to grasp what is most important – the mental states of the human being, the structure of the soul, which ultimately influence the motives of human action and define what is unique and unrepeatable.

Slightly earlier, in the *Jahrbuch für Philosophie und Phänomenologische Forschung* (*Yearbook for Philosophy and Phenomenological Research*) (1922, no. 5), Stein published the essay *Über die Möglichkeit einer Deduktion der psychischen Kategorien aus der Idee einer exakten Psychologie* (*On the Possibility of a Deduction of the Psychic Categories from the Idea of an Exact Psychology*) (Stein 2010, 87–90), in which – in the phenomenological spirit – she defined psychology in the strict sense of the word "as the science of the psyche and its actual states, as the science of pure consciousness" (Stein 2010, 87–90). Most important, however, was the definition of psychology as a science based on laws analogous to those governing the natural sciences. In this sense, psychology would be the science *par excellence*, the science relating to the human being. It would be, in Stein's words, "a practical knowledge of man, a history of individual psychic events on the basis of universal laws and data derived from experience" (Stein 2010, 88).

The solution to the problem of empathy required the mastery of a phenomenological method with which to grapple with psychological issues, one of the dominant currents of thought at the time. In brief, the method used by Stein was based on three rules. One was to take "things themselves" as the starting point, that is, to reject everything that seems secondary to things (theories, descriptions, suppositions, etc.) and to aim directly at things themselves. Another principle was to "direct the gaze to the essence" relying only on direct inspection. The notion of looking at things did not mean only, a narrow sensuous empirical sense, but a looking at relating both to the here and now of things and to the properties that constitute the essence of things. The third principle concerned "spiritual viewing" of an intuitive nature as a component of any elementary experience (Stein 2015, 84–85). Edith Stein, like Husserl, focused on the intentional act as the condition for interpersonal cognition of others, as well as the basis for empathic knowledge of the world.

Phenomenological studies and the doctoral thesis consequently led to a broader study of psychology and to the sublimation of this issue in the further development of Edith Stein's thought. It can therefore be said that the type of psychology practised in Breslau became the starting point for a better, phenomenological understanding of psychology and the emergence somewhat later of an original conception of philosophical anthropology, already in a purely Christian spirit, as exemplified by the lectures on philosophical anthropology in Münster (1932/1933).

There is another important aspect that directly connects Stern and Stein – the attitude towards psychoanalysis. Stern clearly, as a university professor and experimentalist, stood in opposition to the non-academic and "non-scientific," non-experimental, methods that psychoanalysis had developed. He criticized both the "fantasies of psychoanalysts" (Stern 1935, 453) and its main representatives Sigmund Freud and Karl Gustav Jung (Stern 1935, 49, 427). Edith Stein adopted this attitude and invariably remained in the position of academic psychology. Significant in this context is an excerpt from the *Lecture in Philosophical Anthropology – The Image Derived from Depth Psychology and Its Impact* (Stein 2015, 49–52). Stein defended the objective character of psychology and, consequently, the objective sense of "cultural creativity," "the spiritual unity of humanity," and "personal unity" (Stein 2015, 50). Psychoanalysis enters into spaces that cannot be grasped in the form of conceptual knowledge: drives, that is, "the power hidden in the depths of the soul that, as an insurmountable power, determines life" (Stein 2015, 51). *Lecture in Philosophical Anthropology*, in contrast to the psychoanalytic approach, has the character of a positive philosophy of human beings – with all the complexity of anthropological description – being soteriologically oriented: "The image of man in the circle of depth psychology is that of fallen man, also viewed statically and ahistorically: his past and his future possibilities and the fact of redemption remain unaccounted for" (Stein 2015, 61). Stern, a practising Jew, and Stein, a Jewish-Catholic, shared the same belief in the human being and anthropological orientation, expressed by the fundamental category of "person."

Subject or person?

William Stern, as noted at the beginning, was concurrently conducting empirical research on the developmental psychology of children and adolescents and working on the project *Person und Sache. System der philosophischen Weltanschauung* (*Person and Thing: System of the Philosophical Worldview*), considered a general philosophy of humanity. When Edith Stein was studying in Breslau, Stern had already published the first volume entitled *Ableitung und Grundlehre* (*Derivation and Fundamental Doctrine*) (1906) and was preparing the second volume, which appeared in 1918 and was entitled *Die menschliche Persönlichkeit* (*The Human Personality*). The third volume was published in 1924 under the title *Wertphilosophie* (*Philosophy of Value*). The original plan was for the whole to take the form of six volumes. In contrast, the extensive treatise *Allgemeine Psychologie auf personalistischer Grundlage* (*General Psychology on a Personalist Basis*) (1935) was an accomplishment summarizing many years of scientific work.

Stern's concept deserves special attention for two reasons. Firstly, it was the first systematic interpretation of personalism, inspiring the reformulation of modern philosophy in an anthropological-scientific direction. Secondly, Stern replaced the abstract notion of subject, commonly used in philosophy, with the notion of person. This seemingly insignificant semantic shift essentially meant a completely new way of understanding the human being, above all in his changing experience of himself, in relation to the world in general, including social relations, historical rootedness, ideological conditions, embeddedness in the world of values, and so on. In this sense, the contradiction between classical subjectivity (to some extent rational and to some extent speculative) and the new conceptualization of the person as grasped in a "system of philosophical worldview" – as the main title puts it – was sharply delineated.

Stern's use of the term "worldview" (*Weltanschauung*) referred to its primary origins in German idealism, particularly Kant, who first used it in the sense of the mind's ability to apprehend the infinite in holistic terms. Similar concepts can be found in Schelling, Humboldt, Schleiermacher. Stern was particularly close to the circulating accounts of the worldview in the various strands of late nineteenth- and early twentieth-century psychology, especially in Fechner and Wundt (Thomé 2010, 453–456). He became acquainted with Dilthey's conception of worldview much later.

The notion of "person" was defined by Stern in his critical personalism as follows – "such an existent thing which, despite the multiplicity of its parts, constitutes a real, specific and intrinsically valuable unity, and as such, despite the multiplicity of its partial functions, is characterized by its own purposive activity" (Stern 1906, 16; Stern 1918, 4–5). The counterpoint to a person would be a thing, which is also "something existing," but in a completely different way – "consisting of many parts, it does not form a real, peculiar and intrinsic unity . . . and does not realize a unified purposive activity of its own" (Stern 1906, 16; Stern 1918, 5).

The juxtaposition of person and thing fully realizes the value of the person as well as the fallacy of the anthropological assumption on which earlier philosophy was based, namely the division into soul and body. According to Stern, the order should have been reversed. A certain holistic structure should have been taken as the starting point: "a uniformly whole, vital personality, which retains its unity in all its innumerable purposive relations with the external world, as well as in the full manifestation of its inner experiences" (Stern 1918, 4). The division into spiritual and corporeal elements would be secondary, stemming from the essence of the person.

Some scholars are inclined to see a structural similarity between Stern and Husserl founded on the common goal that both thinkers assumed, namely "to provide a conceptual basis for the scientific investigation of personal entities" (Lehmann-Muriithi et al. 2016, 216–217), as well as on the so-called "understanding introception" (Lehmann-Muriithi et al. 2016, 218). If Stern recognized the necessity of a method resembling phenomenology, at the same time Husserl recognized the necessity of a personalistic approach as a condition for empathy in relation to another subject. In turn, the understanding psychology, which Stern developed later, would be linked to the Diltheyan conception of experiencing the world in inner experience, which is fundamentally different from scientific description, as Husserl also pointed out. In this sense, the circle of Stern's, Husserl's and Dilthey's thought closes in "the pursuit to grasp the meaning of human being through the study of intentional orientation" (Lehmann-Muriithi et al. 2016, 220). In this context, Edith Stein would be an intermediate link between Stern and Husserl (Lehmann-Muriithi et al. 2016, 217). It is difficult to agree with this type of argumentation. Stein studied Dilthey in depth, whose thought had a significant influence on the conceptualization of the category of empathy and the formation of her doctorate. On many points she agreed with his considerations, but she often remained sceptical and formulated her own stance (Stein 2014, 86–87, 103–105). This area of research was not related to Stern and her studies in Breslau, but to phenomenological studies, primarily Scheler's writings (Stein 1986, 397). Dilthey disappeared from Stein's intellectual horizon rather quickly, namely already in the early 1920s after his conversion to Catholicism, and there is virtually no mention of him.

However, as far as Stern himself is concerned, it is equally difficult to agree that his personalism – with certain similarities to some theoretical solutions – would tend towards phenomenology and hermeneutics. Stern did not modify his concept in substance, but rather painstakingly pursued a preconceived plan, taking into account new interpretations that emerged in contemporary philosophy and psychology. He tried to accommodate them to his system by complementing the structure of experimental psychology he had developed in the three volumes *Person und Sache* – so there are references to Dilthey, Heidegger, Husserl, Jung and many others. But for Stern, it was evidence of the important place psychology occupied in the modern world, how widely accepted its scientific status was. As for the phenomenological work and Husserl himself, their significant role was, Stern argued, that they "also influenced experimental psychological work" (Stern 1935, 368).

If, for example, one considers the definition of person from the *Allgemeine Psychologie auf personalistischer Grundlage*, it is easy to see that, in essence, this formulation does not differ from those quoted above in volumes I and II of *Person und Sache*: "The person is an individual, peculiar whole, acting purposefully, self-centred and open to the world, living, understanding and experiencing" (Stern 1935, 98). Although the last words may suggest Dilthey's understanding and experiencing the world, Stern's point is rather that the determinant of the person is "living" ("existence"), not experiencing. One lives, but not always in full consciousness. For experiencing, consciousness would be necessary (Stern 1935, 99). In the definition quoted, only better wording is used, fitting for the era. Already in the second volume of *Person und Sache* – about 1918 – the notion of "understanding" and "experiencing the world" (Erleben) correlated with the notion of "consciousness" and was within a clearly delineated idealist tradition: Leibniz, Kant, Schelling, von Hartmann (Stern 1918, 223–241). On the other hand, in this context there was an opportunity for a critique of contemporary psychoanalysis based on the "unconscious" (Unbewussten) (Stern 1918, 251–253).

Edith Stein was familiar with Stern's works including *Person und Sache*. She mentions this in her autobiography, but it is not clear whether she was thoroughly acquainted with their contents (Stein 1986, 197). Instead, she mentioned that there were often disputes about his views, vigorously discussed in seminars. She also revealed that the most common argument was "a very decided and resounding 'No!'" Interestingly, Stern gave his students the right to their own opinion and this did not in any way change his benevolent attitude towards them, but at the same time he stubbornly stayed with his position (Stein 1986, 197). Perhaps the whole problem was rooted in a misunderstanding of the complexity of the issues. Edith Stein's main focus was on a critique of experimental psychology and its empirical research tools, and she probably did not take philosophical considerations into account (Piecuch 2013, 214). At the time, only the second volume of *Person und Sache* was being written. Perhaps certain issues were discussed in seminars.

If, therefore, we are looking for elements linking Edith Stein and William Stern, or, in other words, for the inspiration of thought that the Breslau studies may have brought, it was undoubtedly Stern's notion of the "person." It appears as early as in the doctoral dissertation *Zum Problem der Einfühlung* (translated as *On the Problem of Empathy*). Although the classical, phenomenologically tinged "Subjekt" is still frequently used in this work – for the most part, however, the notion of "Person" predominates. The situation is similar in the *Beiträge zur philosophischen Begründung der Psychologie und der Geisteswissenschaften* (*Contributions to the Philosophical Foundation of Psychology and the Human Sciences*), which constitute volume 6 of *Edith Stein's Gesamtausgane*. The situation changes dramatically in *Vorlesung zur philosophischen Anthropologie* (*Lectures on Philosophical Anthropology*), where, apart from a few occasional instances of the use of the term "Subjekt," the technical term for human being is "person," as in *Theological Anthropology* and the lecture collection *Die Frau. Fragestellungen und Reflexionen* (translated as *Essays on Woman*).

The fundamental difference in the understanding of the person between Stern and Stein can be put down to the philosophical interpretation on which the understanding of the human being in both conceptions was based. Stern was starting from the tradition of German idealism – Kant, Hegel, Schelling – with the formula "the True is the whole" (Hegel 1977, 11). For all the peculiarity and distinctiveness of psychology as a field that studies the "person," it is possible to delineate a certain higher level that unifies all possible perspectives – philosophy of humanity, anthropology. Stein, on the other hand, started from the experience of the "person" in the phenomenological sense. Through the phenomenological method, her philosophy of humanity sublimated itself, which, in a philosophical sense, opened her up to the new spiritual experiences that the next stage of her intellectual development brought. In this context, the term "person" already meant "to be a free and spiritual being" (Stein 2015, 8). The concept of "person" thus acquired a broad multidimensional definition, as a living being with a soul and spirit, as an individual, as a cultural being, and above all as a being in search of God (Chojnacki 2015, 42–48).

Summary

From the perspective of Edith Stein's life as a whole, it can be seen that the experience she gained with her professors, William Stern and Richard Hönigswald, contributed immensely to her intellectual independence. Although her studies in Breslau lasted only four semesters, this relatively short but intensive period of work allowed her to build a solid substantive and methodological foundation for her future scholarly work.

Edith Stein became thoroughly familiar with the precise philosophical terminology developed by the Breslau school of neo-Kantianism, became familiar with the subject matter of fundamental philosophical and naturalistic issues, learned to analyze philosophical problems logically and to build clear and adequate argumentative structures based on scientific premises. She mastered the language of philosophical expression characterized by precision, clarity and depth of analysis. In confrontation with experimental psychology, the basic range of her anthropological interests took shape. Her studies in Breslau also allowed her to form an autonomous intellectual attitude, aware of her value, striving for her goal, and defending her position without compromises.

Bibliography

Alechnowicz-Skrzypek, Iwona. 2013. "Philosophy and psychology." In *Commemorative Book for the 200th Anniversary of the Establishment of the State University in Wrocław Volume 2*. Universitas litterarum Wratislaviensis 1811–1945, edited by Jan Harasimowicz, 235–249. Wrocław: Wydawnictwo Uniwersytetu Wrocławskiego.

Chojnacki, Grzegorz. 2015. *Relacyjność osoby Ludzkiej: Studium antropologiczno-teologiczne pism Edyty Stein (Teresy Benedykty od Krzyża)*. Poznań: Pallottinum.

Eckardt, Georg. 2010. *Kernprobleme in der Geschichte der Psychologie*. Wiesbaden: VS Verlag für Sozialwissenschaften.

Hegel, Georg Wilhelm Friedrich. 1963. *Fenomenologia ducha Volume 1*, translated by Adam Landman. Warszawa: Państwowe Wydawnictwo Naukowe.

Hegel, Georg Wilhelm Friedrich. 1977. *Phenomenology of Spirit*, translated by A.V. Miller. Oxford: Oxford University Press.

Kapferer, Norbert. 2001. *Die Nazifizierung der Philosophie an der Universität Breslau 1933–1945*. Münster; Hamburg; Berlin; London: Lit Verlag.

Lehmann-Muriithi, Kolja, Carolina de Resende, Damas Cardoso, James T. Lamiell. 2016. "Understanding Human Being Within the Framework of William Stern's Critical Personalism: Teleology, Holism, and Valuation." In *Psychology as the Science of Human Being: The Yokohama Manifesto*, edited by Jaan Valsiner, Giuseppina Marsico, Nandita Chaudhary, Tatsuya Sato, Virginia Dazzani. [Annals of Theoretical Psychology 13] Heidelberg; New York; Dordrecht; London: Springer.

Lück, Helmut E. 2009. *Geschichte der Psychologie: Strömungen, Schulen, Entwicklungen*, 4. Aufl. Stuttgart: Verlag W. Kohlhammer.

Noras, Andrzej J. 2012. *Historia neokantyzmu*. Katowice: Wydawnictwo Uniwersytetu Śląskiego.

Oost, Katharina. 2004. "William Stern und Edith Stein." W *Edith Stein Jahrbuch* 10 (2004): 203–228.

Orth, Ernst Wolfgang. 1996. "Phänomenologische Motive im Neukantianismus Richard Hönigswalds." W *Studien zur Philosophie Richard Hönigswalds*, edited by Ernst Wolfgang Orth, Dariusz Aleksandrowicz, 133–146. Würzburg: Königshausen & Neumann.

Piecuch, Joachim. 2013. "Edyta Stein i Wrocław." In *Filozofia we Wrocławiu. Dzieje – postacie – problemy Volume 1*, edited by Leon Miodoński, 201–217. Wrocław: Oficyna Wydawnicza Arboretum.

Seidel, Esther. 2013. "Zacharias Frankel und das Jüdisch-Theologische Seminar." In *Zacharias Frankel: Und das Jüdisch-Theologische Seminar: And the Jewish-Theological Seminary*, edited by Hermann Simon, 70–80. Berlin: Hentrich & Hentrich.

Stein, Edith. 1964. *On the Problem of Empathy*, translated by Waltraut Stein. The Hague: Springer Science.

Stein, Edith. 1986. *Life in a Jewish Family: An Autobiography, 1891–1916. The Collected Works of Edith Stein Volume 1*, translated by Josephine Koeppel. Washington, DC: ICS Publications.

Stein, Edith. 1993. *Self-Portrait in Letters, 1916–1942. The Collected Works of Edith Stein Volume 5*, translated by Josephine Koeppel. Washington: ICS Publications.

Stein, Edith. 2010. *Beiträge zur philosophischen Begründung der Psychologie und der Geisteswissenschaften. Edith Stein Gesamtausgabe Volume 6*, edited by Beate Beckmann-Zöller. Freiburg; Basel; Wien: Herder.

Stein, Edith. 2020. *Neuaufgefundene Texte und Übersetzungen VII: Texte zu Philosophie, Politik, Pädagogik: Texte zu Philosophie, Politik, Pädagogik; Übersetzungen: Bonaventura, Karmel-Geschichte: "Judenfrage": Neu aufgefundene Briefe und Dokumente. Edith Stein Gesamtausgabe Volume 28*, edited by Beate Beckmann-Zöller, Ulrich Dobhan, Hanna-Barbara Gerl-Falkovitz. Freiburg; Basel; Wien: Herder.

Stein, Edyta / Teresa Benedykta od Krzyża. 2003. *Autoportret z listów III. Listy do Romana Ingardena*, edited by Hanna Barbara Gerl-Falkovitz, translated by Małgorzata Klentak-Zabłocka, Andrzej Wajs. Kraków: Wydawnictwo Karmelitów Bosych.

Stein, Edyta / Teresa Benedykta od Krzyża. 2014. *O zagadnieniu wczucia. Edyta Stein. Dzieła Volume 5*, edited by Maria Antonina Sondermann, translated by Danuta Gierulanka, Jerzy F. Gierula. Kraków: Wydawnictwo Karmelitów Bosych.

Stein, Edyta / Teresa Benedykta od Krzyża. 2015. *Budowa osoby ludzkiej: Wykłady z antropologii filozoficznej. Edyta Stein. Dzieła Volume 14*, edited by Beate Beckmann-Zöller, translated by Grzegorz Sowinski. Kraków: Wydawnictwo Karmelitów Bosych.

Stein, Edyta / Teresa Benedykta od Krzyża. 2021. *Dzieje pewnej rodziny żydowskiej oraz inne zapiski autobiograficzne. Edyta Stein. Dzieła Volume 1*, edited by Maria Amata Neyer, translated by Immakulata J. Adamska. Kraków: Wydawnictwo Karmelitów Bosych.

Stern, William. 1906. *Person und Sache: System der philosophischen Weltanschauung Volume 1, Ableitung und Grundlehre*. Leipzig: Barth.

Stern, William. 1918. *Person und Sache: System der philosophischen Weltanschauung Volume 2, Die menschliche Persönlichkeit*. Leipzig: Barth.

Stern, William. 1921. *Die Differentielle Psychologie in ihren methodischen Grundlagen Volume 3*. Leipzig: Barth.

Stern, William. 1935. *Allgemeine Psychologie auf personalistischer Grundlage*. Haag: Martinus Nijhoff.

Thomé, Horst. "Weltanschauung." 2010. In *Historisches Wörterbuch der Philosophie*, edited by Joachim Ritter Volume 12, 453–460. Basel: Schwabe.

Zeidler, Kurt Walter. 1995. *Kritische Dialektik und Transzendentalontologie: Der Ausgang des Neukantianismus und die post-neukantianische Systematik R. Hönigswalds*, W. Cramers, B. Bauchs, H. Wagners, R. Reiningers und E. Heintels. Bonn: Bouvier Verlag.

Zyzak, Wojciech. 2015. "Edyta Stein jako fenomenolog." 2015. *W Edyta Stein: Fenomenologia Getyńsko-Manachijska: Aanalizy*, edited by Jerzy Machnacz, Krzysztof Serafin, 161–174. Wrocław: Papieski Wydział Teologiczny.

6

Analogia Liberationis

Divine and Human Freedom in Bonhoeffer's Theology

Philip G. Ziegler, PhD
Professor of University of Aberdeen, Scotland
ORCID: 0000-0003-0389-986X

About the Author

Philip G. Ziegler is Professor of Christian Dogmatics at the University of Aberdeen. His research concerns modern Christian theology generally and the contemporary theological legacies of Karl Barth and Dietrich Bonhoeffer in particular. Among his published writings are *Doing Theology When God is Forgotten: The Theological Achievement of Wolf Krötke* (2006) and *Militant Grace: The Apocalyptic Turn and the Future of Theology* (2018). He is editor of *The Edinburgh Critical History of Twentieth-Century Christian Theology* (2022), and co-editor, with Michael Mawson, of both *The Oxford Handbook of Dietrich Bonhoeffer* (2019), and *Christ, Church and World: New Studies in Bonhoeffer's Theology and Ethics* (2016).

Keywords

Freedom, analogy, Being-for-others, theological anthropology, Christology, Dietrich Bonhoeffer

Abstract

Bonhoeffer offers us a thoroughly theological account of freedom, and this in two senses. First, discursively, he treats of freedom in a consistently theological – rather than a philosophical, sociological, or political – register. Freedom is for him a theme properly at home in *theological* anthropology. But this is so, second and more fundamentally, because Bonhoeffer understands the quality and significance of human freedom to be determined by the reality-making force of God's saving advent in Jesus Christ. Bonhoeffer's account of human freedom involves an *analogia liberationis* established and elaborated christologically in virtue of the Chalcedonian dogma that Christ as God incarnate is "the truly human one" (ἄνθρωπον ἀληθῶς). In this, the concrete form of Christ's own freedom as a *being-for-others* proves decisive. Doing justice to all this is, I suggest, the *sine qua non* of any and all subsequent discussion of freedom in relation to Bonhoeffer's life and thought.

1. Introduction and exposition

There are many possible entrées into the exploration of freedom as a theme in Bonhoeffer's life and legacy. Not the least of these is Bonhoeffer's famous prison meditation *Stations on the Road to Freedom* – a searching and self-reflective dialogue, akin perhaps to the poetry of biblical wisdom, which finally hopes for the apotheosis of human freedom in the death of its disciplined, active, and suffering author (see Henkys 1986, 512–514; Hampe 1977, 70–73; Ulrich 2009, 147–174). However, too-concentrated an interest in this spellbinding introspective text and its dramatic existential setting may keep us from consideration of the Christian doctrine which decisively underpins it. Bonhoeffer rightly fascinates us with his personal integrity, ethical intensity, and profound ecclesial and humane commitment. I would like to suggest that we may and must also acknowledge his *dogmatic acuity* and learn from it. To attempt to do just this in relation to the theme of freedom is the task of this short paper.

In the summer of 1932, Bonhoeffer was a twenty-six-year-old lecturer offering courses on ethics and ecclesiology at the University of Berlin. His last lecture of the semester on the doctrine of the church finished with this claim: "The church can come [through] difficulties only when it sees to it that it stands or falls with the word of *Christus praesens* as its Lord alone" (DBWE 11, 333). The very next morning on Sunday 24 July he preached a service marking the end of the semester at the Trinity church in the Friedrichstadt district. His text – which he announced to be "perhaps the most revolutionary passage in the whole New Testament" – was John 8:32: "You shall know the truth, and the truth will set you free" (DBWE 11, 465 [465–472]). In the pulpit that morning Bonhoeffer exercised just the kind of utter reliance upon the word of the present Christ to which he had called his students the day before. His sermon culminated with this extraordinary claim:

> The human being who loves because [he] has been made free by God's truth is the most revolutionary human being on earth. He is the overturning of all values; he is the explosive material in human society; he is the most dangerous human being, [because] he is ready at any time to let the light of truth fall upon [people] – and that for the sake of love (DBWE 11, 471–472).

This reality of a free human person, liberated, recruited, and empowered as a fifth columnist for the kingdom of God – an arresting vision, to be sure – is a consequence of the event of being "made free by God's truth." Such human freedom owes itself to an event of divine truth understood as "something over which we have no power," something which befalls us, which "*happens*," the advent of the very "power" of "the living God himself and his word, wherever it finds its mark," that is, it owes itself to saving grace (DBWE 11, 468–469). Bonhoeffer identifies this gracious event concretely with Jesus Christ *crucified* in whom divine truth "confronts us in a strange form," *sub contrario*: God's liberating truth suffers our contradiction of it precisely because it seeks and finds those who live and act and are set against it (DBWE 11, 469). When evangelical truth finds us, we are, in Bonhoeffer's view, self-serving in the strong sense of being tyrannically "shackled" to our own selves and so constitutionally at odds with both God and neighbour. This situation – "in which one lives completely" – is our "being in Adam," as the apostle Paul styles it, the condition of the human being turned in upon itself in sin, which Luther designated *homo incurvatus in se* (DBWE 11, 470).[1]

And so, being made free involves liberation *from* just such inhuman autonomy, "from the lie that I am the only one there, that I am the center"; it is the work of God's love and truth to "make us free *from* ourselves" (DBWE

---

1. Cf. DBWE 2, 136–161 on "being in Adam" and "being in Christ," especially:
   > Here is their limit: human beings cling to themselves and thus their knowledge of themselves is imprisoned in untruth. To be placed into truth before God means to be dead or to live; neither of these can human beings give themselves. They are conferred on them only by encounter with Christ in *conditio passiva* and faith. Only when Christ has broken through the solitude of human beings will they know themselves placed into truth. (DBWE 2, 141)

   Bonhoeffer's thinking here very closely tracks Luther's account of the *Bondage of the Will*, and the logic of the early tract *The Freedom of a Christian*.

11, 471).² Elsewhere, Bonhoeffer explains that "Dasein becomes free ... in the sense of escaping from the power of the I into the power of Christ ... having been created anew from untruth to truth" (DBWE 2, 150, 81).³ And at the end of the sermon itself – in his preferred and recurring idiom – Bonhoeffer announces: "God's truth is God's love, and God's love makes us free from ourselves for others" because God's truth alone "allows me to see the other" (DBWE 11, 471).⁴

Something fundamentally important is on display in these claims. Bonhoeffer never speaks of freedom *from* sin without immediately speaking of freedom *for* God and others. Bonhoeffer's theological account of freedom admits no interval between the liberation of the self from itself and its being placed "in truth" or being overtaken by the power of Christ. There is no moment where freedom emerges merely as an indeterminate state, an unrealized possibility to be chosen and exercised – or perhaps not. Rather, our being freed *from* ourselves is coeval and coextensive with our being freed *for* others. This is crucial. The freedom into which Christ sets us free (Gal 5:1) is at once the negative determination that we ought no longer to "be in Adam," bound to ourselves in sin, and the positive determination that we should now "be in Christ" and own "the word of *Christus praesens*" as our sole Lord. As he explains elsewhere, "Through revelation there is only sinful or pardoned existence, without potentiality" (DBWE 2, 97).⁵ In short, "being made free" involves an exchange of lordships, an exodus out of the slavery of the sinful self which just is a passage into the free service of God (DBWE 11, 472).⁶

Now, more can and must be said about the *whence* of this gift of freedom from self and for others, this freedom "in Christ." Bonhoeffer *qua* preacher has

---

2. "Biblical texts consistently refuse all talk of freedom apart from divine actions of deliverance (*Befreiung*) which are presented as exclusively God's. 'Deliverance', insists Ps 3:8, 'belongs to the Lord'. If we understand the *topos* of freedom in biblical terms, then, we can take deliverance to be the most characteristic grammar of God's acts" (Ulrich 2022, 30).

3. The later talk of "untruth / truth" is redolent of John 8:32, but also of course of Kierkegaard's *Philosophical Fragments*.

4. This pairing of freedom *from* and freedom *for* appears repeatedly in these climactic paragraphs of the sermon (DBWE 11, 470–472).

5. The theme – that human existence is determined by the saving work of God in Christ as reality and not merely as possibility – is predominant in his *Ethics*: "There is no human being as such, just as there is no God as such; both are empty abstractions. Human beings are accepted in God's becoming human and are loved, judged, and reconciled in Christ, and God is the God who became human" (DBWE 6, 253).

6. "If a people today really knows that [the path of love leads on to the cross], it will be the only people that can justifiably call itself a free people, the only people that is not the slave of itself but the free servant of God's truth."

told us that it arises from "God's truth." And he has also said that this truth is identical with Jesus Christ. A student of both Luther and Barth, Bonhoeffer is a theologian of revelation whose thinking is marked by an extraordinary christological concentration. The advent of this liberating truth is itself, for Bonhoeffer *qua* theologian, both an enactment of divine freedom and its revelation as such. As early as his *Habilitation* thesis of 1930, wrestling with these ideas leads Bonhoeffer to the following claims about the quality of divine freedom:

> In revelation it is not so much a question of the freedom of God – eternally remaining within the divine self, aseity – on the other side of revelation, as it is of God's coming out of God's own self in revelation. It is a matter of God's *given* Word, the covenant in which God is bound by God's own action. It is a question of the freedom of God, which finds its strongest evidence precisely in that God freely chose to be bound to historical human beings and to be placed at the disposal of human beings. God is free not from human beings but for them. Christ is the word of God's freedom . . . Here the formal understanding of God's freedom is countered by a substantial one . . . a true understanding of God's freedom (DBWE 2, 90–91).

Several things are notable here. Though there is and can be nothing like the problem of sin in God, nevertheless Bonhoeffer speaks here of divine freedom as a "coming out of God's own self," an overflowing movement of self-giving from out of God's self-existence. In doing so he intimates that God is not a prisoner, as it were, of his own aseity or autonomy but a God able to self-dispose.[7] No less than with human freedom, our understanding of divine freedom must distinguish it from counterfeit concepts. Bonhoeffer worries that our thinking of God is, at this point, haunted by abstract and merely "formalistic" accounts of divine freedom as sheer transcendence or *potentia dei absoluta*, accounts which at their worst may be projections of our own egoistic subjectivity (see Ziegler 2019). Against these ideas he sets out a vision of the *potentia dei ordinata*, i.e., a purposed and enacted divine freedom substantiated in the actual exercise of God's self-giving as self-binding to which the biblical language of *covenant* points.

---

7. This idea – that God's freedom is most properly understood positively – is one also developed in Karl Barth's doctrine of God (Barth 1956–75, II/1, 301). This is interesting because this passage from *Act and Being* is offered as a criticism of the early Barth and his heavy "foundational" investments in a "negative" and so "formalistic-actualistic understanding of the freedom and contingency of God in revelation" (DBWE 2, 90).

To claim, as Bonhoeffer does here, that "Christ is the word of God's freedom" is to tether all our theological thinking and speaking about divine freedom to Christ's person and work. Only the practice of this discipline finally warrants the striking claim at the heart of this passage: namely, that "God is free not from human beings but for them." The specific nature of that freedom which God ordains for himself is to be *for* that which is not God, for that which is other than God, i.e., to be for humanity. It is in this act of self-binding for the sake of the other – in short, in the divine decision to be for us in Jesus Christ – that the indelible quality of divine freedom decided. Once again, for Bonhoeffer, there is no interval between the negative and positive determinations of divine freedom: Christian theology has no proper interest in a notion of divine "potency" as such, but takes an exclusive interest in the positively ordained disposition of divine power in *this* act of self-giving in Christ for the sake of God's beloved creatures. Such *is* divine freedom as revealed in the gospel witness to Jesus Christ.

In the absence of a detailed doctrine of God in Bonhoeffer's work, it is chiefly in christological contexts that these claims are elaborated further. Lecturing in Berlin in the fraught summer of 1933, Bonhoeffer stresses that while God and humanity "cannot be drawn together [in this relationship] as a necessity," the God who is revealed to us in this way "is identical with God himself" such that we might say "God in his timeless eternity is *not* God" but that "in the human being Jesus Christ, God *is* God" (DBWE 12, 337, 350, 313). In accordance with the "ontological structure" of the person of God incarnate, Bonhoeffer contends that the being of Christ's person is "his being-for-me. This *pro-me* is . . . the being of his very person . . . I can never think of Jesus Christ in his being-in-himself, but only in his relatedness to me" (DBWE 12, 304, 314). God in the outworking of his divine freedom is met in Christ, and Christ is met as the one who *is* for me; the force of this claim is ontological: in Christ's humble being-for-me, Bonhoeffer contends, we encounter the reality and revelation of God's own self-humbling for us.[8] So fundamental is this, any theology which does not "say right from the beginning that God and Christ can only be Christ *pro-me*" has, Bonhoeffer says, simply "deserted its God" (DBWE 12, 314–315).

This claim concerning God's freedom *for* us in Jesus Christ receives a final reiteration in Bonhoeffer's prison letters. Here, in the "Outline for a Book" of 1944 we read of an

---

8. For further discussion here of Bonhoeffer's use of the important reformational concept of *promeity* see Ziegler, 2013.

Encounter with Jesus Christ. Experience that here there is a reversal of all human existence, in the very fact that Jesus only "is there for others" [*für andere da ist*]. Jesus's "being-for-others" [*Für-andere-dasein*] is the experience of transcendence ... Faith is participating in this being of Jesus ... the "human being for others" [*der Mensch für andere*]! Therefore the Crucified One. The human being living out of the transcendent (DBWE 8, 501; DBW 8, 558–559).

As Eberhard Bethge comments, "Jesus's freedom from self, his concern for others, 'maintained till death,'" provides Bonhoeffer with the answer to his life's question of "who Christ really is for us today?," and with it, to "the question about God," an answer summed up in the "apparently simple and yet so meaningful and new title for Christ: Jesus the man for others" (Bethge 1975, 149). Once again, in the one person of Christ, true humanity and true divinity are both fundamentally characterized by a *positive* freedom for others: Jesus *qua* God, is the humble overreaching of divine transcendence to be God *pro nobis*; while Jesus *qua* man is – precisely in virtue of this same divine overreaching – properly dispossessed of his self and so free to be for others without remainder.[9] In this lies the truth and eschatological character of his humanity.

2. Analysis and conclusions

We have seen that Bonhoeffer offers a thoroughly theological account of freedom.[10] The quality of human liberty as a deliverance unto freedom *for* others derives entirely from the God from whose salutary acts it flows. As a fruit of salvation, true freedom stands in a determinative and parabolic relationship to divine freedom, giving creaturely witness to it precisely in its form as being-for-others. There is, then, what the American theologian Fredrick Herzog calls an *analogia liberationis*, grounded in the fact that human "freedom emerges time and again in what happens to us, to others, and to all creation from 'outside'

---

9. This, I suppose, is the essential meaning of Christ's sinlessness within Bonhoeffer's theology.

10. See Bachtell 1981, 331: "Freedom is a concept that belongs wholly within the realm of theology. For Bonhoeffer, all freedom originates in God, becomes reality through the revelation of the living God, and can ultimately be understood only in relation to the living and personal God." See also Malysz 2014, 47–51 and Bethge 1978, 240–246.

in an overpowering dynamics of justice" which is the outworking of God's own freedom for us.[11]

For Bonhoeffer, the analogy between divine and human freedom is established not in and through the doctrine of creation, but exclusively in and through the doctrines of reconciliation and redemption worked in an ontological register. Indeed, we might say that it is in Jesus Christ himself the *analogia liberationis* is first and decisively made concrete: for here the coming low of the Son of God in gracious freedom for the sake of wayward creatures assumes creaturely shape in the life of a human being who lives and acts and *is* for others; indeed, this divine humiliation is the very source and condition for the analogous human movement that is the life of the man Jesus: a life whose own course through the "stations on the road to freedom" – obedience, action, suffering, death – effectively mediates God's own loving freedom *for* us, to us.

In Christ, the corresponding realities of divine and human freedom truly exist *in actu*. This, for Bonhoeffer, is the significance of the Chalcedonian definition of Christ as *Deum verum et hominem verum* ("truly God and truly human"). For Bonhoeffer, this ancient dogma is indication not explanation. Rather than giving an explanatory account of *how* the incarnation is possible, it instead merely indicates its reality, pointing out *that* it has occurred. On such a view, christological predicates – especially talk of "God" and "human" – are understood to receive their essential definition from the reality of the incarnate one, whose existence instantiates and fills out their primary meaning. In other words, to speak of Christ as "God" is not to offer an evaluative judgment but rather an ostensive definition. Bonhoeffer here moves in line with the spirit of Luther's claim that "You should point to the whole man Jesus and say, 'That is God.'"

So too with "freedom" then. Christ's being-for-others as God incarnate is the definitive actualization of the reality of both divine and human freedom. What takes place in him determines the truth about human existence generally, and about the nature and shape of human freedom in particular. Talk of creaturely freedom without this reality is "abstract" and problematically so. For Bonhoeffer, the peculiar and concrete freedom "into which Christ has set us free" (Gal 5:1) is paradigmatic of true human freedom as such. We should understand this theological judgment as a gloss on the biblical claim that "if the Son makes you free, you will be free indeed" (John 8:36). As Geffrey Kelly explains, for Bonhoeffer, true human freedom "assumes the proportions

---

11. "Man can only be grasped through the analogy of liberation (*analogia liberationis*), in accord with his liberation in Christ" (Herzog 1972, 126). Cf. Herzog 2003, 205.

of utter devotion to others after the manner of Jesus" whose truly human life expresses the divine freedom in which God exists for his creatures (Kelly 1984, 61–62).

Freedom on this view is fundamentally positive, purposive, indeed vocational. Here I might venture a discrete comparison with Edith Stein. For Stein once remarked that, "One cannot desire freedom from the Cross when one is especially chosen for the Cross." What Stein says here specifically concerns avowed religious life and her own personal fate, to be sure. But the truth of this remark, for Bonhoeffer, can and should be extended across all Christian life, and indeed finally proves also to be the "hidden truth" of all human freedom as such.

In his homily on the occasion of the canonization of Stein, Pope John Paul II spoke of how her pursuit of freedom found its *telos* in a final "surprising realization: [that] only those who commit themselves to the love of Christ become truly free" because "the love of Christ and human freedom are intertwined." This concretization of freedom in commitment, the Pope suggested, calls into question the idea of freedom as sheer openness, as the condition of untrammelled possibility and deferred decision: "*Your life is not an endless series of open doors!*," he admonished those present (John Paul II, 1998). With this Bonhoeffer would concur. For freedom's vocation – to live out the truth that our genuine freedom is freedom *for* others – cannot be held in suspense as possibility, but is only honoured – or denied – in act. It is, as it were, always too late to ask about the possibility of freedom, for in virtue of the enactment of perfect freedom for us in Jesus Christ, we find ourselves always already delivered into an analogous freedom for others and so summoned to it as our true vocation of being-responsible-for-others.[12]

To conclude – Bonhoeffer offers us a thoroughly theological account of freedom.[13] He understands the quality and significance of human freedom to be determined by the reality-making force of God's saving advent in Jesus Christ. In the words of Hans Ulrich, "at root, Christian freedom is an impli-

---

12. "The subject's for-the-other, which is this finite freedom, could not be interpreted as a guilt complex, or as natural goodwill (like a "divine instinct"), nor again as a tendency to sacrifice. This finite freedom, which, ontologically, has no sense to it, is the rupture of being unrendable *essance*" (Levinas 2000, 178–79). There might be a sense in which the decisive positive determination of our freedom as freedom *for others* resonates with the priority of ethics over negative freedom in Levinas's own philosophical programme.

13. "Freedom is a concept that belongs wholly within the realm of theology. For Bonhoeffer, all freedom originates in God, becomes reality through the revelation of the living God, and can ultimately be understood only in relation to the living and personal God" (Bachtell, 1981, 331).

cate of God's very own freedom as it appears in His story in Jesus Christ and is fulfilled in Christ as actualized lordship. The essence of the lordship of Christ is to bring deliverance to human beings. Thus" – Ulrich concludes – "to become part of the story encapsulated in his life and death entails a freeing from all other forms of bondage and all other determinations" (Ulrich 2022, 29). Bonhoeffer's account of human freedom, as we have shown, involves an *analogia liberationis* established and elaborated christologically by appeal to the Chalcedonian dogma that Christ as incarnate *God* for others is also "the *man* for others," that is, "the truly human one," and so the truly free one. Conceived in this way, true freedom is always and fundamentally positively determined, a purposeful freedom *for* others, a vocation to eccentric life lived in creaturely correspondence to the ordained and loving freedom of God. Since true human freedom both derives from and relies upon the exercise of divine freedom, theological reflection upon freedom should end in the invocation of God, with prayer. Bonhoeffer's 1932 reflections on John 8:32 with which we began, end with this prayer:

> God, we cry out for freedom. But, O God, keep us from dreaming of a false image of freedom and staying in the lie. Give us the freedom that throws us fully onto you, onto your mercy. Lord, make us free with your truth, which is our [Lord] Jesus Christ. Lord, we are waiting for your truth (DBWE 11, 472).

Bibliography

Barth, Karl. 1956–1975. *Church Dogmatics*. Edinburgh: T&T Clark.
Batchtell, Donald S. 1981. "Freedom in Bonhoeffer" in *A Bonhoeffer Legacy: Essays in Understanding*, edited by A. J. Klassen, 333–344. Grand Rapids: Eerdmans.
Bethge, Eberhard. 1975. *Bonhoeffer: Exile and Martyr*, edited by John W. de Gruchy. London: Collins.
Bethge, Eberhard. 1978. "Freiheit und Gerhorsam bei Bonhoeffer" in *Schöpferische Nachfolge: Festschrift für Heinz Eduard Tödt*, edited by Christofer Frey and Wolfgang Huber, 331–361. Heidelberg: FEST.
Bonhoeffer, Dietrich. 1986–1999. *Dietrich Bonhoeffer Werke*. 17 vols. Edited by Eberhard Bethge, et al. Munich and Gütersloh: Chr. Kaiser-Gütersloher Verlagshaus. Cited as DBW.
Bonhoeffer, Dietrich. 1996–2014. *Dietrich Bonhoeffer Works* 17 vols, edited by Wayne Whitson Floyd Jr., et al. Minneapolis: Fortress Press. Cited as DBWE.
Hampe, Johann Christoph. 1970. *Dietrich Bonhoeffer, Prayers from Prison. Prayers and Poems*, translated by John Bowden. London: Collins.

Henkys, Jürgen. 1986. *Dietrich Bonhoeffers Gefängnisgedichte*. Beiträge zu ihrer Interpretation. Berlin: Evangelische Verlagsanstalt Berlin.
Herzog, Frederick. 1972. *Liberation Theology: Liberation in the Light of the Fourth Gospel*. Chicago: Seabury Press.
Herzog, Frederick. 2003. "Freedom," in *New and Enlarged Handbook of Christian Theology*, edited by Donald W. Musser and Joseph L. Price, 203–206. Nashville: Abingdon.
John Paul II. 1998. "Homily of John Paul II for the Canonization of Edith Stein, 11 October 1998." Dicastery for Promoting Christian Unity. http://www.christianunity.va/content/unitacristiani/en/commissione-per-i-rapporti-religiosi-con-l-ebraismo/atti-commemorativi/pope-john-paul-ii/1988-homily-for-canonization-of-edith-stein.html.
Kelly, Geffrey B. 1984. *Liberating Faith: Bonhoeffer's Message for Today*. Minneapolis: Augsburg Press.
Levinas, Emmanuel. 2000. *God, Death, and Time*, translated by Bertina Bergo. Stanford: Stanford University Press.
Malysz, Piotr J. 2014. "Freedom and Suffering in Bonhoeffer's Theology." *Lutheran Forum* 48.1: 47–51.
Ulrich, Hans G. 2009. "'Stations on the Way to Freedom': The Presence of God – The Freedom of Disciples," in *Who Am I? Bonhoeffer's Theology Through His Poetry*, edited by Bernd Wannenwetsch, 147–174. London: T&T Clark.
Ulrich, Hans G. 2022. *Transfigured not Conformed: Christian Ethics in a Hermeneutic Key*. Edited by Brian Brock. London: T&T Clark.
Ziegler, Philip G. 2013. "Christ For Us Today: Promeity in the Christologies of Bonhoeffer and Kierkegaard." *International Journal of Systematic Theology* 15.1: 25–41.
Ziegler, Philip G. 2019. "God," in *The Oxford Handbook of Dietrich Bonhoeffer*, edited by Michael Mawson and Philip G. Ziegler, 137–149. Oxford: Oxford University Press, 2019.

7

Absolute Human Freedom in Zen Philosophy (D. T. Suzuki) and Evangelical Theology (D. Bonhoeffer)

Piotr Lorek, PhD Hab.
Professor of Evangelical School of Theology in Wrocław
ORCID: 0000-0003-4345-5235

About the Author

Piotr Lorek is the academic dean at Evangelical School of Theology, Wrocław, Poland (2007–). He is a graduate of Biblical Theological Seminary, Poland (1999) and University of Glamorgan, UK (2000). In February 2004, he defended his PhD thesis in the field of biblical theology at the University of Wales, UK. In 2015, he obtained a habilitation from the Christian Theological Academy in Warsaw, Poland. He specializes in NT theology and interreligious dialogue between Christian theology and Zen philosophy.

Keywords

Human freedom, D. T. Suzuki, zen, D. Bonhoeffer, Christianity

Abstract

Two argumentative models defending the absolute freedom of a human being are presented. Both come from the twentieth century; one represents Far

Eastern Zen (Daisetz Teitaro Suzuki), and the other European Protestantism (Dietrich Bonhoeffer). The conclusion of the paper shows the basic convergence of both models in the fact of relativization of the human being in the name of defending their absolute freedom. Both systems of thought turn out to use the paradoxicality of philosophical-theological concepts. The conducted analysis results in the inconclusiveness and unverifiability of the thesis on the absolute freedom of a human being in both systems of thought.

Introduction

Are humans free? It is not a question of a sense of limited freedom, for this is usually available and does not need to be proven. Instead, it is about that freedom of humans which transcends human limitations, that is, absolute freedom. Humans have an awareness of their limitations of doing what they would like to do. This state of understanding raises the question of whether the human individual is or can be ultimately free, despite the experience of accidental limitations.

Philosophical and religious systems of thought have posed the question of human freedom for centuries. This paper will juxtapose two argumentative models presenting the concept of absolute human freedom. Both date from the twentieth century. One represents Far Eastern Zen, the other European evangelicalism. The selected representatives of Zen Buddhism and evangelical Christianity are well-known and respected thinkers. Their views on human absolute freedom will be reconstructed on the basis of selected excerpts from their works and then compared in order to bring out basic similarities and differences.

The conclusions aim to show the fundamental convergence of the two models in terms of relativizing the human being in the name of defending their absolute freedom. Both systems of thought turn out to use the paradoxicality of philosophical-theological concepts. The analysis will also show the inconclusiveness and unverifiability of the thesis on the absolute freedom of a human being in both anthropological postulates.

Zen philosophy (D. T. Suzuki)

Daisetz Teitaro Suzuki (1870–1966) brought Zen Buddhism to the West. In one of his lectures, entitled *East and West*, he somewhat schematically, though heuristically, juxtaposes two types of mind. He describes the Western mind as: "analytical, discriminative, differential, inductive, individualistic, intellectual, objective, scientific, generalizing, conceptual, schematic, impersonal, legalistic, organising, power-wielding, self-assertive, disposed to impose its will on others, etc." (Suzuki 1960, 5). The Eastern mind, on the other hand, he describes as: "synthetic, totalizing, integrative, nondiscriminative, deductive, nonsystematic, dogmatic, intuitive (rather, affective), nondiscursive, subjective, spiritually individualistic and socially group-minded, etc." (Suzuki 1960, 5).

In this juxtaposition, it is to the West that the Japanese philosopher attributed "impersonal" thinking, in spite of its individualistic tendencies, while the East, in spite of its collectivist tendencies, he credited with subjectivism and spiritual individualism. As a founder of *The Eastern Buddhist Society* (1921),[1] expounding Zen thought to the West, he undertook to defend the freedom of the human person.

Machine

Suzuki noted that it is due to the Western mind that science has developed and with it the concept of the machine. In the industrialized world, the machine begins to influence the perception of the human being, as personal labour is transformed into mechanical labour. The West seeks to reconcile the concept of person and machine, but according to a secular Zen practitioner, this results in a misperception of the person (Suzuki 1960, 8). In one of his lectures Suzuki postulates several theses from the Zen perspective.[2] These centre on the relationship between the person and their rationality and freedom.

The starting point of Suzuki's argument is to grasp that the machine is a product of *rationalisation* and *generalisation*, while the person is a free and responsible individual. If one looks at the person as a *rationalised* machine, the individuality, freedom and responsibility are lost. Suzuki insists that "in logic there is no freedom, for everything is controlled by rigid rules of syllogism" (Suzuki 1960, 9). What follows from these words is the thesis that maintaining the freedom of the person requires transcending the understanding of the person in terms of the rationally determined rules of logic. It is not only the rationalist understanding of the person that deprives the person of freedom. Suzuki adds that humans' biological determinism, impulses, stimuli and social conditioning make it difficult for the West to speak of a human being as a free person. A rationalistically conceived person is no different from a machine.

---

1. The Eastern Buddhist Society, *About the Society*, https://ebs.otani.ac.jp/society.html.
2. This lecture was delivered in 1957 at the Department of Psychoanalysis of the School of Medicine of the Autonomous National University of Mexico. See also Fromm, 1960, vii.

Rationality, determined by the necessity of inference, prevents creativity, ensuring only reproducibility, which undermines human freedom (Suzuki 1960, 9).

Paradox

How, then, can one free oneself from the rules of logic, from a machine-minded approach to personhood, and thus keep the person from losing their freedom? In order to preserve the freedom, responsibility and spontaneity of the person, one must transcend the framework of classical logic and introduce paradoxical thinking, thinking by means of apparent contradictions. This is how Suzuki describes the freedom of the person: "The person is free only when he is not a person. He is free when it denies himself and is absorbed in the whole. To be more exact, it is free when it is himself and yet not himself" (Suzuki 1960, 9). It can be seen in this postulate that Zenist thought situates the concept of person in a paradoxical juxtaposition of separateness and wholeness.

In a similar vein, Suzuki makes another statement. He argues that the affirmation that transcends assertion and denial is capable of liberating a person:

> When we say "yes," we assert, and by asserting we limit ourselves. When we say "no," we deny, and to deny is exclusion. Exclusion and limitation, which after all are the same thing, murder the soul; for is it not the life of the soul that lives *in perfect freedom* and in perfect unity? There is no freedom or unity in exclusion or in limitation. Zen is well aware of this. In accordance with the demands of our inner life, therefore, Zen takes us to an absolute realm wherein there are no antitheses of any sort (Suzuki 1964, 67–68, emphasis added).

In the context of a discussion of a human being as a free person, it is typically argued that either a human being is realistically separate from the whole (and thus presumably free), or that a human being is realistically inseparable from the whole (and thus presumably unfree/enslaved). By transcending the principle of non-contradiction, Zenist thought claims that a human being is both separate and inseparable from the whole (and thus presumably free). Thus, paradoxically, the connection between separateness/inseparateness and freedom would be abolished, as would the categories of separateness and inseparateness.

Is such an endeavour to rescue and establish the freedom of the individual effective? The fact of a person's actual freedom does not necessarily follow from the observation of a human being as an individual. By analogy, the opposite thesis can also be questioned. From the paradoxical inclusion of a human being in the whole, the conclusion about their freedom does not automatically emerge. Moreover, when one relativizes separateness in relation to the whole, freedom can theoretically be postulated, for there is no longer anything either internal or external that could deprive a person of it. However, the question then arises as to who is supposed to be free when individuality has been relativized. One can also ask whether the whole is free. One might just as well postulate a thesis of a non-free whole.

Subjectivity

As has been shown, Suzuki abolishes classical logic as an inadequate tool for describing human freedom and introduces paradoxical language. He also questions the possibility of machine-like objectification of human beings. Another aspect of Suzuki's proposal concerns a departure from the logical and the objective, and thus proposes to situate human freedom in the subjective. Suzuki writes: "Freedom is a subjective term and cannot be interpreted objectively. When we try, we are surely involved inextricably in contradictions. Therefore, I say that to talk about freedom in this objective world of limitations all around us is nonsense" (Suzuki 1960, 10). In these words, he argues for the non-existence of objective freedom.

Suzuki thus suspends rationality and objectivity and seeks human freedom in subjectivity. But by maintaining freedom only on the subjective plane, does it realistically succeed in preserving it? The possibility of evaluation is further complicated if one considers that, since Suzuki relativizes the distinction between the individual and the whole, the distinction between the objective and the subjective is simultaneously blurred. In a text dated three years later (1960) than the lecture discussed here, Suzuki speaks of the self being emptied of egocentricity in the name of unity with all reality.[3] What is subjective and internal in the human being, therefore, is not understood as unique and separate from the external.

---

3. "The self, therefore, emptied of all its so-called psychological contents is not an emptiness as is generally supposed. No such empty self exists. The emptied self is no other than the psychological self cleansed of its ego-centric imagination. It is just as rich in its contents as before; indeed it is richer than before because it now contains the whole world in itself instead of having the latter stand against it. Not only that, it enjoys itself being true to itself. It is free in the real sense of the word because it is the master of itself, absolutely independent, self-relying, authentic, and autonomous" (Suzuki 1970, 2).

Absolute freedom

One can now move on to Suzuki's main thought behind the theses, namely the claim of human "absolute freedom." It proclaims that "the Western ideas of individual freedom and personal responsibility run counter to the Eastern ideas of *absolute freedom*" (Suzuki 1960, 8, emphasis added). In light of the proposals introduced above, this claim becomes clearer. If one paradoxically incorporates the individual into the whole and frees him from classical logical thinking, one then arrives at his "absolute freedom."

Suzuki considers these theses the phenomenology of human consciousness. The objectified world, the mechanized processes destroy the freedom of the person. The subjective level, on the other hand, properly understood, becomes the gateway to absolute freedom. This freedom contains the paradoxical nature of its separateness and its capacity to rationalize.

Emptiness

In his final thesis, Suzuki completes his apologia for the freedom of the person by invoking the concept of emptiness (Sanskrit *śūnyatā*), central to Mahayana Buddhism, including the Zen tradition. The basic concept of emptiness assumes that all beings are *de facto* empty – they do not have their own separate identities. This makes them appear separate on the one hand, while on the other hand they are part of a whole; thus they are and are not at the same time.

It is from here that the individual-whole paradox takes its inspiration and the paradoxical logic is introduced. This logic subjectively pulls from the objectifying necessity of reality as perceived by classical reason recognizing human beings' personal and social enslavement. The concept of emptiness becomes the key to explaining the Zenist perspective and advancing the argument for absolute freedom.

Incarnation

In the final thesis of Suzuki's lecture, the concept of emptiness becomes a fundamental distinction between classical Christianity and Zen. If a human being's nature is not substantial, then their liberation contradicts the Western concept of the incarnation of Christ constituting theologically the distinctiveness of a human being. One then needs to escape from the logicality of the word into silence and paradox. It is about breaking free from the locality of the flesh and realizing the whole. The idea is to stop contrasting the temporal with the eternal and experience the infinite *hic et nunc*. In this way one is to experience "absolute freedom." Suzuki concludes: "Christianity, which is the religion of the West, talks of Logos, the Word, the flesh, and the incarnation, and of tempestuous temporality. The religions of the East strive for excarnation, silence, absorption, eternal peace. To Zen incarnation is excarnation; silence roars like thunder; the Word is no-Word, the flesh is no-flesh; here-now equals emptiness (*śūnyatā*) and infinity" (Suzuki 1960, 10).

God

The Zenist departure from the substantiality of beings, from the concreteness of incarnation and the locality of the individual, results in a corresponding relation to God. In his classic work, *An Introduction to Zen Buddhism*, Suzuki draws an important contrast between the God of Christian mystics, conceived as a concrete object, and the experience of the totality of so-called creation. To grasp God is automatically to reject everything else, which deprives man of absolute freedom. Suzuki writes: "whereas with the God of mysticism, there is the grasping of a definite object; when you have God, what is no-God is excluded. This is self-limiting. Zen wants *absolute freedom*, even *from God*" (Suzuki 1964, 97).

In the same lecture in Zen philosophy, Suzuki emphasizes the need to free oneself from abstract concepts. The avoidance of thoughts detached from the commonness of experience, including thoughts about God, is to become the way to achieve freedom:

> To meditate, a man has to fix his thought on something; for instance, on the oneness of God, or his infinite love, or on the impermanence of things. But this is the very thing Zen desires to avoid. If there is anything Zen strongly emphasizes it is the attainment of freedom; that is, freedom from all unnatural encumbrances. Meditation is something artificially put on; it does not belong to the native activity of the mind. Upon what do the fowl of the air meditate? Upon what do the fish in the water meditate? They fly; they swim. Is not that enough? Who wants to fix his mind on the unity of God and man, or on the nothingness of this life? Who wants to be arrested in the daily manifestations of his life-activity by such meditations as the goodness of a divine being or the everlasting fire of hell? (Suzuki 1964, 41, cf. also similar motif on page 78).

To conclude, the Zen philosopher believes that absolute human freedom is possible. Possible when one moves away from objectifying cognition into the subjective, and this is properly grasped and concrete. Absolute freedom is possible when one suspends the division between individual and whole, temporal and eternal, in paradoxical thinking.

Evangelical theology (D. Bonhoeffer)

The period of Dietrich Bonhoeffer's life (1906–1945) partly overlaps with Suzuki's life. The evangelical theologian was born thirty-six years after the Zenist philosopher, but died a martyr's death twenty-one years before the latter's demise. The two thinkers were not contemporaries, however Suzuki was living throughout the thirty-nine years of Bonhoeffer's life. Bonhoeffer is a representative of evangelical Western thought, which never got caught up in the utopian propaganda of Nazism that deprived its enemies of the right to freedom and life. Bonhoeffer, like Suzuki, defends human freedom; like Suzuki he postulates what he also calls absolute human freedom. He understands this freedom, however, in a different way.

In the second chapter of Bonhoeffer's doctoral thesis (completed in 1926), entitled *Sanctorum Communio: A Theological Study of the Sociology of the Church*, the future Lutheran clergyman refers to the "absolute will." One needs to extract this passage from the entire dissertation in order to grasp how Bonhoeffer establishes human freedom in its absolute sense (cf. Bonhoeffer 1998, 54–55).

In an attempt to reconstruct an understanding of freedom in Bonhoeffer's thought, it is important to bear in mind that this theme does not occupy a prominent place in his work. Even in *Sanctorum Communio*, the concept of freedom is treated superficially.[4] However, nearing his thirtieth year of age, the theologian reflects on the relationship between God, the human person and society. Bonhoeffer states: "The I comes into being only in relation to the You; only in response to a demand does *responsibility* arise. 'You' says nothing about its own being, only about its demand. This demand is absolute" (Bonhoeffer 1998, 54). Implicit in these words is the thesis that the personality of the individual does not emerge ontically as such, but socially in contact with the other

---

4. Cf. Csepregi 2003, 134: "Bonhoeffer never turned to the theme of freedom as a central topic of one of his studies," 132: "In *Sanctorum Communio* the concept of freedom plays only a marginal role."

individual. From this encounter a responsibility towards the other is born.⁵ This responsibility is of an absolute nature, that is, one that cannot be annulled in human experience. The concept of freedom functions in Bonhoeffer's work in conjunction with responsibility; freedom is understood positively, not as freedom from something, but freedom to someone, as ethical responsibility for the other (Csepregi 2003, 142). The person becomes Christ for the other person (Bonhoeffer 1998, 55).

Absolute responsibility towards the other has its reference to God. Maria Zwiefka comments: "Since such responsible, absolute free action is already always fraught with the risk of guilt, so paradoxically the one who does the will of God at the same time comes under His judgment" (Zwiefka 2008, 91). Guilt is coupled to the possession of absolute freedom: "Any substitutionally responsible action, together with the acceptance of guilt, can only be done in absolute freedom. This is why its role in the structure of the responsible life is so important. Freedom is always understood by Bonhoeffer as freedom for one's neighbour" (Zwiefka 2008, 91).

In the mere social encounter between an I and a you, a human being is not constituted and the absolute responsibility concerning this being cannot be established. The absolute nature of the demand from a you and the responsibility present in an I must therefore have a transcendent source, transcending individual and social conditions. Bonhoeffer puts it as follows: "One human being cannot of its own accord make another into an I, an ethical person conscious of responsibility. *God or the Holy Spirit joins the concrete You; only through God's active working does the other become a You to me from whom my I arises. In other words, every human You is an image of the divine You.* You-character is in fact the essential form in which the divine is experienced; every human You bears its You-character only by virtue of the divine" (Bonhoeffer 1998, 54–55).

But does not such an account of the establishment of a human being, its absolute demand and responsibility, automatically abolish the human subject and present it only as a divine manifestation?⁶ Bonhoeffer distances himself from such a conclusion and defends the human person as having been assumed by God: "Rather, the divine You creates the human You. And since the human

---

5. Cf. Zwiefka, 2008, 88: ". . . as for Emmanuel Lévinas or Joseph Tischner . . . the very presence of the other is for Bonhoeffer that claim which obliges one to respond."

6. Csepregi similarly identifies the difficulty in distinguishing between human persons and the human and divine person: "Besides the lack of a clear difference between the I and the You, on the other hand, Bonhoeffer's concept of You is also fluid in the sense of being unable to mark the difference between God's person and the human person" (Csepregi, 2003, 149).

You is created and willed by God, it is a *real, absolute, and holy You*, like the divine You. One might then speak here of the human being as the image of God with respect to the effect one person has on another" (Bonhoeffer 1998, 55).

Bonhoeffer thus argues that he does not abolish the human "you," replacing it with a divine "you." The absolute value of the human "you" remains, but it is established through God's creation of it and God's acceptance of it. This act is the source of its reality, its sacredness, in absolute terms because of the absoluteness of God.

Paradox

In the last two passages of Bonhoeffer's argument cited above, one can see the paradoxical nature of the language used. The theologian juxtaposes the human you with the divine you. The human you itself is not established. It is established by the you of the divine. On the other hand, the human you exists as such and is not identical with the divine you. The logic of such a discourse reveals the paradoxical nature of representations of the divine and the human. From one perspective, the two types of you are being fused with each other, while on the other hand they are clearly separated. This contradiction is not absolute, but it is not difficult to identify as apparent.

God's calling and acceptance does not change the human person, which proves that one's true identity has its source directly in God himself. The human person receives absolute reality, holiness, but also absolute will, not through social interactions or own efforts, but through God himself. Bonhoeffer continues: "Since, however, one person's becoming You for an other fundamentally alters nothing about the You as person, that person as I is not holy; what is holy is the You of God, the absolute will, who here becomes visible in the concrete You of social life" (Bonhoeffer 1998, 55).

To sum up Bonhoeffer's claims, it should be noted that he wished to establish a basis for the existence of the human individual and his absolute duty towards the other. He argues that social relations single out individuals in relation to each other and demonstrate their mutual absolute claim and responsibility. Bonhoeffer no longer accepts the establishment of the individual's freedom and responsibility on the basis of social relations, that is, of the immanent. Of course, he allows for the relative value of the individual's freedom in its social conditioning.[7] He argues, however, the human being, its individuality, sacredness, freedom, responsibility and dignity (a demand from the other) are established transcendentally. This occurs through the fact of God creating humans, making them like himself and receiving them in a way that paradoxically communicates himself to them. This affirmation of humans by God does not fundamentally transform them as such. It means that the absolute God remains the source of a human being's absolute will and therefore of their freedom and responsibility. It is God, and not humans of themselves, who is the basis for their individuality, freedom and responsibility. These have their absolute character because they have their basis in the absolute.

Bonhoeffer ultimately does not establish the unity and separateness of the person in question on the basis of his horizontal relations. The concreteness of the person derives from the establishment by the divine you. Therefore, Bonhoeffer opposes the abolition of social individuality and thus the deprivation of individual freedom and responsibility for a human being. He concludes:

> In summary, the person is willed by God, in concrete vitality, wholeness, and uniqueness as an ultimate unity. Social relations must be understood, then, as purely interpersonal and building on the uniqueness and separateness of persons. The person cannot be overcome by a personal spirit; no "unity" can negate the plurality of persons. The social basic category is the I-You-relation (Bonhoeffer 1998, 10).

Summary

Both Suzuki and Bonhoeffer affirm a human being as a free person. Both thinkers defend a person's freedom, a freedom understood absolutely. Their arguments, stemming from different preconceptions – different mentalities (Eastern and Western), different religious inspirations (Zenistic Mahayana Buddhism and evangelical Christian theology) – are developed differently. Let us point out in conclusion the main differences and similarities.

Both Suzuki and Bonhoeffer, when they look at human individuals in their horizontal, immanent and social conditioning, perceive their relative freedom,

---

7. Cf. an excerpt from Bonhoeffer's later work *Ethics*: "It is of crucial importance that this relative freedom shall not be confused with an absolute freedom for God and one's neighbour such as only the imparted word of God itself can create and bestow; yet this relative freedom is still important even for him to whom Christ has given the freedom for God and for his neighbour" (Bonhoeffer 1995, 144).

limited by the individuals themselves as well as by external factors. In order to establish absolute freedom, however, individuals must transcend the order of perception. Suzuki introduces the category of emptiness, while Bonhoeffer introduces God. The former frees himself from determined individuality by demonstrating its insubstantiality, while the latter establishes his substantiality with the divine being. The first solution is a move towards the extensionality of immanence, while the second is a move towards the uniqueness of transcendence. Both scholars in this procedure are forced to depart from classical logic based on the principle of non-contradiction. Suzuki introduces a paradox between the individual and the immanent whole, while Bonhoeffer introduces a paradox between the human individual and the divine individual. In the first case, the individual is horizontally liberated through continuity with the whole; in the second case, the individual is vertically liberated through union with the divine individual. Both treatments enter the realm of conceptual and ontological speculation. For it is not possible to demonstrate rationally or empirically either the reality of insubstantiality (emptiness) or the reality of the person of God. It appears that the unprovable preconceptions of both cultures and mentalities are used for the apologia of human freedom.

Both Suzuki and Bonhoeffer intend to bring individuals out of their immanent entanglement based on the mere experience of the human self, which is aware of its limitedness and relativity of freedom. As individuals, human beings are subject to internal and external factors, which demonstrate their inability to do what they want. This framing of the human self threatens its self-determination and can lead to a complete loss of the conviction of his or her freedom as well as situating him or her only at the level of a sense of limited freedom. Zen – like evangelical thought – wants to transcend this sense of threat to human freedom. Suzuki chooses the path of immanent relativization of the individual, while Bonhoeffer chooses transcendent relativization. In defence of humans' absolute freedom, their insubstantiality is relativized and replaced by immanent insubstantiality or transcendent substantiality respectively. It can thus be seen that both authors do not establish the absolute freedom of a human being as such. This absolute dimension of freedom becomes available only when we paradoxically unite the individual with an immanent totality or transcendent subject. Human beings, then, do not remain in themselves. Viewing them as such becomes a reminder to individuals of their limitedness and introduces the threat of the absence of absolute freedom. In both cases, subjectification is introduced to protect the individual from the limitation of freedom imposed by experience. The acceptance of the conviction of being part of a whole or being caught up in God is recognizable not on the level of mere observation, but on the level of personal insight (Zen) or faith (evangelicalism).

Concluding the juxtaposition of the two thinkers' views, let us further translate them into the categories of incarnational Christology familiar in our cultural circle. Suzuki proposes absolute freedom through de-incarnation and de-individualization, while Bonhoeffer proposes absolute freedom through incarnation and individualization. Suzuki encourages a paradoxical silencing of words, while Bonhoeffer encourages a paradoxical reformulation of the human word, the word of God. They both silence the human logos, with Suzuki remaining in silence, while Bonhoeffer allows the divine Word to resound. The muted human logos is to be given absolute freedom in exchange for its silence. Its source is either ontological horizontal blurring or theological vertical sharpening. Human individuality as such is relativized and relegated to the background.

The final evaluation of the two argumentative strategies, both of the Zenist philosopher and the evangelical theologian, remains dependent on the adopted cognitive stance. Certainly, human beings have within themselves the conceptual potential to produce a conception of absolute freedom. Perhaps this concept – variously derived – reflects the ultimate nature of a human being, or perhaps it is the result of a poignant conviction of his or her own limitation and a conceptual attempt to transcend it.

Bibliography

Bonhoeffer, Dietrich. 1995. *Ethics*. New York: Touchstone.
Bonhoeffer, Dietrich. 1998. *Sanctorum Communio: A Theological Study of the Sociology of the Church. Dietrich Bonhoeffer Works Volume 1*, edited by Clifford Green, translated by Rheinhard Krauss and Nancy Lukens. Minneapolis: Fortress Press.
Csepregi, András. 2003. *Two Ways to Freedom. Christianity and Democracy in the Thought of István Bibó and Dietrich Bonhoeffer*. Budapest: Acta Theologica Lutherana Budapestinensia.
The Eastern Buddhist Society. n.d. *About the Society*, https://ebs.otani.ac.jp/society.html [accessed: 11.06.2023].
Fromm, Erich. 1960. "Foreword." In Erich Fromm, D. T. Suzuki, Richard De Martino, *Zen Buddhism and Psychoanalysis*. New York: Harper&Brothers, vii–viii.
Suzuki, Daisetz Teitaro. 1960. "Lectures on Zen Buddhism." In Erich Fromm, D. T. Suzuki, Richard De Martino, *Zen Buddhism and Psychoanalysis*. New York: Harper&Brothers, 1–76.
Suzuki, Daisetz Teitaro. 1964. *An Introduction to Zen Buddhism*, foreword by C. G. Jung. New York: Evergreen Black Cat.

Suzuki, Daisetz Teitaro. 1970. "Self the Unattainable," *The Eastern Buddhist*, 3.2, October, 1–8.

Zwiefka, Maria. 2008. "Miejsce rzeczywistości i odpowiedzialności w etyce Dietricha Bonhoeffera." In *W odpowiedzialności za drugiego człowieka*, edited by Joel Burnell, Marcin Orawski, Janusz Witt. Wrocław: Wydawnictwo c2, 85–99.

Part 3

Bonhoeffer and Stein: Freedom in Personal Context

8

Edith Stein and the Jews

Janusz Królikowski, PhD Hab.
Pontifical University of John Paul II in Krakow
ORCID: 0000-0003-3929-6008

About the Author

Janusz Królikowski – professor, priest of the Diocese of Tarnów. In 1996–2009 lecturer in Eastern Theology at the Pontifical University of the Holy Cross in Rome; since 1997 lecturer in Dogmatic Theology at the Faculty of Theology, Tarnów Section, of the Pontifical University of John Paul II in Krakow; since 2010 lecturer in Mariology at the Marian and Kolbian Institute "Kolbianum" in Niepokalanów (UKSW). Member of the Polish Mariological Society (since 2021 President), Society of Dogmatic Theologians, member of the Committee of Theological Sciences of the Polish Academy of Sciences, ordinary member of the International Pontifical Academy of Mary in Rome. Consultor of the Marian Commission of the Polish Bishops' Conference.

Keywords

Jews, conversion, faith, cross, expiation, church, Carmel, Nazism

Abstract

Edith Stein's relationship to the Jews has two aspects that always deserve attention and reflection when we look at her life in an attempt to understand it. She comes from a Jewish family, but then this natural origin is covered by her conversion, which makes this relationship acquire new aspects that take root more and more in her spiritual experience. These new aspects are first expressed in her discovery of what is common in Judaism and in Christianity, but then they are taken to a mystical level, which is expressed to the greatest extent in her deep conviction of the need to give her life as a kind of expiation for her people. In this second aspect, she saw the fulfilment of her spiritual quest and also the way forward for others, both Jews and Christians. Whatever happened in her life she was deeply convinced of the link between faith and the cross of Christ.

Introduction

The life of Edith Stein (Saint Benedicta Teresa of the Cross) has received attention from many points of view (cf. Matre Dei 1963; Posselt 1963; Neyer 1987; Herbstrith 1987; Adamska 1988; Meester 2013. Polish bibliography: Mikołajczyk 2016). Along with her sainthood, which has been recognized by the Catholic Church (beatification on 1 May 1987, canonization on 11 October 1998) (Królikowski 1998, 26–42), we owe to her one of the very interesting attempts to graft onto the old trunk that constitutes *philosophia perennis* the method and issues of modern thought, especially phenomenology. It is undoubtedly to Edith Stein's credit that she developed – at least within German Catholicism – a solid foundation for the elaboration of a Christian pedagogy and a healthy feminism. "European" spirit in addressing philosophical and political problems had in her an intelligent harbinger. All this was appreciated by Pope John Paul II when he called Saint Edith Stein, who was the "the symbol of Europe's tragedies" in the twentieth century, one of the three co-patrons of Europe, alongside Saint Brigid of Sweden and Saint Catherine of Siena (John Paul II 1999).

Here, leaving aside other issues, we will deal with Edith's relationship with the Jewish world from which she came, drawing primarily on her biography (cf. Stein 1986)[1] and letters (Stein 1993). This is key for understanding the whole life and personality of this woman, along with her spirituality and her approach to her religious life in Carmel (Herbstrith 1998; Sleiman 1999). Apart from its biographical value, Edith Stein's Hebrew background also provides an important paradigm for the dialogue between the Jewish world and the Christian world. She foreshadowed and embodied in her life those profound themes that bring Jews and Christians together and that were sought by the Second Vatican Council, whose teachings recent popes have attempted to implement. Edith is

---

1. This autobiography is an indispensable source for understanding the family environment and Edith's youth.

a figure of Christians who can legitimately and fruitfully propose Christianity to their Jewish siblings, not so much in an attempt to convert them, but to show one of the great daughters of the Jewish people. She is a new Rebecca, who experienced in herself the mystery of the "two peoples" who had disputes with each other over centuries – church and Synagogue – until the act of reconciliation which in her case took the form of shedding the same blood in the same manner for both peoples.

Returns home

In the spare moments between her teaching work and the enthusiastic preaching at conferences, Edith, also as a Catholic, would go to her native Breslau to absorb the invigorating spirit of the family atmosphere, even if it was at first disturbed by her Catholic faith. She asked questions, observed, and shared the daily chores. Since childhood, she had been paying attention to what went on in the house, and it was as a kind of sacred liturgy, of which her mother was a rigorous "priestess," otherwise extremely gentle in family matters. Her autobiographical notes collected in *Life in a Jewish Family* provide an illustration of Edith's childhood and the people who shaped her environment.

Edith was born, the last of eleven children, on 12 October 1891, into a family of Jewish tradition. The coincidence of dates seems to mark her entire destiny from birth, as she was born on the Day of Atonement (Yom Kippur), which also made her her mother's favourite daughter. Her ancestors held prominent positions in the various Jewish communities in which they lived. Her mother, Augusta Stein, née Courant, born in Lublinitz (present-day Lubliniec), was almost an embodiment of the spirit of the Old Testament. She was pious, strict (at the age of eighty, she kept complete fasting on the Day of Atonement), and after the untimely death of her husband, she brought up her children according to a principle taken from old Tobias: "You will have great wealth, if you fear God" (Tb 4:21 USCCB).

Edith had a quiet childhood, protected to some extent from external influences; she was self-centred, but this did not save her from some internal crises. Although she was taken gentle care of, she felt the loneliness of her childhood world. It was not until she went to school that she began to be "taken seriously"; she had opportunities to explore and develop, which she availed herself of enthusiastically and abundantly. Then she took an unexpected decision: on the eve of becoming a junior secondary school student, she discontinued her education. She resumed it a year later and would be consistent in her studies for the rest of her life, with success.

At the age of thirteen, Edith put her Jewish faith completely aside; she would grope in the religious darkness, being for all practical purposes an atheist until she turned twenty-one. A friend would later testify that at school Edith was completely indifferent to religion. The motives behind it are obscure; one thing appears certain: that attitude was not caused by the positivist and anti-religious spirit of the school at the time. Edith was too intellectual to succumb to such influences. Still, her Jewish faith was like the winter sun, which radiates but does not warm. Faded, disconnected from everyday life and the future, the Jewish religion as practised then had little to offer an adolescent in terms of enlightenment or support; an adolescent could not help challenging the multitude of rabbinic practices, rituals and traditions as they failed to define the purpose of life and justify the strictness of the duties imposed. Death, for one, appeared absurd and entailed boundless sadness and hopelessness. Edith's subsequent life was fraught with these shortcomings that hindered her from opening herself up to the divine.

Having successfully graduated from secondary school, Edith enrolled at the University of Breslau, taking an interest in German studies and experimental psychology. Very soon she became disillusioned with psychology in particular, due to the positivism that pervaded it at the time, which – unable to offer a satisfactory explanation – drove the problem of the spirit out of the discipline. On holiday that year she delved enthusiastically into Husserl's *Logische Untersuchungen (Logical Explorations)*, which led her to decide to go to Göttingen and to study under Husserl. "Beaming, I told [Professor Hönigswald], 'I'm going to Göttingen in the summer. Oh, if only I were advanced enough to do this kind of work myself'" (Stein 1986, 219). Husserl, discouraged by idealism, insisted on the necessity to "go back to the things themselves" in a new spirit (cf. Depraz 2010). At the time, this was something genuinely new in German philosophy, and it enthralled Edith, so that she soon forgot about her planned doctorate in psychology, which she "shrugged off," as she noted in her memoirs (Stein 1986, 172).

It was at Göttingen where Edith's intelligence flourished and where she developed her character, which easily won her friends. She became one of Husserl's favourite students and entered the circle of the most distinguished phenomenologists (cf. Machnacz 2019). Among them, she met and particularly appreciated the young philosopher Adolf Reinach, who had not long earlier converted to Christianity and, together with his wife, had become a deeply religious man. His personality stirred Edith's soul, sensitive to human kindness and to the nobility of a pure conscience. When Husserl was appointed to the

University of Freiburg in Breisgau, he chose Edith Stein as his assistant, even though she had not yet completed her doctorate.

The First World War was underway, claiming numerous casualties. Adolf Reinach was killed at the front in Flanders. His wife asked Edith to come to Göttingen to help her sort out the notes left by her husband. She obliged her, full of fear and anxiety. She had to face a question to which neither her Jewish faith nor her later atheism had given an answer, namely: the hopelessness of death. With deep anxiety, she wondered what she was supposed to say to a young widow, crushed by the burden of bereavement. She was in for a big surprise. Edith was struck by the widow's inner peace and reconciliation with reality, by her Christian acceptance of the cross, all of which left a deep impression on Edith and directed her attention to another, unknown world. That was the first time that she was attracted to Christ.

Conversion

After this first religious surge, Edith slowly progressed towards conversion along the way marked by a painful but persistent search for the truth. She kept reflecting on the divine meticulously during the years spent in Freiburg beside the Master, which would prove its effectiveness later, when, announcing to an unexpecting priest that she wanted to be baptized, she calmly revealed to him her accurate and deep knowledge. Her intelligence was somewhat ahead of her will, marked by an exceptional readiness to follow the path of faith. Edith's experience is like that described by St. Augustine (2024, 8, 5) in the *Confessions*: "Nor had I now any longer my wonted excuse, . . . because my perception of the truth was uncertain; for now it was certain."

In the history of the church, there are many converts who are similar to Edith Stein in their journey to Christ. There is a clear overlap between her conversion and that of St. Augustine. A comparison of the two cases provides a number of much the same points that call for a broader analysis. Edith, like Augustine, fell into the embrace of God, seeking the truth (cf. Pryba 2015). This search for truth was sincere, courageous and as such influenced the decision-making. Augustine said to God: "panting under which for the breath of Your Truth, I was not able to breathe it pure and undefiled" (Augustine 2024, 5,11), and Edith stated with deep conviction: "My search for truth was a constant prayer" (Spiritu Sancto 1952, 55).

It was not intelligence that brought these two eminent "intellectuals" into the realm of truth, but example. Augustine's acute religious turn begins with an overheard story about the conversion of the rhetor Victorinus and two imperial officials, who had abandoned their careers, left their brides and consecrated themselves to God in the wake of reading the life of St. Anthony the hermit. Edith experienced this moving power of example in the empty house of her friend Reinach. The "Take and read" that one day turned the troubled Augustine into a believer was still missing from her life. For Edith, this "take and read" did not take place in a garden setting, but in the country house of a friend, also a philosopher, Hedwig Conrad-Marius. On a summer evening in 1921, Edith was left alone in the house, reached for a thick book from her friend's library and began to read avidly. It was the autobiography of St. Teresa of Avila. She read all night and in the morning closed the book stating: "This is the Truth!" (Posselt 1963, 100), thus ending the long years of spiritual restlessness she had painfully experienced. From that moment on, Edith belongs completely to Christ. In Bergzabern, on 1 January 1922, she was baptized; she beamed with an extraordinary joy that deeply moved the witnesses of the event.

At this point, it is important to note a remarkable, somewhat paradoxical thing. Edith's conversion to the Christian faith became for her at the same time a conversion to Judaism. Her discovery of Christ leads her to a new discovery of Hebraism – a discovery that will gradually develop and deepen until it assumes mystical depths under external persecution. In this sense it is not strictly to speak of conversion. The Jew who converts does not have to go backwards, does not have to destroy anything of his past, as the pagan, for whom conversion must be a break with the past. A Jew needs only to go forward in order to come to Christ, with whom the law was permeated, as the fathers of the church, led by St. Augustine, emphasized.

When Edith came home after a period of uncertainty and knelt before her mother, openly confessing that she had become a Catholic, a shocking drama erupted. The mother was pierced by pain, but she loved her daughter too much to accuse her of anything, so she expressed her reaction in tears. Brothers and sisters froze in disbelief. How come? Edith, the genius, the ornament of the family, a Catholic? To understand this reaction one has to take into account the tradition of Jewish faith in the family, which saw this conversion above all as an unacceptable and unforgivable betrayal. Of course, one must also bear in mind the vision of the Catholic faith that was held in Jewish circles at the time, namely that it was seen as the cultivation of superstition and servility. Only the great mutual love and respect that Edith enjoyed allowed the family to accept the whole affair in patient silence, albeit marked by pain. Faith, in turn, revived in Edith the experience of Abraham, to whom the calling God said: "Go forth from your land, your relatives, and from your father's house to a land that I will show you" (Gen 12:1). For her, too, it was to be a journey to an unknown country, marked by difficulties but also by unexpected spiritual discoveries.

Edith's new attitude towards the Jewish world is very instructive. Above all, she was free from any kind of distancing herself from it or from escapism. She spontaneously accompanied her mother in prayer in the synagogue and with her breviary joined her in reciting the psalms. Her mother, observing Edith's prayer, confessed one day: "I have never seen anyone praying like Edith and – even more strangely – she can connect with our prayers with her book" (Spiritu Sancto 1952, 97).

If previously it meant virtually nothing to Edith to belong to the Jewish world, now she is proud of it – as were the Jewish philosophers of her time: Husserl, Bergson, Meyerson – repeatedly saying, "We Jews." One of her friends said that one had the impression of hearing Saint Paul's cry on her lips: "Are they Israelites? So am I" (2 Cor 11:22). During this time, she developed a friendship with a Jewish woman from Breslau who came to her to take phenomenology lessons. On this occasion, Edith's great gentleness and respect for the religion of her fellow countrymen became apparent. She never took any action that might have induced her friend to abandon her religious convictions. She herself justified her actions by a principle she had strongly expressed on Husserl's death in a letter to her sister Adelgundis Jaegerschmid:

> I am not at all worried about my dear Master. It has always been far from me to think that God's mercy allows itself to be circumscribed by the visible church's boundaries. God is truth. All who seek truth seek God, whether this is clear to them or not (Stein 1993, 388).

She herself had experienced this in her life, and was therefore all the more convinced of such a judgment.

This extraordinary respect, however, did not prevent Edith from rejoicing when she learned that there was someone else in the family to whom Jesus had addressed the call, "Follow me!" It was her sister, Rose. The conviction that this was the right choice made Edith strongly support her sister, and all the others who were making this choice. She found undoubted consolation in being able to lead, as it were, by the hand, a number of Christ's disciples.

The road to the monastery

Edith, like St. Augustine, was quick to see the double requirement in her conversion, namely to break with the world and to serve God alone. She could not, however, immediately consecrate herself entirely to God, choosing a monastic life in the Carmelites, since such an unpleasantness could have led her mother to death. She did, however, give up teaching at the University of Freiburg as an assistant to Husserl, and went to Spira, where she took up a job as a teacher at a female high school run by Dominican nuns. She acted like St. Augustine, who left teaching rhetoric in Milan and went to Cassiciacum, at the foot of the Alps. She taught there for ten years in the silence of the monastery, until fame snatched her from this enclave of peace to share her thoughts through conferences preached in Germany, Switzerland, Vienna, Paris and Prague.

Edith revealed herself as a forerunner of Christian feminism, striving for the inclusion of women in various areas of society without diminishing their maternal vocation. It is safe to say that she was the first woman to speak as a woman to women in this way. The German writer Gertrude von Le Fort (1876-1971), author of the unforgettable *Dialogues of the Carmelites*, kept a photograph of Edith on her desk while she was writing her pioneering work *The Eternal Woman*.

In 1932, under some pressure from German Catholics, Edith began to seek work at German universities so that she could present her new philosophical orientation from her university chair, but this became increasingly difficult because she was not an Aryan. The rejection she encountered became, as it were, her first warning against Nazism (cf. Bello and Chenaux 2005). Then came the increasingly aggressive persecution of Jews and Christians in Germany. There was a repeat of what had already happened under the Roman Empire: "*Non licet esse vos!* It is not lawful for you to exist," as recorded by Tertullian (2024, 4). The Jews became *Lebensunwert* for the German Nazis.

In 1932, Edith was appointed a docent at the German Institute of Scientific Pedagogy in Münster, but had to resign from teaching after a year because of her Jewish background. Like few others in Germany from 1932 onwards, Edith was aware of the impending extermination of the Jews. She sought a private audience with Pope Pius XI to encourage authoritative intervention against the persecution of the Jews, but the times were still too immature for such action. Even in Germany, her gloomy assumptions were not believed and her clerical father Abbot Raphael Walzer advised her against such intervention, although at the same time he helped her to obtain an audience with the Pope (cf. Bellino 2018, 154-155). Later, Edith herself realized how such an intervention would be unhelpful and even harmful. However, she wrote a letter to Pius XI (1933) in which she expressed her concerns:

> ... not only Jews but also thousands of faithful Catholics in Germany, and, I believe, all over the world, have been waiting and hoping for the Church of Christ to raise its voice to put a stop to this abuse of Christ's name.

Recognizing that her tasks in the world had come to an end, Edith returned to her former intention and chose the life of a Carmelite nun in a convent in Cologne. On 13 October 1933 she said goodbye to her family and on 15 April 1934 she took the name Teresa Benedicta of the Cross at the monastery. After three years at the monastery, on 21 April 1938, she took her perpetual vows and on 1 May received the black Carmelite veil from the hands of Bishop Strockums. After a terrible round-up in the monastery on the night of 9 November 1938 in search of Jews and their belongings, the superiors concluded that even Carmel was no longer a peaceful place for Edith to stay. When the Nazis came to the convent to make the nuns swear an oath of loyalty to the Führer, they asked about Edith, among other things, and, leaving the convent, noted that she was not an Aryan. On 31 December 1938, a friend of the convent took her by car abroad, to the Dutch Carmel in Echt.

From as early as 1942, anti-Semitic persecution also took place in the Netherlands. From there too, as from other countries conquered and occupied by the Germans, trains full of Jews were leaving for the concentration camps. Faced with this fact, on 17 February 1942, representatives of the Catholic Church and Protestant communities in the Netherlands sent a telegram to Reich Commissioner Arthur Seyss-Inquart, in which they wrote:

> Deeply moved by the information about the mass arrests of Jews ... and the ruthless treatment of those arrested, ... we cannot suppress the cry of conscience. ... In the name of humanity and Christian principles, we loudly protest in defence of the inalienable right of human conscience (Phayer 2011, 156).

The German Nazis did not succumb to the admonitions and not only continued the extermination of the Jews, but escalated it. At that time, the Dutch bishops and other Christian community leaders jointly drafted a pastoral letter containing a protest and admonition to be read in all churches in the Netherlands, in which they included the quoted text of the telegram. Under pressure and threats from Seyss-Inquart, some leaders of the Christian communities withdrew from this initiative. The Catholic bishops, led by the Archbishop of Utrecht, and other Christian communities did not cave into the pressure and the letter was read out to all the faithful on 26 July 1942.

It has been debated much and repeatedly whether the position of the church authorities could have stopped the extermination of the Jews by Hitler and his collaborators. Much was generalized and hypothesized. In this case we have a concrete case with which to verify the Nazi reactions to the intervention taken by church authorities. Rolf Hochmut's belief that local interventions by church authorities had positive results is not historically true. The pastoral letter of the Dutch bishops, important as a document expressing courage and Christian convictions, sadly contributed to the deaths of many innocent victims. The Germans immediately executed merciless retaliation, arresting and deporting all members of Jewish religious communities and around three hundred baptized Jews.

Two representatives of the Gestapo turned up at the gate of the Echt Carmel on the Sunday afternoon of 2 August 1942. Edith Stein and her sister Rose were told to go with them. They had little time to take their personal belongings or food. They had to leave Carmel if they did not want to endanger the whole convent. Thus began Edith's way of the cross. From Echt they were taken to the camp at Amersfort and from there, on 4 August, to the concentration camp at Westerbork, where Edith became directly acquainted with the unheard-of suffering inflicted on the Jews in a climate of apocalyptic terror. Women, separated from their husbands, fell into numbness and stupor. Children, taken away from their mothers and shot for fun, as we read in the files of the beatification trial, crawled towards Edith, who fed and soothed them. Witnesses in the beatification process confirmed her heroic devotion to her fellow human beings in the camp at Westerbork (Herbstrith 1987, 167–168).

At the Westerbork camp, the prisoners were loaded onto a train in which they were mercilessly squeezed and sent "east." "East" meant only one thing at the time – Auschwitz – where Edith, her sister Rose and the other Jews would die in the gas chamber on 9 August 1942. Before the martyrdom of blood, Edith experienced the martyrdom of the heart, the cause of which was the destruction of her family. Her elder brother was deported with his family and later killed; also her sister Frieda was deported and died; other relatives dispersed in America (Stein 1993, 497). The mother died in 1936. When her beloved daughter was in the convent, she would write letters to her – bearing the signatures of Edith's sisters – every week. This was consistent with her mother's faith. After her death, there were claims that she had finally converted, but the daughter challenged such assumptions in a letter to Kaliksta Kopf dated 4 October 1936:

> The news of [my mother's] conversion was a totally unfounded rumor. I have no idea who made it up. My mother held to her faith to the very last. The faith and firm confidence she had in her God from her earliest childhood until her 87th year remained steadfast, and were the last things that stayed alive in her during the final agony. Therefore, I have the firm belief that she found a very merciful judge and is now my most faithful helper on my way, so that I, too, may reach my goal (Stein 1993, 341–342).

"For the nation"

This somewhat general biographical information makes it possible to situate Edith Stein's attitude towards Hebraism during the persecution brought about by Hitler in a relatively comprehensive way.

Edith's disclosure of her intention to enter a convent caused a drama in the family even greater than her conversion. Edith described it all in her moving autobiographical text *How I entered the Carmel in Cologne* (Stein 1994, cf. eadem 1950). When Edith tried to explain that this is what Christ wants of her, her mother fearfully asked her: "Why have you learnt [about Christ]?" This peculiar admonition evoked a deep sadness in Edith, which probably recurred later in difficult moments. After all, she might have expected the reaction that while her people were being persecuted, she was abandoning them to take safe refuge in a monastery.

Edith's approach to this fact, however, was entirely different. She was inspired by the biblical tradition associated with the figure of Esther, in whose story she saw the reflection of her life and her destiny in relation to the Jewish people. She wrote to her friend Petra Brüning:

> I keep having to think of Queen Esther who was taken from among her people precisely that she might represent them before the king. I am a very poor and powerless little Esther, but the King who chose me is infinitely great and merciful. That is such a great comfort (Stein 1993, 413).

Edith knew that she had apparently abandoned her own kinsfolk only to accept its destiny and lay it before Christ, combining it with her personal prayer and expiation.

This "revelation" appeared to Edith supernaturally when she prayed before the Crucified One, even before entering the monastery, in the chapel of the Carmel in Cologne. This is what she wrote about it in one of her letters:

> By the Cross I understood the destiny of God's people which, even at that time [in 1933 – J.K.], began to announce itself. I thought that those who recognised it as the Cross of Christ had to take it upon themselves in the name of all. Certainly, today I know more of what it means to be wedded to the Lord in the sign of the Cross. Of course, one can never comprehend it, for it is a mystery" (Stein 1993, 418).

The conviction of an expiatory mission, expressed here very clearly, accompanied Edith all the time in the monastery. In her will drawn up at Echt on 9 June 1939, she wrote: "I already accept with joy the death that God has destined for me, in full submission to His most holy will. I ask the Lord to accept my living and dying to His honour and glory" (Herbstrith 1987, 156). She went on to list all the intentions that were important to her, which included "expiation for the unfaithfulness of the Jewish people and that the Lord may be accepted by His own" (Herbstrith 1987, 156). As Edith and Rose were leaving the convent in Echt to set off on their final journey, Edith was to say to her terrified sister: "Come, we are going to suffer for our people" (Stein 1967, 136).

The mystical experience of the crucified one did not prevent Edith from bleeding inwardly at the sufferings of her countrymen. Out of this pain came her tragic cry: "It is necessary for Cain to be persecuted, but woe to him who touches Cain" (Herbstrith 1987, 167). Her usually calm and youthful countenance, which we see in Edith's photographs, also experienced deep sadness. In the Westerbork camp she was to say, "I would never have thought that my brothers and sisters had to suffer to such an extent" (Herbstrith 1987, 167). The sight of this suffering moved her to the depths, causing her the most personal suffering.

In adopting the Christian faith, Edith did not distance herself in any way from the Jewish world, nor did she shut herself off from the world of her new faith. For her, the monastery did not mean isolation, but a fuller participation in the affairs of the world at that time. Her awareness of the need for expiation inscribed her profoundly in the tradition and framework of Israeli life, which is why she always considered herself one of the persecuted Jews. It must be emphasized at this point, on the basis of the testimonies we have, that the persecutions triggered in Edith an ever more far-reaching deepening of her inner solidarity with the Jewish people, to whom she belonged both in spirit and in body, also by virtue of her bond with Jesus Christ himself.

Her conversion and entry into the monastery gave Edith a new and deepened motive for solidarity with the race to which she belonged. She was enabled to do so by feeling the blood of Jesus Christ himself pulsating in her veins. She could therefore conclude that the persecution of the Jews was a persecution of the humanity of Christ. German Nazism never forgave Jesus for not being an Aryan, which is why, immediately after the Jews, the Nazis cruelly persecuted the Christians. Gradually escalating facts confirmed the suppositions which, from Hitler's rise to power onwards, were awakening in Edith. Her mystical experience in the Cologne monastery became a fact that affected her personally, and its consequences became shared by the church, which also drew on what she went through.

Summary

Pope John Paul II (1998), at the time of the canonization of Edith Stein – Teresa Benedicta of the Cross – summarized her life and her spiritual experiences in the following way:

> The mystery of the Cross gradually enveloped her whole life, spurring her to the point of making the supreme sacrifice. As a bride on the Cross, Sr Teresa Benedicta did not only write profound pages about the "science of the Cross," but was thoroughly trained in the school of the Cross. Many of our contemporaries would like to silence the Cross. But nothing is more eloquent than the Cross when silenced! The true message of suffering is a lesson of love. Love makes suffering fruitful and suffering deepens love. Through the experience of the Cross, Edith Stein was able to open the way to a new encounter with the God of Abraham, Isaac and Jacob, the Father of our Lord Jesus Christ. Faith and the Cross proved inseparable to her. Having matured in the school of the Cross, she found the roots to which the tree of her own life was attached. She understood that it was very important for her "to be a daughter of the chosen people and to belong to Christ not only spiritually, but also through blood."

The papal statement can also serve as the conclusion of this article, which shows Edith Stein's bond with her people, a bond completed in the Christian faith and in the mystery of Christ's cross, with which she was ultimately united in this ultimate experience, which is martyrdom.

Bibliography

Adamska, Janina I. 1998. *Błogosławiona Edyta Stein*, Kraków 1988. Kraków: Wydawnictwo Karmelitów Bosych.

Augustine. n.d. "Confessions." *New Advent*, https://www.newadvent.org/fathers/1101.htm [accessed: 11.06.2024].

Bellino, Alessandro. 2018. *Il Vaticano e Hitler. Santa Sede, Chiesa tedesca e nazismo (1922–1939)*. Milano: Guerini e Associati.

Bello, Angela A., and Philippe Chenaux, eds. 2005. *Edith Stein e il nazismo*. Rome: Città nuova.

Depraz, Natalie. 2010. *Zrozumieć fenomenologię. Konkretna praktyka*, translated by Agata. Czarnecka. Warszawa: Oficyna Naukowa.

Herbstrith, Waltraud. 1987. *Das wahre Gericht Edith Steins*. Aschaffenburg: Kaffke-Verlag.

Herbstrith, Waltraud. 1988. *Edith Stein. Jüdin und Christin*. Munich; Zurich; Vienna: Verlag Neue Stadt.

Jan Paweł II. 1998. "Homilia podczas Mszy świętej kanonizacyjnej (11 października 1998)." *L'Osservatore Romano* 19 (1998) 12: 19–20.

Jan Paweł II. 1999. "Homilia na rozpoczęcie Synodu Biskupów poświęconego Europie (1 października 1999)." *L'Osservatore Romano* 20 (1999) 12: 22–23.

John Paul II. 1998. "Homily of John Paul II for the Canonisation of Edith Stein (11 October 1998)." *The Holy See*. https://www.vatican.va/content/john-paul-ii/en/homilies/1998/documents/hf_jp-ii_hom_11101998_stein.html [accessed: 11.06.2024].

John Paul II. 1999. "John Paul II, Second Special Assembly for Europe of the Synod of Bishops (1 October 1999)." *The Holy See*. https://www.vatican.va/content/john-paul-ii/en/homilies/1999/documents/hf_jp-ii_hom_01101999_sinodo-europa.html [accessed: 11.06.2024].

Królikowski, Janusz. 1988. "Od filozofii do męczeństwa. Kanonizacja Teresy Benedykty od Krzyża – Edyty Stein." *W drodze* (1998) 12: 36–42.

Machnacz, Jerzy. 2019. "Edyta Stein – św. Teresa Benedykta od Krzyża. Osoba, fenomenolog, metafizyk (ontolog), teolog mistyk, świadek (martyr)." In *Splendor Personae. Św. Edyta Stein, Patronka Europy*, edited by Bogumił Gacka, and Cezary Ritter, 63–94. Warszawa: Wydawnictwo Naukowe UKSW.

Meester, Conrad de. 2013. *Edith Stein. Eine Frau auf der Suche nach der Wahrheit*. Vienna: Christliche Innerlichkeit.

Mikołajczyk, Mirosław. 2016. *Edyta Stein – św. Teresa Benedykta od Krzyża. Bibliografia polska 1933–2013*. Wrocław: Papieski Wydział Teologiczny.

Neyer, Maria A. 1987. *Edith Stein. Ihr Leben in Dokumenten und Bildern*. Würzburg: Echter Verlag.

Phayer, Michael. 2011. *Kościół katolicki wobec holokaustu 1930–1965*, translated by Jacek Lang. Poznań: Axis, Replika.

Posselt, Teresia R. 1963. *Edith Stein. Eine große Frau unseres Jahrhunderts.* Freiburg: Herder-Bücherei.
Pryba, Andrzej. "'Great Daughter of Israel and Carmel,' Searching for the Truth Every Day," *The Person and the Challenges* 5 (2015) 1: 85–99.
Sleiman, Jean. 1999. "Edith Stein, martire di Cristo per il suo Popolo." *Teresianum* 50 (1999) 1–2: 359–384.
Spiritu Sancto, Teresia R. de. 1952. *Edith Stein – Lebensbild einer Philosophin und Karmelitin.* Nürnberg: Glock und Lutz.
Stein, Edith. 1933. "Letter to Pope Pius XI (1933)." *Council of Centers on Jewish-Christian Relations.* https://www.ccjr.us/dialogika-resources/primary-texts-from-the-history-of-the-relationship/stein1939april [accessed: 11.06.2024].
Stein, Edith. 1950. "The road to Carmel: how I entered the Carmel in Cologne." *Life of the Spirit* 4.44: 354–366. https://www.jstor.org/stable/43703437 [accessed: 11.06.2024].
Stein, Edith. 1967. *Edith Stein. Briefauslese 1917–1942. Mit einem Dokumentenanhang zu ihrem Tode.* Freiburg; Basel; Vienna: Herder Verlag.
Stein, Edith. 1986. *Life in a Jewish Family: An Autobiography, 1891–1916. The Collected Works of Edith Stein Volume 1*, translated by Josephine Koeppel. Washington, DC: ICS Publications.
Stein, Edith. 1993. *Self-Portrait in Letters, 1916–1942. The Collected Works of Edith Stein Volume 5*, translated by Josephine Koeppel. Washington: ICS Publications.
Stein, Edith. 1994. *Stein E., Wie ich in der Kölner Karmel kam*, edited by M. A. Neyer. Würzburg: Echter 1994.
Stein, Edyta / Teresa Benedykta od Krzyża. 2000. *Dzieje pewnej rodziny żydowskiej*, edited by Maria Amata Neyer, translated by Immakulata J. Adamska. Kraków: Wydawnictwo Karmelitów Bosych.
Stein, Edyta / Teresa Benedykta od Krzyża. 2002. *Autoportret z listów I. 1916–1933*, edited by Maria A. Neyer, translated by Immakulata J. Adamska. Kraków: Wydawnictwo Karmelitów Bosych.
Stein, Edyta / Teresa Benedykta od Krzyża. 2003. *Autoportret z listów II. 1933–1942*, edited by Maria A. Neyer, translated by Immakulata J. Adamska, and Anna Talarek. Kraków: Wydawnictwo Karmelitów Bosych.
Teresia a Matre Dei. 1963. *Edith Stein. Auf der Suche nach Gott.* Kevalaer: Butzon und Bercker.
Tertullian. "Apology." n.d. *New Advent.* https://www.newadvent.org/fathers/0301.htm [accessed: 11.06.2024].

9

Bonhoeffer 1941: Peace Aims for the Time after the War in an Ecumenical Perspective

God's Command in a Secular World

Rev. Emeritus Gottfried Brezger
Bonhoeffer House, Berlin

About the Author

Gottfried Brezger, theologian, church musician and graduate sociologist, pastor emeritus of the evangelical church Berlin-Brandenburg-schlesische Oberlausitz, since 1998 honorary chairman of the Bonhoeffer-Haus Memorial and Place of Encounter, Marienburger Allee 43, Berlin. Publications include "Dynamics of Dietrich Bonhoeffer's inclusive Christology in the footsteps of Martin Luther in contradiction to the dynamics of political exclusion" (*Theologia Wratislaviensia*).

Keywords

Bonhoeffer House, Bonhoeffer and ecumenism, God's reality in the reality of the world

Abstract

Against the backdrop of the Bonhoeffer family home in Berlin, this paper discusses sources for resistance in Bonhoeffer's life and upbringing, including his family, his ecumenical relationships, and his faith in God's reality in the reality of the world.

The Bonhoeffer family house

Many visitors who come to the Bonhoeffer House in Berlin from the ecumenical world ask us: "From where did Dietrich Bonhoeffer get his strength to resist even unto death?" Three sources were of particular importance for him: his family, his ecumenical relationships and his faith in God's reality in the reality of the world.

First I would like to invite you to the home of his family, which since 1987 is a Memorial and Place of Encounter of the evangelical church. As a historical place of learning the Bonhoeffer House is a topography of resistance in the city of the "Topography of Terror." In 1935, Karl and Paula Bonhoeffer moved into the house they had built for their retirement. Dietrich Bonhoeffer got his study room under the roof. During his time at the preacher's seminary in Finkenwalde near Stettin (Szczecin), his travelling, and his work with his brother-in-law Hans von Dohnanyi in the counterintelligence of the Supreme Command of the Wehrmacht, the family home became a place of retreat for him, a place to work on his "Ethics" and to conspire with like-minded people. On 5 April 1943, Dietrich Bonhoeffer was arrested here, in the house. In the restored study room with his desk, copies of his books, and his clavichord, the encounter with Bonhoeffer's story becomes vivid and alive.

Of the many moving situations I have experienced in the study room with visitors since 1998, one is particularly emphatic for me: during the visit of a small group from England, an elderly woman approached me and tearfully told me that her father, who was a pilot in the Royal Air Force, had taken his irreconcilable hatred against the Germans to his grave. She hugged me and explained that, representing her father, she wanted to reconcile at the place where Dietrich Bonhoeffer had lived. For her, Dietrich Bonhoeffer represented the "other Germany."

1. First source of resistance: family

As the sixth of eight children, Dietrich Bonhoeffer grew up in an upper middle-class family characterized by mutual respect, a sense of justice, solidarity, culture and education. His father Karl, head of the Department of Psychiatry and Neurology at the Charité, and his mother Paula, a trained teacher, fostered in the four sons and four daughters respect, an alert and empathetic perception, understanding of political processes and civil courage. They were resistant to Nazi ideology. Later, in the political resistance the siblings, joined by their friends and partners – together with Dietrich's closest friend Eberhard Bethge and Dietrich's bride Maria von Wedemeyer – they knew that they could trust each other and rely on each other. "Who stands firm?"[1] asks Dietrich Bonhoeffer in his account of resistance at the turn of the year 1942–43 (Bonhoeffer 2010, 38). Learning civil courage with the Bonhoeffer family is a special opportunity in the encounter today in their historic house.

2. Second source of resistance: ecumenical relationships

The resistance to National Socialism of Dietrich Bonhoeffer as one of the representatives of the "other Germany" depended on reliable, courageous and empathetic cooperation with representatives of the ecumenical movement. George Bell, bishop of Chichester, and Visser 't Hooft, designated General Secretary of the World Council of Churches (WCC), which was then in the process of being established, took up the challenge for ecumenism to be *one* church in confession.

As youth delegate of the World Alliance for International Friendship of Churches, Bonhoeffer participated in the meeting of the World Alliance together with the Ecumenical Conference of Life and Work on the island of Fanø/Denmark, 18–30 August 1934. In his address "The Church and the Peoples of the World" he urgently called for peace. He confronts the Conference with the fundamental question:

> How does peace come about? . . . There is no way to peace along the way of safety. For peace must be dared. It is the great venture. It can never be made safe . . . Peace means to give oneself altogether to the law of God, wanting no security . . .
>
> Battles are won, not with weapons, but with God. They are won where the way leads to the cross. Which of us can say he knows what it might mean for the world if one nation should meet the aggressor, not with weapons in its hand, but praying,

---

1. From "An Account at the Turn of the Year 1942–1943. After Ten Years," written for Eberhard Bethge, Hans von Dohnanyi, and Hans Oster. Dietrich Bonhoeffer wrote this account in his family home, where it was hidden and later found after the war.

defenseless and for that very reason protected by "a bulwark never failing"?

Once again, how will peace come? Who will call us to peace so that the world will hear, will have to hear? so that all peoples may rejoice? The individual Christian cannot do it. When all around are silent, he can indeed raise his voice and bear witness, but the powers of this world stride over him without a word . . . Only the one great Ecumenical Council of the Holy Church of Christ over all the world can speak out so that the world, though it gnash its teeth, will have to hear, so that the peoples will rejoice because the Church of Christ in the name of Christ has taken the weapons from the hands of their sons, forbidden war, and proclaimed the peace of Christ against the raging world (Bonhoeffer 2007, 308f).

Bonhoeffer has a clear vision of the challenge for the church to speak up on behalf of the silent and excluded when the state disenfranchises people and groups and violates its duty to protect the weak. His call is reminiscent of the biblical message of the prophets. A prophet or prophetess does not predict what will happen but says the right word at the wrong time; and that person stands for this with his or her actions and life. If this message remains unfulfilled, later generations can remember the resistant prophetic word and draw strength for their resistance from it. This was already the case with Isaiah, Deutero-Isaiah and Trito-Isaiah. And it also happened in the 1980s when peace movement groups in the German Democratic Republic referred to Bonhoeffer's call for the church to "to seize the wheel itself" (Bonhoeffer 2009, 365).

In the summer of 1939, when Dietrich Bonhoeffer could no longer avoid his obligation as a soldier for the impending war of the Nazi state, he fled to the USA. But he abandoned the exile he had been offered at Union Theological Seminary in New York, USA after just four weeks (12 June–7–8 July 1939) and returned to Berlin with uncertain prospects for the future. His double life in the ecumenical as well in the military resistance began in October 1940 when his brother-in-law Hans von Dohnanyi arranged for him to work as an undercover agent for the Foreign and Defence Office of the Supreme Command of the Wehrmacht (OKW). Through his collaboration in the conspiracy, he, who on Fanø wholeheartedly advocated the non-violent proclamation of peace through a council of the churches, participated in the planning of a violent tyrannicide. Dietrich Bonhoeffer was aware of the ethical dilemma: he recognized that his actions were tainted with great guilt. But if he did not resist the Nazi state, the tyranny against the Jews and others who were declared enemies of the people, and against the continuity of the war of extermination, he would also incur guilt.

Keith Clements asks the question "how and why [Dietrich Bonhoeffer] the ecumenist became a conspirator?" and examines the links between the two roles of Bonhoeffer. As a courier for the resistance group in the counterintelligence around Colonel Oster and Hans von Dohnanyi, covered by Admiral Canaris, Bonhoeffer traveled to Switzerland three times in 1941–42 with the secret service ID of a courier. The aim of his talks with ecumenical interlocutors in neutral foreign countries was to come in contact with political leaders of the Western Allies with the intention to move them to guarantee fair conditions for peace negotiations in the event that a coup would succeed. This was of crucial importance for the resistance groups working towards an end to the Nazi war and terror. Bonhoeffer was probably unaware of the parallel efforts from the "Kreisau Circle," through Adam von Trott zu Solz from the Foreign Office, who also communicated confidentially with Visser 't Hooft, and Helmuth James Graf von Moltke from the Supreme Command of the army.

With Visser 't Hooft in Geneva, Bonhoeffer had a strong partner who, like him, came from the theology of Karl Barth. Visser 't Hooft, who set up in Geneva a conspiratorial agency between underground activists in occupied Netherlands and the Dutch government-in-exile with Queen Wilhelmina in London, had already in January 1940 analyzed the causes of the war and set the course for the behaviour of Christians, the churches and ecumenism. He recalled – in the face of danger to the foundations of human coexistence – "God's claim to sovereignty over the whole world." Visser 't Hooft (1973, 317f) demanded that the church "lift up its voice against the violation of whole nations, against the attacks by big nations of small ones, against the suppression of national and international freedom."

Bonhoeffer's second trip on behalf of the intelligence service to Switzerland from 29 August to 26 September 1941 took place ten weeks after the invasion of the Soviet Union by the German Wehrmacht on 22 June 1941. Despite the rapid advance of German troops, Bonhoeffer was convinced, as he told Visser 't Hooft, that the course of the war had turned. All the more reason for both of them to be alert to the discussion of peace aims in the English churches in the midst of the pursuit of war aims. They took the publication of the book by William Paton (1941), a friend of George Bell and secretary of the WCC in England, "The Church and the New Order" as an opportunity to write a memorandum as a "highly political book review" (headline in: Bethge 2000).

In his remarks on the aims of peace after the war and the end of Nazi tyranny, Bonhoeffer became specific:

> What matters is whether a state order in Germany is realised that acknowledges its responsibility to the commands of God. That will become evident in the total removal of the Nazi system, including and especially the Gestapo; in the restoration of the sovereignty of equal rights for all; in a press that serves the truth; in the restoration of the freedom of the church to proclaim the word of God in command and gospel to all the world (Bonhoeffer 2006, 532, cf. Theological Declaration of Barmen 1934, 6th Thesis).

3. Third source of resistance: faith in God's reality in the reality of the world

What does "a state order . . . that acknowledges its responsibility to the commands of God" mean? Is the general agreement to God's commands for life and living together not an imposition on secular political consciousness, which has stepped out of the shadow of ecclesiastical paternalism? There are four ways of dealing with the church and the world: (1) sacral re-Christianization by means of state authority and autocracy; (2) secular understanding of religion and adaptation in the spirit of a liberal attitude; (3) limiting religion, faith and the message of the church to private sphere; (4) "The claim of Jesus Christ on the world that has come of age" (Bonhoeffer 2010, 457, and 425–429).

Bonhoeffer's path leads between the Scylla of "liberal anarchy" and the Charybdis of the totalitarian Nazi state. He trusts in the ultimate reality of God revealed in Jesus Christ in the penultimate reality of the world. "Your kingdom come. Your will be done, on earth as it is in heaven." God's claim to sovereignty calls for responsible action in secular society and sets on the one hand clear limits against any form of state clericalism. Pope Francis responded to Patriarch Kyrill, who presented Putin's arguments for the war of aggression in Ukraine to him: "Brother, we are not state clerics, we are shepherds of the people" (Vatican News 2022).

On the other hand, Bonhoeffer, in the sense of the dynamism of the Word of God, overcame the dualism that is fatal to Christian ethics and firmly opposed the sacred and the secular, church and world.

> In Christ we are invited to participate in the reality of God and the reality of the world at the same time, the one not without the other. The reality of God is disclosed only as it places me completely into the reality of the world. But I find the reality of the world always already borne, accepted, and reconciled in the reality of God. That

> is the mystery of the revelation of God in the human being Jesus Christ. The Christian ethics now asks, then, how this reality of God and of the world that is given in Christ, becomes real in our world (Bonhoeffer 2005, 55).

In closing, I think that in his faith in the reality of God in the reality of the world under the sign of the cross, Dietrich Bonhoeffer's dialectic and Edith Stein's mysticism come close to each other. Bonhoeffer (2005, 57) contradicts the "division of the whole of reality into sacred and profane" and thus challenges the secular understanding of the world historically founded in the Enlightenment. Two opposition circles, the "Kreisauers" and the "Freiburgers," also formulated a reference to God in their ideas for a peace order. However, Bonhoeffer explicitly does not seek the basis of the legal order in the ideal of the individual's right to personality or human rights, but in God's command to protect the other. The dignity of the other is guaranteed in God's otherness (1st commandment) and can be experienced in Christ as the "man for others."

> Whoever confesses the reality of Jesus Christ as the revelation of God confesses in the same breath the reality of God and the reality of the world, for they find God and the world reconciled in Christ (Bonhoeffer 2005, 62).

What does this Christian confession mean today for the ideas of the rule of law in Europe in interreligious dialogue in the context of religious-cultural plurality? On what normative foundation can the "common house of Europe" exist in stormy times and also withstand the imperial warlike attacks of the clerically transfigured "Russki Mir" ("Russian World") and any imperial claims? Certainly not only through the demonstration of military strength to the outside world, but fundamentally through the internal strengthening of civil, state and international law. Mutual response and mutual responsibility, effective border demarcation against the aggressor on the one hand and sustainable overcoming of borders in the interest of a common future on the other hand belong together in principle – even if it is not possible at all times – like now. But times of discussion of war aims should at the same time be times of discussion of peace aims. If the dignity of "the other," which is grounded in the "otherness" of God (first commandment) is to be respected, violations of dignity through aggression, hatred, disrespect and exclusion must be sanctioned. But when openness to one another, willingness to learn and dialogue in respect, empathy and solidarity blossom, the fulfilment of the commandment of love becomes the sign of the reconciled reality in the unreconciled one. Bonhoeffer experienced the realization of this command of God, which demonstrates its reconciling power in Christ in the "universal Christian brotherhood which rises above all national hatreds" (Bonhoeffer 2006, 468 f). These were the last recorded words of Dietrich Bonhoeffer in his message to Bishop George Bell.

The question of our faith in God's reality in the reality of our world is also relevant today: How responsible and relevant, independent, courageous and clear is the church to "proclaim the word of God in command and gospel to all the world" and thus to establish justice and peace and the sovereignty of independent law in the secular state and between peoples?

Bibliography

Bethge, Eberhard. 2000. *Dietrich Bonhoeffer: Theologian, Christian, Man for his Times*, edited by Victoria J. Barnett, translated by Eric Mosbacher et al. Minneapolis: Fortress Press.

Bonhoeffer, Dietrich. 2005. *Ethics. Dietrich Bonhoeffer Works Volume 6*, edited by Clifford J. Green, translated by Reinhard Krauss, Charles West, and Douglas W. Stott. Minneapolis: Fortress Press.

Bonhoeffer, Dietrich. 2006. *Conspiracy and Imprisonment 1940–1945. Dietrich Bonhoeffer Works Volume 16*, edited by Mark Brocker, translated by Lisa Dahill. Minneapolis: Fortress Press.

Bonhoeffer, Dietrich. 2007. *London. 1933–1935. Dietrich Bonhoeffer Works Volume 13*, edited by Keith Clements, translated by Isabel Best. Minneapolis: Fortress Press.

Bonhoeffer, Dietrich. 2009. *Berlin 1932–1933. Dietrich Bonhoeffer Works Volume 12*, edited by Larry L. Rasmussen, translated by Isabel Best and David Higgins. Minneapolis: Fortress Press.

Bonhoeffer, Dietrich. 2010. *Letters and Papers from Prison. Dietrich Bonhoeffer Works Volume 8*, edited by John W. de Gruchy, translated by Isabel Best, Lisa E. Dahill, Reinhard Krauss, and Nancy Lukens. Minneapolis: Fortress Press.

Paton, William. 1941. *The Church and the New Order*. London: Student Christian Movement Press.

The Theological Declaration of Barmen. 1934. https://cathedralofhope.org/wp-content/uploads/2019/03/The-Theological-Declaration-of-Barmen.pdf [accessed: 11.24.2022].

Vatican News. 2022. "Papstinterview: 'Das ganze Drama des Krieges sehen.'" Papst. https://www.vaticannews.va/de/papst/news/2022-06/papst-interview-civilta-cattolica-krieg-ukraine-kyrill-weltkrieg.html.

Visser 't Hooft, Willem A. 1973. "Main Points for statement to the churches. 7 January 1940." In *Kirchenkampf und Ökumene 1939–45. Darstellung und Dokumentation*, edited by Armin Boyens, 317–318. Munich: Chr. Kaiser.

10

"Today" Moments in the Troubled Life of Dietrich Bonhoeffer

March 1939 and His Commendation of the Catholic Modernist Friedrich von Hügel as an Example

Rev. Dr. Keith Clements, PhD
Former General Secretary of the Conference of European Churches
ORCID: 0000-0001-8183-4987

About the Author

Rev. Dr. Keith Clements (PhD Bristol). An ordained minister of the Baptist Union of Great Britain. Former General Secretary of the Conference of European European Churches. Emeritus member, Board of the International Bonhoeffer Society. Keith Clements has written extensively on Bonhoeffer, his books including *A Patriotism for Today* (1984, 2nd edition 2011), *Bonhoeffer and Britain* (Churches Together in Britain and Ireland 2006), *Dietrich Bonhoeffer's Ecumenical Quest* (World Council of Churches 2011), and *Appointments with Bonhoeffer: Personal Faith and Public Responsibility in a Fragmenting World* (2022). He is also editor of *London 1933–1935* (DBWE Vol. 13, 2007).

Keywords

History, crisis, faith, church struggle, ecumenism, Bonhoeffer, von Hügel, Barth

Abstract

This paper seeks to highlight how Bonhoeffer typically responds to moments of crisis in his own life, in the world and in the church, not by taking flight into abstract, intellectual generalities about history, but by plunging into that specific historical moment in all the risk and vulnerability of decision. Through venturing into the act of decision, however, he lays bare underlying theological issues and enables reflection on wider – even universal – features of faith.

Introduction

"Heute" – "Today" is how he begins his letter to Eberhard Bethge on the fateful day 21 July 1944, in which he produces those remarkable sentences about what it means to have faith, to be a truly human being, by sharing in the sufferings of God in the world. Other examples include: his sermon preached in London 21 January 1934 during a critical early phase of the church struggle; his sermon of 8 July 1934 just after the "Röhm putsch," and moreover his sermon on Trinity Sunday, 27 May 1934, just as the Barmen Synod was meeting. Bonhoeffer does not in every case make direct reference to the critical context, but it is quite clear what was in his mind and how it bears on his words.

In March 1939 Bonhoeffer was in London for several weeks, with Eberhard Bethge, engaged on behalf of the Confessing Church with leading figures in the British churches and the ecumenical movement. In an incident noted only relatively recently, he told a small group that if they had read the Catholic Modernist Friedrich von Hügel, "You would not have needed to read Karl Barth." This may seem a surprising statement, but seen against the background of the fraught discussions Bonhoeffer was having with certain ecumenical figures in London it becomes understandable. Bonhoeffer during these weeks was a deeply troubled soul about his church, the ecumenical movement, his country and his own personal future in face of the coming war. With the notable exception of Bishop George Bell, the measured, idealistic Anglican theology typically sought consensus in ecumenism above everything else, and saw the German church struggle as an affair of different "parties within the church." Bonhoeffer was still maintaining the exclusive claim of the Confessing Church to be the true witness in Germany over against the "German Christians" and the Reich church, and he grew increasingly frustrated and angry at the nebulous "Anglo-Saxon" view which refused to acknowledge the decisive issues at stake. Von Hügel had retained a Kierkegaardian insistence that in face of the transcendent, holy God, humans are called to *decision*. Von Hügel, whose writings were well known in Britain, evidently impressed Bonhoeffer as one to whom the British might pay attention if they found Barth too difficult! I deal with this episode more fully in my book *Appointments with Bonhoeffer: Personal Faith and Public Responsibility in a Fragmenting World* (2022).

Thus Bonhoeffer responds theologically to critical events, not by detached rationality, not by inventing theological escape mechanisms, but by engagement and decision in communion with God. "Now we are no longer bystanders, onlookers, judges of these events, but we ourselves are being addressed, we are affected. This has happened for us, God is speaking to us, this is all about us" (Bonhoeffer 2007, 369).

For some of us who have been in the circles of Bonhoeffer scholarship over the years, one of our greatest privileges was our friendship with Bonhoeffer's closest friend and biographer, Eberhard Bethge and his wife Renate. For me, one particularly memorable moment was one day in 1985 when visiting the Bethges at their home Wachtberg-Villiprott. In the course of conversation in his study I asked Eberhard where the originals of Bonhoeffer's prison letters were now kept. "Oh," he said casually, pointing to his desk, "in here. Would you like to see some of them? Any of them in particular?" A minute later I was holding in my hand that most precious and moving letter of 21 July 1944, the day after the failed attempt on Hitler's life, the day when Bonhoeffer surely knew that his eventual fate was now sealed: the letter in which he penned those profound reflections on what it means to become "a human being, a Christian," sharing the sufferings of God in the world. Eberhard pointed to the very first word in that letter: *Heute*, "today." *Heute will ich Dir nur einen kurzen Gruss schicken.* In both the older and the newer English translations this is rendered "This short greeting is all I want to send you today" (Bonhoeffer 2010, 541). Eberhard however believed that Dietrich intentionally began the letter with *Heute*, to emphasize the fateful significance of that day, and therefore adding immeasurably to the meaning of all the thoughts that follow.

Bonhoeffer was never so engrossed in the immediate here and now as to forget the wider world and the historical dramas of human existence. But neither did he allow himself to rest in a realm beyond time and temporality. His emphasis on the "this-worldliness" of faith includes a sense that here and now, today, matters. It is of course a note that sounds throughout the Bible: "O that today you would listen to his voice" (Ps 95:7); "Today is born to you in the city of David a Saviour"; "Today this scripture has been fulfilled in your hearing" (Luke 4:21). What is happening now, this moment, this day, is decisive.

Prophetic "today" proclamation

There are points in Bonhoeffer's writing and preaching, as in the 21 July 1944 letter, where the significance of "today" is very evident, even if he himself does not make it explicit. We see it several times, for example, in the sermons he preached while as pastor in London during 1933–35. On 21 January 1934, he preached on the text Jeremiah 20:7: "O Lord, you have enticed me, and I was enticed; you have overpowered me, and you have prevailed." The prophet's sense of enchainment by God's command is, says Bonhoeffer, being paralleled in Germany; "Today in our home church, thousands of parishioners and pastors are facing the danger of oppression and persecution because of their witness for the truth. They have not chosen this path out of arbitrary defiance, but because they were led to it . . . They followed it because God had become too strong for them." (Bonhoeffer 2007, 351–352). In fact Bonhoeffer was also full of anxiety about the outcome of a meeting between Protestant church leaders and Hitler, due to take place just four days later. On 8 July 1934 he preached on the incident in Luke's Gospel, when Pilate had "mingled the blood" of some Galileans with their sacrifices (Luke 13:1–5). Just days before that sermon, there had taken place in Germany the infamous "Röhm putsch" when upwards of two hundred Nazi "storm troopers" had been massacred on Hitler's orders, an event which sent shockwaves throughout Germany and well beyond. Bonhoeffer does not actually mention it in his sermon: he would not have needed to, as he spoke to his congregation about events so fearful that people shrank even to hear of them, and perhaps looked to church as a means of escape from such traumas. But for Bonhoeffer the terror of such a day cannot be evaded by averting one's gaze, still less simply blaming others. He has a stern message, based upon Jesus's reported words, "unless you repent, you will all perish as they [the Galileans] did." It is, says Bonhoeffer, we ourselves who are under judgment here: "This is the fruit of what I and my brothers have sown – and these people here, these Galileans and Pilate, are my brothers in sin, in hate and evil and lovelessness, my brothers in guilt" (Bonhoeffer 2007, 369).

Then there is his sermon preached in London on 27 May 1934, Trinity Sunday, not always a preacher's favourite day in the Christian year. But Bonhoeffer has no hesitation in confronting his congregation with the glorious paradox of mystery combined with revelation – that it is precisely in God's hiddenness that his glory is revealed. Bonhoeffer bases his sermon on 1 Corinthians 2:7–10:

"But we speak God's hidden wisdom, secret and hidden, which God decreed before the ages for our glory. None of the rulers of this age understood this; for if they had, they would not have crucified the Lord of glory." In his own words Bonhoeffer says:

> But the world is blind to this mystery. It wants to have either a God whom it can calculate and exploit or else no God at all. The mystery of God remains hidden from the world. The world does not want it. Instead, it makes its own gods according to its wishes and never recognizes the mysterious and hidden God who is near at hand . . . the Rulers of this world live by calculation and exploitation; that is how they come to be great rulers in the eyes of the world. But they do not understand mystery; only children do (Bonhoeffer 2007, 362).

It is, says Bonhoeffer, the mystery of Jesus Christ in whom "God became poor and lowly, small and weak, out of love for humankind . . . That is the one God, Father and Creator of the World, who in Jesus Christ loved us even unto death, who in the Holy Spirit opens our hearts to receive and love that one God." Nowhere in the sermon is there a reference to any contemporary event: but we now know the event which was about to happen and was certainly on Bonhoeffer's mind. Two days later, at Barmen in Germany, the Free Synod would gather and with Karl Barth's help draw up and declare the church's confession in opposition to the German Christian heresy: "Jesus Christ, as he is made known in Holy Scripture, is the one word of God whom we are to hear, trust and obey in life and in death." Bonhoeffer was not present in person at Barmen, but the resonances of his sermon with what was to be formulated and declared there show that he would certainly be there in spirit at the birth of the Confessing Church.

March 1939: Bonhoeffer, England and von Hügel

Now to one of the most intriguing peculiarly intriguing episodes in Bonhoeffer's life. Or rather, an incident which I only heard of by chance some years ago, and which genuinely puzzled me until, more recently, it dawned on me that this could well have been a "Today" moment for him.

Just over thirty years ago I was in conversation with the notable Anglican bishop and ecumenist Oliver Tomkins (1908–1992). He surprised me by saying that in 1939, while working for the Student Christian Movement (SCM) in London, he had actually met Dietrich Bonhoeffer at a small lunch party attended by several notable church figures. Someone asked Bonhoeffer which English theologian he thought most worth reading, and his reply was "Friedrich von Hügel," on the grounds that "if you English had read him you would not have needed to read Karl Barth!" (Clements, 2022).

This was, to say the least, surprising. Despite his Germanic name the Austrian-born von Hügel (1852–1925) was a naturalized Englishman. But there were genuine grounds for my surprise at this report of Bonhoeffer's choice, because as far as I knew (and still know) there is absolutely no mention of von Hügel in any of Bonhoeffer's published works or in his preserved unpublished writings. A Roman Catholic layman, von Hügel had played a leading role in the Catholic Modernist movement of the early 1900s. Until his death in 1925 he continued to write, to wide acclaim in both academic and popular circles in the English-speaking world, in his chosen fields of philosophy of religion, spirituality and church history. Oliver Tompkins was sufficiently impressed by Bonhoeffer's remark to start reading von Hügel for himself, and found there an exposition of "the mystery and sovereign grace of God over the proud pretensions of man" (see Hastings 2001, 20), which liberated him from the rather naïve theological liberalism in which he had been nurtured.[1]

Bonhoeffer was indeed in London at this time (see Bethge 2000, 635–648). On 12 March, accompanied by his close friend Eberhard Bethge, he arrived in London for a five-week visit to England. He had several objects in view. The first was to discuss with ecumenical contacts, including Bishop George Bell, and Canon Leonard Hodgson of Oxford, future relationships between the Confessing Church and the ecumenical movement in view of the formation of the World Council of Churches which was now under way. The second was to confide in George Bell the agonizing personal choices now facing him as war approached, on whether to stay in Hitler's Germany where he was likely to face the military call-up as well as the mounting suspicions of the Nazi authorities. Third, he wished to visit his twin sister Sabine and her "non-Aryan" husband Gerhard Leibholz and their two young daughters. The Leibholzes had got out of Germany the previous year and with George Bell's assistance found refuge in London. Meetings with all these mentioned figures took place during the visit, and are well chronicled as are two others: with W. A. Visser 't Hooft, recently-appointed secretary of the new World Council of Churches who happened to be in London briefly; and with the American theologian Reinhold Niebuhr who was delivering lectures in Edinburgh and came south to meet

---

1. For a fuller account and more detailed discussion of this episode than given here see: Clements 2022.

Bonhoeffer at St. Leonards-on-Sea, and discussed actual possibilities for him to get away to America at least for a time. But nowhere, not even in Bethge's account of these London days, is there a mention of this lunch meeting. But it would be sheer presumption to assume that there is nothing whatever to be known about a person or event beyond what is on paper or in print, and even the most incidental piece of oral transmission may prove significant.

What Bonhoeffer found in von Hügel

Let us suppose that Bonhoeffer opened von Hügel's two-volume magnum opus, *The Mystical Element of Religion*. He would have found von Hügel expressing appreciation of a whole range of religious and philosophical thinkers past and present, including St. John of the Cross and Søren Kierkegaard. For von Hügel, Kierkegaard especially is a model for writing "*existentially*, pricked on by the exigencies of actual life, to attempt their expression in terms of that life, and in view of its further spiritual development" (von Hügel, 1908 Vol. I, XVII). Further, says von Hügel, Kierkegaard discomforts idealist thought with the "jealousy" of God, saying, "the Absolute is cruel, for it demands *all*, whilst the Relative continues to demand *some* attention from us" (von Hügel 1908 Vol. II, 353). In Volume II of *The Mystical Element in Religion* von Hügel engages in a complex discussion of asceticism as seen in St. John of the Cross, Catherine of Genoa, Blaise Pascal and Kierkegaard. Sufficient for our purpose here is what he says about Kierkegaard, "who pushed the doctrine of the qualitative, absolute difference between God and all that we ourselves can think, feel, will or be." For Kierkegaard, von Hügel recognizes, the soul's relation to God "is a relation to a Being absolutely different from Man, who cannot confront him as his Superlative or Ideal, and who, nevertheless, is to rule in his inmost soul" (von Hügel 1908 Vol. II, 345). The result is a suffering asceticism.

Bonhoeffer's remark to Oliver Tomkins, that if the English had read von Hügel they would not need Karl Barth, can be interpreted more than one way. It could mean that he thought von Hügel had been grossly neglected or unknown in Britain hitherto, an unlikely scenario given that Bonhoeffer must have known of von Hügel's relative and continuing popularity. But it could also imply that Bonhoeffer was aware of how difficult, intimidating or simply baffling, even educated Anglo-Saxons often found Barth's language and ideas even in English translations, and that Bonhoeffer sensed von Hügel could provide a less intimidating approach to the divine mystery. Perhaps Bonhoeffer felt that having been lured into reading von Hügel, and if they *really and thoroughly* read him – beyond those comforting passages assuring them that faith, science and historical criticism could be blended in a harmonious whole – and had dared to journey with Kierkegaard and St. John of the Cross to face the radical otherness of God, then indeed they might be excused having to drink the severe Barthian medicine. Bonhoeffer himself, as we have seen, expresses the divine transcendence in terms of mystery as seen in that Trinity Sunday sermon of 1934.

Von Hügel does not lessen the Kierkegaardian discontinuity between God and humankind, between heaven and earth. This discontinuity brings the ultimate disturbance to the synthetic life, jealously confronting the beautiful synthesis of relative relations with what lies beyond yet seeks to claim it *absolutely*. In the context of prayer this leads von Hügel, with the aid of St. Augustine, to be as brusque as Barth in opposing the sentimental, easy-going familiarity between the human and divine which had marked much recent religious thought. Von Hügel for his part maintains the ever-present mystery of God who does not promise increased "understanding" but demands faith and obedience – *decision*. And it was decision that Bonhoeffer was striving after in March 1939.

March–April 1939: a troubled Bonhoeffer

It is fully understandable, therefore, that Bonhoeffer would have commended von Hügel to his friends in London as a surrogate Barth to counter the still-prevailing idealism pervading theology (at least in the Anglican church), as exemplified by the outstanding Anglican churchman and thinker of the time, Archbishop William Temple. But there is also a very specific and existential reason why he might have felt constrained to do this in March–April 1939. His visit to London was prompted by severe anxieties for the future of the Confessing Church and for himself, and some of his experiences during the visit increased those anxieties still further. The Confessing Church maintained that because at Barmen it had declared itself against the racial and nationalistic heresies of the so-called German Christian Movement, the Confessing Church alone should be recognized as having a rightful German place at the ecumenical table.

Bonhoeffer had taken a rigorous line on this since the inception of the Confessing Church in 1934. In 1935 he had received an invitation from the noted Anglican theologian Leonard Hodgson, secretary of the Faith and Order movement, to a meeting of the committee preparing the 1937 Faith and Order Conference. On learning that Theodor Heckel, head of the foreign relations department of the Reich Church, would also be attending, he refused. If the meeting was indeed to comprise representatives of churches which "accept our Lord Jesus Christ as God and Saviour," Bonhoeffer declared, it would be impossible for a Confessing Church representative to attend, since the Reich Church, as shown by its teachings and practice, did *not* recognize Christ as its head (see Clements 2015, 166). Rather, the Reich church government was "an instrument of the Antichrist" and should be judged accordingly by the ecumenical conference. In a frank exchange of correspondence, Hodgson stated and repeated that according to its statutes Faith and Order was obliged to invite "all branches of the Christian Church" to the meeting. This of course did not meet Bonhoeffer's claim that the Reich Church was *not* part of the Christian Church. The matter ended in stalemate.

Four years after that exchange, the attitude of the Confessing Church leadership had changed somewhat. Now, evidently feeling that continuing to make an exclusive claim to ecumenical participation had to be weighed against the dangers of total isolation from the ecumenical movement, they deputed Bonhoeffer to see if there might at least be *a* place for a Confessing German either as a staff person or a member on one of the ecumenical governing bodies. Accordingly, Bonhoeffer secured a meeting with Leonard Hodgson, secretary of Faith and Order, in Oxford, on 29 March (Clements 2015, 166). It was a long, fraught and fruitless meeting in the course of which, Hodgson reported later, Bonhoeffer grew very heated. Hodgson was adamant, his position no different from that of 1935. The Faith and Order committee could co-opt additional representatives, but this would require the Germans to apply to Faith and Order via a central German body having the confidence of all the "groups" within the German Evangelical Church, and there was not of course any such body in Germany. Hodgson's mind was as far removed as could be imagined from the situation that Bonhoeffer believed the Confessing Church, and he himself, to be in: a battle to the point of suffering for the truth of the gospel, not an academic discussion or a game of inter-church politics. It was not a matter of being fair to all "groups," but of acknowledging which was the true as distinct from the heretical church in Germany. Bonhoeffer was yet again meeting a refusal to see the issue as one of truthful witness in Germany. He returned from Oxford to London dispirited and frustrated. The official ecumenical leadership's stated wish to act "impartially" was once again simply playing into the hands of the Reich Church. He would no doubt have been even angrier had he known that William Temple, chair of the WCC Provisional Committee, on receiving Hodgson's report on the meeting strongly agreed with the line Hodgson had taken. The desire for inclusivity and impartiality at all costs was shielding the ecumenical bodies from taking a *decision* about what was happening to the gospel in Germany: the resonances with today's debates about the place of the Russian Orthodox Church within the ecumenical fellowship, due to its stance on the war in Ukraine, are inescapable. English (or at any rate Anglican) reasonableness, and a framework of philosophical idealism, were fine when the path to be followed lay through green pastures and beside still waters. But in 1939 Bonhoeffer and his Confessing cohorts in Germany were on a steep and rugged climb where there were no clear maps to guide, with hazardous ravines to negotiate or leap across, and before long a perilous descent into a valley as dark as death. He was not wanting easy answers, but had hoped at least for recognition of the plight of those making the costly witness in Germany. He did not find it in Oxford.

He did find that recognition in his closest English friend, George Bell, to whom he wrote while in London with similar ideas to those he put to Hodgson, and whom he visited at Chichester. But to Bell Bonhoeffer also wanted to unburden himself of his most pressing personal dilemma: whether to leave Germany or not. Bell's wife Henrietta noticed the change in Bonhoeffer since she had seen him during 1933–35: "He was much quieter, much more serious and labouring under great personal strain. He wanted to stay in his own country... and he wasn't sure of his whole attitude to war" (see Clements 2006, 100). The only alternative to conscription or conscientious protest would be service outside Germany, or perhaps on behalf of the Confessing Church within the ecumenical movement, or maybe with one of the British missionary societies. Afterwards Bonhoeffer wrote gratefully to Bell, thanking him "for the great help you gave me in our talk at Chichester... I do not know what will be the outcome of it all, but it means much to me to realize that you see the great conscientious difficulties with which we are faced" (Bonhoeffer 2011, 160). He also found recognition in an unexpected encounter with the Dutchman, Willem Visser 't Hooft, the secretary of the infant WCC (Bethge 2000, 645–647). Then there was the meeting with Reinhold Niebuhr from which arose the invitation for Bonhoeffer to go to the USA in the summer, a visit which led him into even more heart-searching and his eventual, fateful decision to return to Germany for good.

It was, then, a very troubled Bonhoeffer who was in London in March and April 1939. He was not in need of a comprehensive understanding of the world situation set within a comforting philosophic idealism, but rather of costly grace in making drastic decisions. Four years earlier in his London vicarage, he had written to his brother Karl-Friedrich on the need for a new Christianity based on the Sermon on the Mount and uncompromising discipleship: "Things do exist that are worth standing for without compromise. To me it seems that peace and social justice are such things, as is Christ himself" (Bonhoeffer 2007, 285). Now in London again, he was in search of a community which recognized this challenge. That, I dare to suggest, is why he wanted to direct his English friends to Friedrich von Hügel, the one who, from within their own midst, and sympathetic to much in their religious and intellectual ethos, had nevertheless pointed to the overriding claim of the transcendent God, the call to face the ultimate point, the beyond in the midst, where personal faith and public responsibility meet in the hour of crisis. In that "today" moment nothing else mattered.

Bibliography

Bethge, Eberhard. 2000. *Dietrich Bonhoeffer: A Biography*. Minneapolis: Fortress Press.
Bonhoeffer, Dietrich. 2007. *London. 1933–1935. Dietrich Bonhoeffer Works Volume 13*, edited by Keith Clements, translated by Isabel Best. Minneapolis: Fortress Press.
Bonhoeffer, Dietrich. 2010. *Letters and Papers from Prison. Dietrich Bonhoeffer Works Volume 8*, edited by John W. de Gruchy, translated by Isabel Best, Lisa E. Dahill, Reinhard Krauss, and Nancy Lukens. Minneapolis: Fortress Press.
Bonhoeffer, Dietrich. 2012. *Theological Education Underground: 1937–1940. Dietrich Bonhoeffer Works Volume 15*, edited by Victoria J. Barnett, translated by Claudia D. Bergmann, Peter Frick, and Scott A. Moore. Minneapolis: Fortress Press.
Clements, Keith. 2006. *Bonhoeffer and Britain*. London: Churches Together in Britain and Ireland.
Clements, Keith. 2015. *Dietrich Bonhoeffer's Ecumenical Quest*. Geneva: World Council of Churches.
Clements, Keith. 2022. *Appointments with Bonhoeffer: Personal Faith and Public Responsibility in a Fragmenting World*. London: T&T Clark.
Hastings, Adrian. 2001. *Oliver Tomkins: The Ecumenical Enterprise*. London: SPCK.
Hügel, Friedrich von. 1908. *The Mystical Element of Religion as Studied in Saint Catherine of Genoa and Her Friend Volume 1 and 2*. London: J.M. Dent.

Part 4

Dietrich Bonhoeffer: Reception of Freedom in New Contexts

11

The Testimony of the Polish Publicist Anna Morawska about the Theologian Dietrich Bonhoeffer

Consequences for the Present[1]

Marek Prawda, PhD
Lecturer at Collegium Civitas, Warsaw

About the Author

From January 2024 Marek Prawda served as Undersecretary of State in the Ministry of Foreign Affairs. From 2016 to 2021, he was director of the Representation of the European Commission in Poland. Previously, he served as the permanent representative of the Republic of Poland to the European Union (2012–2016), and before that as the Ambassador of the Republic of Poland to Sweden and Germany. From 1992 to 2016 he was an employee of the Ministry of Foreign Affairs: first, as deputy director (1998–1999) and then director (until 2001) of the Department of Western Europe and director of the secretariat of the Minister of Foreign Affairs (in 2001 and 2005–2006). In the 1980s, he was active in the Solidarity Citizens' Committee and worked at the Polish Academy of Sciences (1979–1992), where in 1984 he defended his doctoral thesis

---

1. This paper was read in Görlitz on 6 June 2022, as part of the program for *Lausitzkirchentag* (Lausation Church Day).

in the field of the sociology of work. He is a lecturer at Collegium Civitas in Warsaw, at the Paweł Adamowicz Civic Center in Gdańsk and at the European University Viadrina in Frankfurt (Oder).

The Polish adventure with Bonhoeffer

Twenty-two years ago I was invited, together with a German diplomat, to the Reconciliation Center in Glencree (Centre for Peace and Reconciliation) near Dublin. Our task was to tell representatives of two parties involved in the historical conflict, Sinn Fein and the Unionists, about Polish-German relations after World War II, more specifically, to speak about how the churches had worked to find a common language and a way to be able to come closer step by step. I was surprised that those present, based on their own experiences, primarily saw churches and religions as part of the problem and not part of the solution. One immediately had to think about the words of the German theologian, Dietrich Bonhoeffer: "Cheap grace is the preaching of forgiveness without repentance . . . is communion without confession of sins."

It is similar to reconciliation, which requires effort and willingness, and which must be a "costly grace." I can remember that I talked a lot about Dietrich Bonhoeffer back then in Glencree, especially about the phenomenon of the Polish encounter with Bonhoeffer in the 1970s.

In 1970 Anna Morawska published a book about this theologian in Poland, *A Christian in the Third Reich*. The author could not have dreamed that her work would attract so much attention and influence. But the explanation probably lies in her ability on the one hand to build bridges between two communities, and on the other hand to formulate refreshing ideas for oppositional action in communist Poland. Bonhoeffer's personal fate and writings provided an excellent basis for this.

Although we are talking about an internal Polish phenomenon, the bilateral dimension should also be mentioned here. Because a striking number of people in Poland were interested in Bonhoeffer, circles in the former GDR began to take an interest in this Polish phenomenon. This is how the Anna Morawska Seminar, which many of you are probably familiar with, came about. Over time it became an increasingly important part of German-Polish communication.

Initially, Morawska's book became key reading for critical Catholic intellectuals. A surprising number of members of the Polish opposition, who had little to do with religion, quickly commented on this. A lively debate developed in the semi-independent Catholic magazines and underground newspapers. Bonhoeffer fascinated Poles: he was seen as the lonely hero, the individual in a totalitarian dictatorship, with his pangs of conscience and his ethical responsibility.

While fighting the enemy is a morally clear matter, individual ethical choices usually have backing in institutional authorities like church or nation. In contrast, Bonhoeffer represented an extreme variant of heroism, because he acted without the support of large social groups. The basic consensus of the silent majority of society was against him. Nonetheless, he decided to act. He declared that it wasn't enough to have clean hands. As a pastor, he could not content himself with comforting the bereaved when a madman in his car drives people into the abyss. You have to grab the wheel from him first.

Morawska informed the Poles that they should not look for a closed religious system in Dietrich Bonhoeffer, but rather "a direction of questioning and a type of experience" in which "the people living today recognize themselves." Like Bonhoeffer, "they are looking for a Christian interpretation of the actual circumstances of their time."

The author encouraged her Polish readers to engage with the German perspective of the time, and not to understand the actions of the people living at that time based on the circumstances of the time. Their encounter with Bonhoeffer was an encounter with the private, tragic fate of a German, and this was meaningful for the strained bilateral relations. The discovery of "the other Germans" made many Poles curious about "the other Germany." Therefore, one sought dialogue in the time of monologues and language in a time of speechlessness.

Reading Morawska's book was important for debates between different wings of the nascent [Polish] democratic opposition. It was a "must-read" book that you read voluntarily. She gave her fellow Poles a common spiritual ground beyond their ideological and denominational borders. In studying [Bonhoeffer's] extreme situation, the activists sought guidance on how to act against an unfree system that was not foreign rule (a homemade dictatorship, so to speak).

Leftists, ex-Marxists, found a way to understand the Christian faith. Bonhoeffer's courageous thesis of "religionless Christianity" was helpful in understanding that Christian morality is about something more than the fear of punishment and the desire for reward. They felt at home in a world, perhaps without God, but where his commandments should nevertheless be lived out. The "other person" can also become the foundation of ethics. Clearly, a tactical alliance was also sought with the Catholic Church, which was the only pluralistic alternative in Poland.

This is how the Polish opposition consolidated itself – heterogeneous but pulling in the same direction, making it strong. The discussion triggered by Catholic publicists contributed significantly to the alliance between Christian circles and the liberal opposition. Between "Catholics" and "lay people," if one may put it somewhat simply. This is why the Solidarity movement emerged much later, where as many people as possible could feel at home and in good hands.

Consequences for the present
1. Democracy must not be defenseless

Quite recently, we thought that we now live in a world where it doesn't matter how many tanks you have. However, there is much to suggest that the war in Ukraine will herald a longer phase of confrontation between authoritarian and democratic states.

Europe must prepare for this development with its own strategy. Because, as we know from history, a weak Europe would only be an invitation for the great powers to settle their conflicts of interest on our continent. We must defend peace and freedom with all severity, otherwise, we will feel the harshness of others. Democracies must be capable of deterrence and be able to win wars. It is not enough to settle into a world of natural prosperity and unimpeded progress. Today, learning from Bonhoeffer means sharing his view that uncompromising defense of the limit behind which the autonomy and freedom of other people is infringed, no matter how rationally motivated this is.

Bonhoeffer warns against taking refuge in the shadow of the authority of an ideology or institution. There is little point in continually making compromises for the "good of the people," or "the good of the church." The totalitarian system does not recognize partial concessions. It demands everything, you have to give yourself completely to it; if you are not completely with it, you are against it. And so those who began with innocent compromises ended up with shameful compromises (such as the German churches on the question of the Jews; or the incomprehensible reluctance of the Polish church in 1968).

2. Values-based foreign policy

Bonhoeffer teaches us that there are situations where skeptical distance is not enough. He argued that values should become the basis of political action. He would ask us, or our politicians, today: in the name of which values should conformism be rejected?

My interpretation is this: Given recent events and the clear evidence that raw materials were used as a political weapon, one could not credibly defend the claim today that applying a "politics of two drawers" – one for interests, the other for values, which exist completely independent from each other – makes any sense. It turns out that companies that stand on their own can't make it in the market. Autocrats strive for supremacy while disregarding European rules. To defend against autocrats, strength must be built. We must be willing to pay an economic price today, lest we pay incomparably more in the future. And because these questions are of existential importance, it means that a foreign policy based on values must also be possible.

3. Unity in the EU

Bonhoeffer's ecumenical thought was not directed towards comparing theories. Instead, according to Morawska, he saw the commonality of all heirs of the Christian tradition in the attitude, hope and religious imagination of living people. What can we say about European unity today? And about citizens' will to strive for it? What areas of tension are we confronted with today? I would like to briefly discuss this using Germany and Poland as examples.

After her defeat and discrediting in 1945, Germany was able to join the democratic community of states. Foreign policy followed a path of self-restraint. Marked by a heavy complex of guilt, Germany also believed that credit similar to that which the world had given it after World War II should also be given to Russia. Thus a policy of change through rapprochement should be pursued with Russia. That fitted into a certain distribution of roles in the relationship between the world and Russia: some rely on deterrence with proportionate dialogue, others on dialogue with proportionate deterrence. In stable times this could even work.

For Putin's Russia, however, it has become a welcome opportunity to drive a wedge between Western countries. In doing so, Putin used "anti-Nazism" as moral blackmail, which was particularly successful in relation to Berlin. But following the wars in Chechnya and Georgia and the annexation of Crimea, at the latest, it was difficult to understand why Berlin stuck to its stance of avoiding anything that could have made dialogue with Putin more difficult. Finally, Putin had made clear that he did not want dialogue. In the meantime, German companies were able to draw on these political scruples without restriction and thus make Berlin extremely dependent on Russia in terms of raw materials policy.

Germany is currently undertaking a strategic reorientation of its Russia policy. A new normal has been proclaimed, in which the mantra of "security only together with Russia" is being abandoned. Instead, it is now necessary to oppose Russia, especially because Russia uses violence to destroy the international order and create zones of influence. In addition, blackmail using anti-Nazism has lost its meaning, because in the eyes of the world the terrible war and the attitude of the Ukrainians have deprived the Russian aggressors of any right to claim the defeat of German Nazism exclusively for themselves.

There are clear signs of change, such as our western neighbour is undergoing. These changes and the maintenance of European unity must be of fundamental importance for a country on the frontlines, which Poland has now become. This is not the time for escalating disputes with our western neighbours and capitalizing on anti-German hysteria for domestic political ends.

Moreover, we must note the wrong notes that are being struck in Polish domestic politics. Resistance to Putin's Russia is based not only on moving away from oil and gas imports, but also on rejecting what is at the heart of Putinism: trampling on the constitution, undermining the rule of law, patronizing democratic institutions and free media, or babbling about "Gayropa." And these things are exactly what Putin's verbal critics have big problems with here in their own country.

4. Bonhoeffer and peaceful revolutions

In 1989, many in East Central Europe strengthened each other and developed a sense of togetherness. This is the story we should tell ourselves today. A story about how the wall didn't fall by itself. That the system change was preceded by a long phase of oppositional movements throughout our region. For example, before Adam Michnik became a legend for us, courageous Russian dissidents had been his role models. Roland Jahn, a former civil rights activist from Jena, often says that on 9 October 1989, *Solidarity* symbolically took part in the famous freedom demonstration on the Leipzig inner city ring road. We in Warsaw, on the other hand, had been following the prayers for peace in Leipzig's Nikolaikirche with excitement and hope since June of the same year. We prayed symbolically. This is how Europe is created – we thought at the time. It therefore seems more than appropriate to break out of the narrow national-heroic perspective as we commemorate the events of 1980 and 1989. To recall the words of Ludwig Mehlhorn, "the revolutions of 1989 were a gift that we gave each other" (*Der politische Umbruch in Mittel- und Osteuropa und seine Bedeutung für die Bürgerbewegung in der DDR / The*

Political Upheaval in Central and Eastern Europe and Its Significance for the Civic Movement in the GDR).

If we want to go beyond the narrow horizon of the national-heroic narrative today, then who better than Dietrich Bonhoeffer should move us to do so? After all, the history of the Polish opposition under communism cannot be fully told without him. That being the case, he can also be the inspiration for our current efforts to establish a new German-Polish presence in Europe.

The most important finding from the Year of Miracles (1989) is that people can make history themselves. If we push society into the background and confine ourselves to the role of politicians, then we overlook the most important thing that characterized these revolutions: that round tables replaced the guillotine.

Sometimes the meaning of 1989 is reduced to a collapse of the ineffective systems on the periphery. It is added that in the GDR, for example, the state was already dead. The real performance of the citizens thus tends to be explained as a small thing.

There are good arguments for speaking of a double founding of the European Union, one after 1945 and one after 1989. If we know the European tradition in its entirety, we are better equipped to deal with our crises and remain more resistant to attempts at division. Furthermore, the non-inclusion of the Eastern European perspective often serves as a pretext for some politicians from this part of Europe to denounce the alleged Western misunderstanding of the East. The Hungarian Prime Minister, for example, praised his specifically Eastern view of the rule of law, which is not understood in the West because the East is not known and despised there. As if the principles of the rule of law were up for debate and could be reduced to a kind of local custom.

To be sure, the complex and confused European past is still told primarily from a Western perspective. That is why concepts of Europeanization have a noticeably Western trait. Moreover, not all criteria of European collective identity, as they are often formulated in the context of German history, can be transferred to Polish reality. Aleida Assmann, for example, speaks of this: "Denationalization seems to me to be a specific German dream that responds to the specific German nightmare of National Socialism."

5. Europe's third founding

The war in Ukraine has accelerated the erosion of our previous certainties. Take for example the belief that economic relations can exclude our conflicts with third countries. We thought we were exporting values, instead, we were importing chaos. The advantage of entering a "Fluid Reality" is that we become more open to system changes. For example, Germany has increased defense spending and responded positively to French calls for more European government bond issuance. In this way, you can support Ukraine and achieve autonomy in energy policy. Green transformation and supply chain shortening are no longer costly pipe dreams. They are a condition for surviving and successfully resisting dictators.

Europe in need discovers its potential. A Europe is emerging before our eyes that will become more than a factory of rules. So far, we've been fine just managing "collective happiness." This has proven to be a kind of "cheap grace." Now we understand that our geopolitical vacation is over. The Union has to also make strategic political decisions and deal with existential threats. Europe, as a power among powers, must clearly determine what defines it, what it stands for and what price it is willing to pay for it. In Bonhoeffer's language, Europe is now attempting to reinvent itself as "costly grace."

The war is a test of whether the West will leave the Ukrainians to their own devices with their aspirations for freedom and integration into Europe, or whether it will be willing to provide assistance. As a result, it inevitably puts its own safety at risk. But there is no other way to prove that our stand for freedom is sincere and not opportunistic. The visits of the President of the European Commission were an attempt to provide this evidence. With this, Ukraine was included in an EU understood as a community of destiny.

This symbolic acceptance of Ukrainians into the EU is largely thanks to cities and municipalities. In the beginning it took place primarily through spontaneous activities. International partnerships proved to be lively and effective. From them, the Union is learning that it is not as helpless and sluggish as some have made it out to be. European citizens discovered Ukraine for themselves. But it's more than that. After correcting its relations with Russia, the EU is becoming more "Eastern" in a genuine sense. It was understood that the previous focus on Moscow was not evidence of European-Eastern competence. In fact, the opposite was true. Only the (albeit somewhat belated) perception of other eastern neighbours as subjects constitutes this competence.

There is much to suggest that we are living through a process comparable to the events of 1989. Therefore, it would even be legitimate to speak of a third founding of Europe.

Here in Görlitz, I would like to add that our rapidly changing Europe must have a particularly good ear for the border regions. Voices of all those who understand well the nature of the area, which is the borderland of regional as well as national identities, will gain in importance. The war has revealed that these identities are essential to salvaging our universal values. Before we wake up in a truly "post-national" or "post-heroic" reality, we see how the national identity of Ukraine's neighbours is a crucial source of their fighting spirit. And they fight for the universal values of "post-national" reality.

6. Democracy – costly grace

Critics of the European Union and liberal democracy have said that the war in Ukraine is a setback for those who had a naïve belief in Enlightenment values and a world without wars. They also say the war changes everything and that advocating for the rule of law is now irrelevant.

It's exactly the other way around: First, the war proves what a system that disregards the constitution and the rule of law is capable of. Second, we are witnessing the demise of the claim that the world is one of inevitable wars of all against all. Because we have seen what the world may be like when ruled by those who exclude peaceful coexistence. And third, it made us realize that we must defend democracy in every way we can.

This too is costly grace.

12

Longing for Nature in Confinement
Dietrich Bonhoeffer's Prison Writings

Joel Burnell, PhD
Evangelical School of Theology in Wrocław
ORCID: 0000-0003-2211-6998

About the Author

Joel Burnell is the Chair of the Theology Department at the Evangelical School of Theology in Wrocław, Poland. He is a member of the Board of the Dietrich Bonhoeffer Society – Poland section, and Director of the Jonathan Edwards Center – Poland. Joel specializes in systematic theology, theological ethics, and political theology, and has devoted special interest to the work of Dietrich Bonhoeffer and Jonathan Edwards. He is the author of *Poetry, Providence and Patriotism: Polish Messianism, in Dialogue with Dietrich Bonhoeffer*, as well as numerous articles in his areas of specialization. He has organized and co-organized numerous national and international academic conferences and congresses. He writes poetry (mostly in Polish), preaches at First Baptist Church of Wrocław and the International Church in Wrocław, and is an active participant in Polish civil society.

Keywords

Bonhoeffer, love of nature, prison experience, bio-theoacoustics, ecotheology, nature mysticism

Abstract

This paper examines Bonhoeffer's experience in prison of being deprived of normal contact with the natural world. Rather than surveying his theological works to develop the trajectory of a Bonhoefferian theology of nature, it explores his own descriptions of his prison experience, contained in *Letters and Papers from Prison, Fiction from Prison,* and *Love Letters from Cell 92*. In the context of his imprisonment, this focus on his feelings of being cut off from nature yields an image of Bonhoeffer which is surprisingly intimate and deeply personal. His love for nature lost is woven intricately into his thoughts and feelings towards other loves and losses, from the loss of freedom in general, to being denied regular contact with his fiancé Maria. Bonhoeffer's primary love language, it seems, is the language of nature.

Bonhoeffer truly embodies what Dahill has called bio-theoacoustics. His love for nature was a form of communion and prayer, and as his visceral descriptions of "sun-worship" attest, it enabled him to understand and experience God in ways he could not otherwise experience, truly as a "bigger and wilder Thou." These texts contribute little in a direct way to a Bonhoefferian ecotheology that leads, as Dahill and Rayson argue persuasively, to advocacy for the beleaguered creation which we humans call home. Nevertheless, his embodied love for nature, on full exhibit in these letters and poems, provides strong anecdotal support to their claim that Bonhoeffer's theology, and his experience of nature as a form of prayer, does indeed lead to a reimagined relationship with the natural world and responsible action on its behalf.

Introduction

Dietrich Bonhoeffer experienced the loss of freedom, not merely as a threat but as an experienced reality. Facing death at the hands of Nazi Germany, he described death, when faced responsibly, with discipline, purpose, and acceptance of suffering, as "the highest of feasts on the way to freedom eternal" (Bonhoeffer 2010b, 571). One looks at freedom differently when it is threatened, restricted or taken away. This paper focuses on a particular aspect of Bonhoeffer's prison experience of freedom lost, namely the longing for nature while in confinement. Although touched upon, this subject has not received adequate attention, which is surprising given the number of books and articles on the implications of Bonhoeffer's thought for ecotheology.

Many poets and writers have written on the experience of confinement. Their observations and descriptions were often fueled by their personal experience of isolation or incarceration. Similar reflections appear in the memoirs and autobiographies written by individuals who were imprisoned for their actions or beliefs, including social activists, progressive thinkers, political figures, religious leaders, and members of ethnic and other minority groups. As could be expected, these works poignantly describe their intense longing for freedom.

While there are differences in such accounts, several consistent themes emerge. One of the more notable experiences many prisoners share is that of yearning for nature. Oscar Wilde described it well in "The Ballad of Reading Gaol" (Wilde 1898), a poem he wrote upon release from prison in 1887, where he had been held since 1886 on charges of "Gross Indecency" for homosexual behavior. His poem was inspired by the execution of a fellow prisoner who, on the day Wilde was imprisoned, was hanged for killing his wife. The lengthy poem explores deeper issues, such as the guilt we all feel and all share ("each man kills the things he loves"), and the question of punishment and justice. In this wider context, Wilde's description of the prisoners' longing for nature remains telling. He writes:

> I never saw a man who looked
> With such a wistful eye
> Upon that little tent of blue
> Which prisoners call the sky,
> And at every drifting cloud that went
> With sails of silver by (Wilde 1898, I).

Wilde here describes the glimpse of sky that prisoners have through the windows of their cell as "a little tent of blue." Their longing for freedom is awakened by the clouds that drift by on "sails of silver" – a stark contrast to the lack of freedom they experience in prison. It is easy to imagine that what Wilde sees in the "wistful eye" of the condemned man is a projection, or at the very least a reflection, of the longing for nature he himself felt in his prison cell.

Solitary Watch is a website dedicated to telling the stories and advocating for humane treatment of prisoners subjected to solitary confinement. In their short article about Nelson Mandela, who spent twenty-seven years in prison during his struggle against apartheid, including eighteen years on Robben Island and six years in isolation in Pollsmoor Prison (Cassella and Ridgeway

2013), the editors quote Mandela's own description of life in Pollsmoor Prison, taken from his autobiographical work, *Long Walk to Freedom*.

> I found solitary confinement the most forbidding aspect of prison life. There is no end and no beginning; there is only one's own mind, which can begin to play tricks. Was that a dream or did it really happen? One begins to question everything. Did I make the right decision, was my sacrifice worth it? In solitary, there is no distraction from these haunting questions (Mandela 1994a, 416).

Mandela often connected his longing for freedom with his longing for nature. The following passage, in which he relates his struggle to maintain his dignity, suggests that one of the things that kept him going while in prison was the vision that one sunny day he would walk on green grass again as a free man.

> Prison and the authorities conspire to rob each man of his dignity. In and of itself, that assured that I would survive, for any man or institution that tries to rob me of my dignity will lose because I will not part with it at any price or under any pressure. I never seriously considered the possibility that I would not emerge from prison one day. I never thought that a life sentence truly meant life and that I would die behind bars. Perhaps I was denying this prospect because it was too unpleasant to contemplate. But I always knew that someday I would once again feel the grass under my feet and walk in the sunshine as a free man (Mandela 2008, 391).

Mandela often describes isolation from the natural world as one of the most difficult aspects of his imprisonment. This deprivation of nature symbolized the broader loss of freedom and humanity that Mandela and his fellow prisoners endured during their years of incarceration. In contrast, even the smallest contact with nature brought new hope to the prisoners. Mandela writes:

> During the harsh days of the early 1970s, when the ANC seemed to sink into the shadows, we had to force ourselves not to give in to despair. In many ways, we had miscalculated; we had thought that by the 1970s we would be living in a democratic, non-racial South Africa. Yet as we entered the new decade my hopes for that South Africa rose once again. Some mornings I walked out into the courtyard and every living thing there, the seagulls and wagtails, the small trees, and even the stray blades of grass, seemed to smile and shine in the sun. It was at such times when I perceived the beauty of even this small, closed-in corner of the world, that

I knew that someday my people and I would be free (Mandela 2008, 506).

In this harsh environment, Mandela found joy in the act of gardening. Tending a garden brought a sense of personal fulfilment as well as a taste of freedom. What is more, Mandela drew valuable lessons for leadership from his gardening experience

> A garden was one of the few things in prison that one could control. To plant a seed, watch it grow, to tend it and then harvest it, offered a simple but enduring satisfaction. The sense of being the custodian of this small patch of earth offered a small taste of freedom.
>
> In some ways, I saw the garden as a metaphor for certain aspects of my life. A leader must also tend his garden; he, too, plants seeds, and then watches, cultivates, and harvests the result. Like the gardener, a leader must take responsibility for what he cultivates; he must mind his work, try to repel enemies, preserve what can be preserved, and eliminate what cannot succeed (Mandela 1994, 489).

The examples of longing for nature in prison given above illustrate the phenomena which this article explores in the prison writings of Dietrich Bonhoeffer. The texts referred to are contained in *Letters and Papers from Prison*, *Fiction from Prison*, and finally *Love Letters from Cell 92*, containing the correspondence between Bonhoeffer and his fiancé Maria von Wedemeyer. But before we consider Bonhoeffer's own texts, a look at two recent articles shows the relevance of Bonhoeffer's own experience of nature for today, and raise important questions about how our relationship to the natural world relates to our spirituality and praxis.

Theology, spiritual practice and nature in Western Christianity

In "Bio-Theoacoustics: Prayer Outdoors and the Reality of the Natural World," Lisa Dahill argues for the need to reconnect spirituality in general, and prayer and meditation in particular, with the natural world. In describing the disconnect that exists between Western Christianity and the natural world, Dahill proposes what she calls "bio-theoacoustics," which she defines as "the practice of listening in prayer to what of G*D is perceptible outdoors, on various levels" (Dahill 2013, 293). Bio-theoacoustical prayer involves reflective encounters with nature, which go beyond observing the wonders of God's creation to deepen our very experience and understanding of God. To illustrate what she means, Dahill recalls her own near encounter with a bear while hiking in Washington, which caused her "to sense a bigger and wilder Thou than the human world alone can mediate" (Dahill 2013, 293). She suggests that such encounters "with this divine/animal wildness" might themselves be a form of prayer, which leads to the question of "what it means to pray when the Earth ... is profoundly endangered by human action?" (Dahill 2013, 293). Dahill makes it clear that reconnecting spiritually with nature, and specifically with God in nature, leads to proactive praxis that protects and preserves nature, of which we as human beings are an integral part.

Dahill recalls Bonhoeffer's statement in *Ethics*, that "all concepts of reality that ignore Jesus Christ are abstractions" (Bonhoeffer 2005, 54), and argues that "the natural world stands in the place today of the Jews and other non-Aryans in Bonhoeffer's time" (Dahill 2013, 295). From this premise it follows that "Christian prayer that does not participate fully and explicitly in the union of God and the natural world in Christ today is on some level an abstraction" (Dahill 2013, 295). Such prayer takes the form both of "indoor abstraction," when it is cut off from the natural world, as well as "outdoor abstraction," which views nature apart from "the meaning, beauty, and vision revealed in Jesus Christ" (Dahill 2013, 296). In response, Dahill declares that "living, Christian faith – encounter with Jesus Christ in all his fullness today – requires sustained conscious bodily-sensory encounter in prayer with the natural world" (Dahill 2013, 294).

In her discussion of "outdoor prayer" (Dahill 2013, 297), Dahill fleshes out how encounters in prayer with the natural world might look in today's world. Prayer can begin to overcome the disconnect of spirituality with nature by moving outdoors, where it can learn to once-again listen to the "more-than-human world" (Dahill 2013, 297). "Bio-theoacoustics" thus imagined and practiced "means broadening the scope of our attention beyond the human world, to both attend to the existence of – and slowly begin to communicate with – the Word incarnate in our Earth's changing climate *and* in the furry or scaled or winged others in our local worlds" (Dahill 2013, 298). This attention and communication is deepened when not only prayer but baptism and Eucharist also move outdoors, "in ways that make explicit the sacramental connection between our bodies, the natural world, and Jesus Christ" (Dahill 2013, 299). Even prayer and sacraments that take place indoors can be oriented towards the world outdoors, through the use of appropriate texts, images and symbols (Dahill 2013, 300).

Dianne Rayson takes the theme of action in solidarity with the natural world that is present in Dahill's paper to the next level. Following in the footsteps of others (Rasmussen 2012), Rayson has written perhaps the definitive book to date on Bonhoeffer and ecotheology (Rayson 2021). In her recent article, "From Pacifism to Tyrannicide: Considering Bonhoeffer's Ethics for the Anthropocene" (Rayson 2023b), she asks how Bonhoeffer's ethics, which she once described as Christonomy, can be applied to the challenge posed by climate change in the Anthropocene. Like Dahill, she calls on Bonhoeffer's reflections of the incarnation of Christ to argue that there can be no separation between the spiritual and the earthly (Rayson 2023b, 145). Drawing on the work of Lovat (Lovat 2006) and others, she describes Bonhoeffer as a "practical mystic," drawing out the implications of Bonhoeffer's famous declaration in *Letters and Papers from Prison* that "we can be Christians today only in two ways, through prayer and in doing justice" (Bonhoeffer 2010b, 389). And she answers her own question regarding how Bonhoeffer would have responded if faced by the present threat of climate catastrophe.

> True to form, he would have contemplated deeply on the problem and striven to address it theologically. His activism, the practical outreach of his mystical experience, would be encased in a theological argument and proposition (Rayson 2023b, 150–151).

Rayson sketches the outlines of a Bonhoefferian response to climate change that is grounded in his view of Christ as the foundation of all creation. In the incarnation the "transcendent, other and divine" God became "immanent, an integral part of creation." She describes Bonhoeffer's view of the relation between humanity and creation as one of sociality rather than dominion. As human beings we participate in what Bonhoeffer called the "one reality," which is modelled for humanity by the "Suffering Christ," the God who entered a suffering creation (Rayson 2023b, 151). Rayson writes that "as the Suffering Christ is present throughout all creation . . . we acknowledge and respond to the Suffering Christ in the face of the 'other', regardless of the 'otherness' of that being" (Rayson 2023b, 151). She argues that Bonhoeffer himself recognized that his theology, which is characterized by "the sense of interrelatedness of all creation, living and nonliving," implies that humanity's relationship to God includes "a role in bringing about restoration and reconciliation with the world" (Rayson 2023b, 152).

Dahill and Rayson based their work in large part on Bonhoeffer's theology and praxis. This paper, which examines what Bonhoeffer wrote about nature from his prison cell, will focus on his own experience of the natural world, and how he fought against the disconnection from nature he felt as a prisoner. It explores whether his own experience of nature allowed him "to sense a bigger and wilder Thou" (Dahill 2013, 293). And it asks whether *for Bonhoeffer* experiencing nature was a form of prayer that – given the opportunity which was largely denied to him in prison – leads to a reimagined relationship with the natural world and responsible action on its behalf.

Before we begin, one more introductory comment relates to Lovat's description of Bonhoeffer, which Rayson refers to in her article, as a *practical mystic*. Although the distinction between a "lover of nature" and a "nature-mystic" is subjective at best, the texts discussed below argue strongly for Lovat's position. In fact, they go further, suggesting Bonhoeffer can be understood as *practical* nature-mystic.

Although mysticism has a long history in Christianity, in particular in the Roman Catholic and Orthodox traditions, where it enjoys a certain prominence and place of honour, it appears less frequently in Protestant circles. As Spencer has argued, this results from a number of factors, among them the association of mysticism with Catholicism, a preference for "objective" truth versus "subjective" experience, and not unfounded fears that mystical experiences will override the authority of Scripture (Spencer 2021, 1028–1029). This can lead to a sense of discomfort, even among those who are arguably nature mystics themselves. As a result, Protestant nature mystics may appear uneasy or apologetic when describing their experiences, and we find them often seeking to "baptize" their experience through the use of biblical "proof-texts." Even Bonhoeffer fell victim to this in a letter to his fiancée Maria, when he qualifies his declaration that he "almost could be a sun-worshipper" by quickly citing a verse identifying Christ as the Sun/Son (Bonhoeffer 1992, 68–69). It is hoped that this paper makes its own contribution to the de-mystification and greater acceptance of (nature) mysticism, particularly in its more practical expressions that seek to engage with this world rather than to escape from or transcend it.

Bonhoeffer's prison reflections on nature in *Letters and Papers from Prison*

Bonhoeffer was arrested on 5 April 1943, and taken to Tegel prison in Berlin. Three letters from prison, in which Bonhoeffer describes and reflects upon his experience of being deprived of direct contact with nature, show a natural progression. On 24 June 1943, in a letter to his parents, Karl and Paula Bonhoeffer, he wrote about the strawberries and raspberries his mother had sent him, noting how they made him feel "that summer has really arrived" (Bonhoeffer

2010b, 105). He also speaks of the joy he felt watching a bird and her nestling chicks in the prison courtyard, and how shocked he was to find them lying dead on the ground, destroyed by a fellow prisoner. In this context he reflects on the special feelings prisoners have about their relationship to nature.

> It is presumably the awareness of nature's undisturbed, quiet, and free life that gives prisoners a very special – probably somewhat sentimental – relationship with animals and plants. Only my relationship with the flies in my cell still remains completely unsentimental. Prisoners are probably inclined in general to react to the lack of warmth and comfort they experience in their environment with an excessive heightening of their emotional side and may easily overreact in all personal and emotional matters. In such cases it is always good to restore one's level headedness and sense of humor by taking a cold shower in order not to lose one's balance. I believe that the Christian faith, properly understood, is especially effective in rendering this service (Bonhoeffer 2010b, 111).

Bonhoeffer here seems uncomfortable with the surprising strength of his own emotions, speaking of them with a certain reserve and suggesting ways to "restore one's level headedness and sense of humour" through Christian faith, if taking a cold shower proves insufficient for this purpose.

Bonhoeffer returns to this theme eight months later, in a letter to Eberhard Bethge dated 12 February 1944. It is now winter, which only heightens his experience in prison of isolation from the natural world. To compensate, he resorts to spending "a good deal of time outdoors" in his imagination, particularly in the forests and glades near the Bonhoeffer holiday home in Friedrichsbrunn.

> I lie on my back in the grass, watching the clouds float across the blue sky in the breeze and listening to the sounds of the forest, so that it seems impossible to me and against my nature that we could have had a house in the high mountains or by the sea! It's the central uplands [Mittelbirge] which are my natural environment – the Harz Mountains, the Thuringian Forest, or the Weser Mountains – and which made me who I am (Bonhoeffer 2020b, 294).

Describing childhood memories of happy times spent with his family in his "natural environment" – the central uplands of Thuringia – Bonhoeffer says, "it's remarkable how our whole outlook is shaped by childhood impressions like these" and goes on to declare that it is these mountains and forests which "made me what I am." He does not apologize for such existential and foundational experiences of nature or attempt to Christianize his intimate connection with the natural world by referring to Scripture. At most, he deflects the potential charge that he is becoming soft and sentimental by suggesting to Bethge that it would be tempting to pursue a "sociological view of natural scenery" (Bonhoeffer 2020b, 294).

Four months later, in Bonhoeffer's letter to Bethge dated 30 June 1944, his longing for nature reaches its peak. It is now summer. Dietrich is still in Tegel prison, while Bethge, who was serving as a conscripted soldier in the Wehrmacht, was in Northern Italy. Bonhoeffer writes:

> Dear Eberhard,
>
> Today was a hot summer day here, and I could only in part enjoy the sun because I could imagine how miserable it must be making you. Most likely you're stuck somewhere in dust and sweat, tired and perhaps with no chance of washing or cooling off. I can imagine that sometimes you begin to hate the sun. And yet, you know, I should really like to feel the full force of it again, burning on one's skin and gradually making one's whole body glow, so that one knows again that one is a corporeal being. I'd like to get tired by the sun instead of by books and thinking. I'd like to have it awaken my animal existence, in the sense not that debases one's humanity but that delivers one from the peevishness and artificiality of a merely intellectual (*geistig*) existence and makes a person purer and happier. I'd like, just for once, not just to see the sun and sip at it a little, but to experience it bodily. The romantic enthusiasm for the sun, which only gets intoxicated over sunrises and sunsets, has no idea of the power and reality of the sun but knows it only as a picture. It can never grasp why the sun was worshipped as a god; for that you need to experience not only its light and colors, but also its heat (Bonhoeffer 2010b, 448–449).

This passage is extraordinary on several levels. If asked to choose texts to defend the claim that Bonhoeffer was a nature-mystic, this would certainly be near the top of the list. Nevertheless, the experience he describes, and which he longs to know once more, which has touched him deeply on an emotional and spiritual level, is an intrinsically *bodily* experience. Only one who has experienced the power and reality of the sun bodily, Bonhoeffer writes, can understand why the sun was worshipped as a god. Rather than shying away from such a bold, and perhaps heretical take on sun worship, Bonhoeffer prefers to bask in its warmth. His encounter with the sun is life-changing; it does not deny reason but transcends it, by allowing one to break out of the confines of the mind and truly be present *in the body*. This is a heady experience, but in contrast to alcoholic intoxication it sharpens the senses rather than dulling them. Since at least the time of Plato, Western thought has largely given preferential treatment to the mind and demonstrated an inherent suspicion of the body. In contrast, Bonhoeffer declares that such encounters with the sun "god" make people purer and happier, by awakening their "animal existence," which in contrast to a life lived in the mind ("a mere intellectual existence") is fully present in the body and in the world.

There is space here for a few more comments on *Letters and Papers from Prison* before we move on to *Fiction from Prison*. In Bonhoeffer's moving poem, "Who Am I" (Bonhoeffer 2010, 459–460), he describes feeling "like a caged bird," "starving for colors, for flowers, for birdsong," "struggling for life breath," and "thirsting for kind words and human kindness." He is torn between hope, rage and fear. Although he declares himself "too tired and empty to pray," his questioning and his longing, which include longing for nature, can perhaps be best understood *as a form of prayer*, a reading that is confirmed by his closing words:

> Who am I? They mock me, these lonely questions of mine.
> Whoever I am, thou knowest me; O God, I am thine!
> (Bonhoeffer 2010b, 460).

Bonhoeffer's prison experiences, including his longing for a physical connection with nature that was largely denied him, enabled him to "grasp something more." His experience of isolation and loss, of separation and estrangement, led to a deeper understanding both of himself ("I am Thine!") and of God ("thou knowest me"). If that is not prayer, then what is?

In another poem, "Night Voices" (Bonhoeffer 2010b, 462–470), Bonhoeffer's hopes, his fears, and his comradeship with his fellow prisoners are expressed in tangible images of night and day, of sunlight and a summer morning. He narrates his inner dialogue, the tormented thoughts of a prisoner during the long, dark night. Wrestling with the awareness of his own guilt and complicity, he hears Night declare, "I am not dark, dark is guilt alone," and in the unseen yet tangible presence of his fellow prisoners, his "brothers," he offers a prayer for endurance, for forgiveness, and for the dawning of a new day.

At last Bonhoeffer sees the morning light of a mild summer day through his window, and feels a gentle summer breeze on his brow. There is no denying that it is a beautiful summer day, even in prison. As his heart stirs with hope, and he wonders what this new day will bring, he hears steps approaching his cell. They stop near his door, and in a moment of prescience he knows they have come to lead a fellow prisoner to his execution. He hears brusque words summoning the condemned man, and his brother's courageous, proud steps as he is led away. Though the words of courage and comfort he whispers to the condemned man fall unheard, they are not in vain; Bonhoeffer is speaking as well to his own heart, and addressing his own hopes and fears. He goes in spirit with the prisoner to the place of execution, and in his mind whispers his last words, as if they were his own: "Brother, when the sunlight I no longer see, do live for me!"

As the summer morning "rises rejoicing," his thoughts go with the condemned man, but this is not his morning; it is not the morning that will at last bring either the freedom of release from prison, or the freedom of death. So he concludes with a declaration of solidarity, or hope, and of resolve.

> Stretched out on my cot
> I stare at the gray wall.
> Outside, a summer morning
> that is not yet mine
> rises rejoicing
> over the land.
> Brothers, until our day breaks
> after the long night,
> we will stand fast! (Bonhoeffer 2010b, 469–470)

In "Outline for a Book" (Bonhoeffer 2010b, 499–500), Bonhoeffer laments the "coming of age of human beings," now commonly referred to as the Anthropocene. In this new age, the goal of modern humans has become reducing the danger that lies in the natural world, in chance, in "the blows of fate." Nature, he argues, "used to be conquered by the soul," now it is conquered through "technological organization of all kinds." Bonhoeffer is describing a phenomenon that has grown only more prevalent and pervasive since his day; we no longer have an unmediated experience of and relationship to nature. We have placed organization, technology, and screens of all types between us and nature, to protect us against the menace of nature. This has two profound consequences; not only is the power of the soul lacking, but there is nothing left to protect us from the menace of organization. Whereas the unmediated experience of nature causes the soul to grow stronger, unmediated experience of organization weakens us and makes us defenceless against "the machine."

This is a powerful call to reconnect with the natural world and to practice what Dahill calls "bio-Theoacoustics."

Bonhoeffer's prison reflections on nature in *Fiction from Prison*

Fiction from Prison contains portions of a novel and a play, both unfinished, which Bonhoeffer was writing during his time in Tegel prison. Both works have strong autobiographical elements, which rather than focusing solely on the main protagonist or another singular character, appear in recognizable form in the lives and thoughts and actions of multiple characters, many of whom reflect certain aspects of Dietrich's own life. This literary device mirrors the various roles that Bonhoeffer himself took on during his intense and all-too short life; he was a son, a brother, and a friend, just as he was a pastor, a theologian and a member of the resistance.

While there are numerous references to nature in this volume, the most notable is a long passage entitled "A Quiet Forest Pond" (Bonhoeffer 2010a, 97–108), which describes an outing in which the younger members of the Brake family tramp through the hills and forests. After a long hike, they come at last to a forest pond where they stop to swim, and to gather mushrooms to cook over a fire for their lunch, along with the new potatoes they brought with them from home. After lunch Christoph and his friend Ulrich relax together.

> On a treeless slope rising gently from the pond in full sun, Christoph and Ulrich lay on their backs in the tall grass, their hands cradling their heads, their gaze directed at times to the sky, at times across the pond, each with a gray linen slouch hat on his head. Their tanned and toughened bodies were impervious to the sun. Anyone seeing the two would have thought they were brothers, as in fact often happened (Bonhoeffer 2010a, 100).

Taken as a whole, "A Quiet Forest Pond" recalls Bonhoeffer's account, contained in his letter to Bethge discussed above, of his own youthful adventures in the hills surrounding their family's holiday house. In the text above he is reliving *in prose* those happy times he relived *in his imagination* ("I lie on my back in the grass, watching the clouds float across the blue sky in the breeze and listening to the sounds of the forest"). His comment that "their tanned and toughened bodies were impervious to the sun" recalls his Letter to Bethge discussed above, where he wrote of his longing to "feel the full force of [the sun] again, burning on one's skin and gradually making one's whole body glow, so that one knows again that one is a corporeal being" (Bonhoeffer 2010b, 448–449).

As might be expected from an eyewitness and participant, Bonhoeffer's description of this adventure is vivid and detailed. Throughout he speaks of the sights and sounds and smells of the forest and its inhabitants, and surprises us with his keen knowledge of wild mushrooms. The conversation between Christoph and Ulrich is at once personal and deep, touching on many subjects that Bonhoeffer wrote about and commented on in his prison letters. For the purposes of this paper, however, the following passage stands out as being almost programmatic:

> This year's new potatoes and the aroma of fresh mushrooms outdoors under the shade trees on the shore of the cool pond made for an incomparable feast. They ate in silence, and along with the nourishing food, each of these young people took in the energy of forest, sun, water, each other's company, their family, their native land, and freedom itself. They received all this more or less consciously as one great gift in the depths of their being (Bonhoeffer 2010a, 98).

Though Bonhoeffer is no stranger to the power of the sun *god*, this passage sounds more like a description of Gaea, the earth goddess whom Bonhoeffer mentions on several occasions with reference to the Antaeus myth (Burnell 2023, 157–158). He writes of the energy of the natural world, of the forest, sun and water, which join with the energy of good friends and family, of their native land and of freedom itself, and which they received "as one great gift in the depths of their being." This is nature-mysticism *from below*, which is experienced directly without any preconceived idea of nature or of nature's relation to human beings, who "more or less consciously" sense the connection shared by all things both living and inanimate – a connection which is as natural as breathing, as nourishing as a mother's milk, and as wholesome as a home-cooked meal.

Bonhoeffer's prison reflections on nature in *Love Letters from Cell 92*

The "love letters" between Dietrich and his fiancé Maria, which remained at her request unpublished until after her death, are a remarkable account of their growing relationship, which was brutally interrupted by his arrest and cut tragically short by his execution in Flossenbürg. They provide a more personal and intimate view of Bonhoffer than we find elsewhere, which is only approached by his correspondence with his close friend Eberhard Bethge.

Reading Dietrich and Maria's letters, it is clear that they both felt a strong connection to the natural world. Their letters contain long descriptions of places that are important to them and that they would like to visit together someday. Among their numerous references to nature, Maria speaks most often of the sky and Bonhoeffer of the sun.

In a letter to Maria dated 29 August 1943, Dietrich spoke of the oppressive summer heat in his cell, and of his "quite earthy and concrete" desire to go swimming with her at a forest lake. His desire to lie there in the shade as he listened to her talk was only matched, he declared, by his "equally natural" aversion to the conditions he was experiencing in prison. This comparison might not sound very romantic, but it speaks powerfully of his longing for contact with the natural world that was denied him. His unspoken desire to embrace his fiancée is expressed in the way he embraces such physical, "earthy" experiences.

It is in this context that Bonhoeffer writes of his visceral attraction to the sun. Noting that human beings were "taken from the earth," and hence consist of more than mind and rational thoughts, Bonhoeffer tells Maria of the recurring temptation, which he first experienced on a trip to Cuba, to succumb to sun-worship.

> The sun has always attracted me, and I've often been reminded by it that human beings were taken from the earth and don't just consist of thin air and thoughts. So much so that once, when I went to Cuba to preach there at Christmas, and exchanged the ice of North America for its luxuriant tropical vegetation, I almost succumbed to sun-worship and could hardly remember what I was really supposed to preach. It was a genuine crisis, and a hint of it assails me every summer when I get to feel the sun. To me, the sun isn't an astronomical magnitude but a kind of vital force which I love and also fear. I think it's cowardly to disregard these realities in a rationalistic way. Do you understand? That's why patience and joy and gratitude and serenity and forgiveness must keep fighting and prevailing over all forms of opposition; and really to perceive and learn and believe what it says in the psalm – "the Lord God is a sun and shield" – is something reserved for moments of merciful exaltation, not a conventional wisdom (Bonhoeffer and von Wedemeyer 1992, 68–69).

The sun as described here by Bonhoeffer is more than a mere object in the physical universe. To him it is a vital force, which he has come both to love and to fear. At first glance one might detect a residual hesitation on the part of the theologian and pastor to confess a proclivity to sun-worship. He is quick to cite Psalm 84:11 ("The LORD God is a sun and a shield"), in what could be taken as an attempt to mitigate his own theological discomfort or defend against potential charges that he is departing from Christian orthodoxy. Yet such hesitation is absent in his letter to Bethge mentioned above (Bonhoeffer 2010b, 448–449). Perhaps Dietrich is unsure of how Maria, who was much younger and less experienced than his theologically astute friend and dialogue partner, might react?

At a more existential level, this is not Bonhoeffer the theologian writing, but Bonhoeffer the lover. In seeking words to tell his fiancée how much he longs to be with her, the first thing that comes to his mind is to compare that longing with his longing for nature. What is more, he connects such experiential moments of sun-worship with moments of "merciful exaltation" that come from experiencing God and from embracing one's calling on this earth. This is a powerful example of what Dahill wrote about, when she described experiencing something more of God through nature than one can experience without contact with nature. Bonhoeffer is describing here how he experiences nature as a form of prayer.

Less than a month later, on 20 September 1943, Dietrich writes to Maria of the hardships that prisoners experience as a result from the changing seasons.

> Autumn begins tomorrow. These last few weeks, whenever people have spoken of Autumn coming early, I've disliked the sound of the word. The changing seasons are harder on one in here than on the outside. You'll be spending a lot of time in the forest hides at dusk and before daybreak. I'm so fond of those autumn mornings when the sun breaks slowly through the mist, but I know that, wherever you are, you'll be waiting with me every day and every hour (Bonhoeffer and von Wedemeyer 1992, 85–86).

Bonhoeffer's reaction to the mention of Autumn goes beyond the suffering that prisoners endure from the heat of summer or the cold of winter. As he tells Maria, the months of separation caused by his imprisonment "have deprived us both of a great deal." He longs to be with Maria, and he longs to enjoy the sun rising on a brisk autumn morning. Deprived of both, his imagination unites these longings in a vision of happiness. This vision remains with him and grows stronger with the passing of time. He shares this vision with her again on 14 January 1944.

> When I picture our first reunion I don't see us talking together in a room; I instinctively see us walking in the woods, seeing and experiencing things together, in contact with the earth and reality. My desire to do so is very great, and I believe and know we share that desire. May God preserve it for us and bring all to fulfilment. My beloved Maria, I am always and will ever be Your Dietrich (Bonhoeffer and von Wedemeyer 1992, 162).

Bonhoeffer would agree with Dahill when she suggests that we can better understand God and more fully experience God through direct contact with nature. In a letter to Maria written on 29 May 1944 he argues that the same is true of the love shared by two human beings. Once again, in searching for ways to describe love, and more specifically to express his love for Maria (or rather the love they shared together), he turns to an analogy with nature.

> Isn't love always, but always, a mutual longing that can never be fully assuaged? What would fulfilment be worth if it robbed us of that longing? It would spell the end of love, not its beginning, its essence. But this mutual longing mustn't always connote frenzy and insensate desire, it mustn't always afflict and torment us, it needn't be forever fretting over what is still denied us. It should surely be like one's longing for a glorious spring morning, when one sees the sky already tinged with red by the sun's first rays. It means waiting, desiring, and yearning, assuredly, but doing so with happiness and utter certainty. That's what our love is like, I believe, and it's all the better for being so (Bonhoeffer and von Wedemeyer 1992, 246).

Bonhoeffer again speaks of love using an analogy with nature in a letter to Maria dated 27 June 1944.

> That ours was no wildly passionate affair and did not become so was dictated by the direction in which we were led, but shouldn't we now be glad of that? How much more intolerable our separation would be, on top of all the anguish it causes us today! If the sun shines on us and warms us, should we complain because it doesn't scorch us? I'm quite content with that warmth, and you must be too (von Bismarck and Kabitz 1992, 254).

There is more to be found in *Love Letters* on our theme, but these passages take us deep into Bonhoeffer's prison experience, and how it impacted his experience of nature, of human love, and of love for God. All these facets of life come together in Bonhoefer's poem "The Past," which he wrote in early June 1944. The selected lines below speak of the emotions Dietrich felt after Maria left following their infrequent meetings in prison, in particular the most recent meeting on 22 May 1944.

> The Past
> You went, beloved happiness and much-loved sorrow . . .
> Just as the sun sinks ever faster over the sea
> As if drawn down into the darkness
> so sinks . . . your image into the sea that is the past
> and is buried beneath a wave or two.
> Just as a puff of warm breath
> dissolves in cool morning air,
> so does your image melt away . . .
> I yearn to inhale the fragrance of your being,
> absorb and linger therein, just as,
> on a hot summer day,
> heady blossoms makes bees welcome
> and intoxicate them,
> and as hawkmoths become drunk on privet.
> But a rude gust scatters scent and blossoms,
> and I stand there like a fool
> before the vanished and the begone . . .
> But I sense
> that all above, beside, below me
> is smiling at me, mysterious and intact,
> smiling at my hopeless endeavor
> to capture the wind,
> and regain what is past . . .
> I stretch forth my hands
> and pray,
> and hear the new tidings;
> The past will be restored to you,
> as your life's most vital part,
> by gratitude and penitence.
> Take hold, in what is past,

of God's forgiveness and grace.
Pray that God may preserve you,
today and on the morrow
(Bonhoeffer and von Wedemeyer 1992, 248–252).

This poem is marked by the pervasive use of images taken from the natural world; it seems that Bonhoeffer's "love language" is indeed the language of nature. It is significant that this is the first poem that we have a record of which Bonhoeffer wrote in prison. It's as if his sense of love and loss for Maria, for nature, for freedom, perhaps even for faith is so strong that a different medium was required to express his thoughts, his feelings, his experience.

Bonhoeffer first sent this poem to Bethge, together with his letter dated 5 June 1944. In the letter he describes the poem as a "confrontation with the past," as an "attempt to hold on to it and get it back, and above all a fear of losing it" (Bonhoeffer 2010b, 416). He felt it would resonate with the thoughts Bethge, who was serving as an army chaplain on the Italian front, had sent to him earlier regarding saying goodbye to his wife Renata (Bonhoeffer's niece). In sharing such intimate thoughts with Bethge, he realizes he must send the letter to Maria as well (Bonhoeffer 2010b, 417). In the cover letter attached to the version he sent to Maria, Dietrich wrote: "My dearest Maria, This is for and you alone" (Bonhoeffer 2010b, 418). This is not strictly true, for he had already shared it with Bethge. Perhaps feeling a bit guilty for this, he tells Maria he had hesitated to send it, for fear it might alarm her, but nevertheless expresses confidence that she will "sense what underlies it." As if to reassure her, he tells her "the last six lines are what matters most; they prompted the rest" (Bonhoeffer 2010b, 418). One may wonder about that; it seems more likely that the poem was triggered by the pain of leaving and loss, which led in the end to Bonhoeffer's expression of faith and God's goodness and providential care. Regardless, the honest wrestling with his own pain and loss, and the growth in his relationship with Maria despite (and in some ways because of) their forced separation, has brought him to a place of greater openness, to a willingness to risk being misunderstood, and to a confidence that regardless of her response to the letter, their relationship will thrive and endure.

In October of 1944, in the aftermath of the failed assassination plot of 20 July 1944, Bonhoeffer was moved from Tegel prison to the Gestapo prison on Prinz-Albrecht-Strasse. Conditions here were much worse, correspondence was limited, and visits were impossible. Here, from his bleak cell in the cellar, he wrote the beloved poem, "By Powers of Good" (*Von Guten Machten*). It is the last poem written by Bonhoeffer that survived. Dietrich included it as part of his 19 December 1944 letter to Maria, prefaced with a note to her that reads: "Here are another few verses that have occurred to me in recent nights. They're my Christmas greetings to you, my parents, and my brothers and sisters" (Bonhoeffer and von Wedemeyer 1992, 269).

Bonhoeffer of course understood that his being moved to Prinz-Albrecht-Strasse greatly increased the likelihood that he would be executed for his part in the conspiracy, which makes this letter to his fiancé even more remarkable and moving. The poem, which has been widely commented upon, largely speaks for itself. The text below is from the Fortress Press edition of *Letters and Papers from Prison*.

1. By faithful, quiet powers of good surrounded
   so wondrously consoled and sheltered here –
   I wish to live these days with you in spirit
   and with you enter into a new year.
2. The old year still would try our hearts to torment,
   of evil times we still do bear the weight;
   O Lord, do grant our souls, now terror-stricken,
   salvation for which you did us create.
3. And should you offer us the cup of suffering,
   though heavy, brimming full and bitter brand,
   we'll thankfully accept it, never flinching,
   from your good heart and your beloved hand.
4. But should you wish now once again to give us
   the joys of this world and its glorious sun,
   then we'll recall anew what past times brought us
   and then our life belongs to you alone.
5. The candles you have brought into our darkness,
   let them today be burning warm and bright,
   and if it's possible, do reunite us!
   We know your light is shining through the night.
6. When now the quiet deepens all around us,
   O, let our ears that fullest sound amaze
   of this, your world, invisibly expanding
   as all your children sing high hymns of praise.
7. By powers of good so wondrously protected,
   we wait with confidence, befall what may.
   God is with us at night and in the morning
   and oh, most certainly on each new day
   (Bonhoeffer 2010, 548–550).

When we remember that *Von Guten Machten* was written first and foremost to Maria, the way Bonhoeffer moves back and forth between thoughts addressed to her and thoughts addressed to God takes on added significance. In the first stanza he writes to Maria of his longing to "live these days with you in spirit," and – perhaps in the flesh? – to enter with her into the New Year. But the perspective quickly shifts in stanza two from the singular to the plural, where it remains to the end. Bonhoeffer is no longer speaking *to* Maria. Now he expresses *with* Maria what he hopes and believes is in both their hearts. Another momentous shift comes in the last two verses of stanza two through the end of stanza five, where Bonhoeffer and Maria address God directly in the plural voice. The final two stanzas contain their joint affirmation of trust in God, their acceptance of whatever fate awaits them, and their confident assurance of God's gracious presence in the darkness of night and the light of each new day.

For the purposes of this paper stanzas three and four stand out:

3. And should you offer us the cup of suffering,
   though heavy, brimming full and bitter brand,
   we'll thankfully accept it, never flinching,
   from your good heart and your beloved hand.
4. But should you wish now once again to give us
   the joys of this world and its glorious sun,
   then we'll recall anew what past times brought us
   and then our life belongs to you alone.

It is in these lines that Bonhoeffer, and by proxy Maria, entrust their love and their final fate to the gracious hands of God. Though Dietrich writes in the plural, he feels the noose closing around his neck and sends what proved to be his final words to Maria. If stanza three serves to comfort and prepare her for the worst, stanza four expresses their mutual hope beyond hope that they may yet have a future together. And here, once again, he envisions the reunion they long for in quite earthly terms, as God returning to them the extraordinary, everyday gift of embracing the "joys of this world and its glorious sun."

Conclusion: some theological implications

This paper examines Bonhoeffer's experience in prison of being deprived of normal contact with the natural world. Rather than surveying his theological works to develop the trajectory of a Bonhoefferian theology of nature, it explores his own descriptions of his prison experience, contained in *Letters and Papers from Prison*, *Fiction from Prison*, and *Love Letters from Cell 92*.

Bonhoeffer's relationship to nature can be described as a practical form of nature-mysticism. His words reveal a connection with the natural world which is direct and intuitive; he neither needs nor provides a developed metaphysical or mystical framework for his experience. Just as his concept of Christ-reality was a lived experience, so his passionate embrace of the physical world embodies a quite earthy aspect of his declaration that "from now on we cannot speak rightly of either God or the world without speaking of Jesus Christ" (Bonhoeffer 2005, 54). As Dahill notes, Bonhoeffer calls all concepts of reality that ignore Jesus "abstractions," and Bonhoeffer's own testimony from prison only serves to strengthen her argument that "Christian prayer that does not participate fully and explicitly in the union of God and the natural world in Christ today is on some level an abstraction" (Dahill 2013, 295). Bonhoeffer practiced Christian prayer in just this way; his prison writings illustrate time and again what Dahill calls bio-theoacoustics. Bonhoeffer's love for nature was indeed a form of communion and a form of prayer. As his visceral descriptions of "sun-worship" attest, it enabled him to understand and experience God in ways he could not otherwise experience, truly as a "bigger and wilder Thou." His encounter with the natural world changed him as well, and visibly impacted his relationships with his closest friend and his fiancé.

Eberhard Bethge first read Bonhoeffer's letters to Maria nearly fifty years after his friend's death. In his "Postscript" to *Love Letters from Cell 92* (Bonhoeffer and von Wedemeyer 1992, 365–368), Bethge notes two ways that his encounter with these letters affected him. First, he writes of his surprise and delight that these are indeed love letters, in which his friend Dietrich said to Maria, again and again, "I want you, only you, and just the way you are." Secondly, he notes how this "unconsummated yet complete relationship formed the culmination of Dietrich's long journey from 'Finkenwalde' to 'Berlin' and back to the world to which he had always belonged" (1992, 366). Bethge's words give testimony to the manner in which Bonhoeffer's personal life journey was intricately woven into the tapestry of his theology.

> Now, by virtue of this correspondence, we can at last see clearly that Dietrich's and Maria's coming together was a prelude to those words which, in the summer of 1944, brought forth a liberated, life-affirming theology whose influence has been more profound and far-reaching than anyone would have expected. The letters also make manifest the experience that wedded Bonhoeffer to the

world more painfully than ever, just when he had to prepare to renounce that world if he wished to keep faith with it (1992, 366).

Bonhoeffer's love for nature is intimately intertwined with his love for God, for life, for Maria, for his family and friends. Time and again we find these other loves expressed in the language of his love for nature. As Bethge argues above in his Postscript to *Love Letters*, Bonhoeffer's seminal thoughts on this-worldly, non-religious Christianity, which took shape in his prison cell, which followed the trajectory of his entire life, and which brought him full circle back to the world, were awakened and strengthened by the unexpected love he experienced late in life with Maria. As this study of his prison writings has shown, that life trajectory, including his lifelong love for nature, was shaped in no small part by the mountains, forests, lakes and fields, that left their indelible mark on his childhood and which had, as he declared, "made me what I am."

On one level this survey of texts concerning Bonhoeffer's love of nature in prison fails to contribute much to a Bonhoefferian ecotheology which leads, as Dahill and Rayson argue, to advocacy for the beleaguered creation which we humans call home. Bonhoeffer was never allowed the luxury of practicing theology in times of peace, and given the challenges he and his generation faced, it is as unsurprising as it is unfortunate that he never found the time to develop his thoughts in this direction in more depth. Nevertheless, his embodied love for nature, on full exhibit in these letters and poems, provides strong anecdotal support to their claim that Bonhoeffer's theology, and his experience of nature as a form of prayer, does indeed lead to a reimagined relationship with the natural world and responsible action on its behalf.

Bibliograpy

Bonhoeffer, Dietrich. 2005. *Ethics. Dietrich Bonhoeffer Works Volume 6*, edited by Clifford J. Green, translated by Reinhard Krauss, Charles West, and Douglas W. Stott. Minneapolis: Fortress Press.

Bonhoeffer, Dietrich. 2010a. *Fiction from Prison. Dietrich Bonhoeffer Works Volume 7*, edited by Clifford J. Green, translated by Nancy Lukens. Minneapolis: Fortress Press.

Bonhoeffer, Dietrich. 2010b. *Letters and Papers from Prison. Dietrich Bonhoeffer Works Volume 8*, edited by John W. de Gruchy, translated by Isabel Best, Lisa E. Dahill, Reinhard Krauss, and Nancy Lukens. Minneapolis: Fortress Press.

Bonhoeffer, Dietrich, and Maria von Wedemeyer. 1992. *Love Letters from Cell 92: The Correspondence Between Dietrich Bonhoeffer and Maria Von Wedemeyer 1943–45*, edited by Ruth-Alice von Bismarck and Ulrich Kabitz, translated by John Brown. Nashville: Abingdon.

Burnell, Joel. 2015. "Mystical Aspects of Dietrich Bonhoeffer's theologia crucis." In *Między Transcendencja a Immanencją – Mistyka Śląska*, edited by Bogdan Ferdek, Leon Miodoński, 179–210. Wrocław: Arboretum.

Burnell, Joel. 2018. "Towards a Theology of the Earth with Dietrich Bonhoeffer." *Teologia Ziemi, Theologica Wratislaviensia* 13 (2018): 77–86.

Burnell, Joel. 2023. "Learning to Sail on the Open Sea: Bonhoeffer on Resilience." In *Resilience in a Troubled World*, edited by John Berry, 151–67. Malta: Kite.

Casella, Jean, and James Ridgeway. 2013. "Mandela in Solitary Watch." *Solitary Watch*, 17 December 2013. https://solitarywatch.org/2013/12/07/mandela-solitary/.

Dahill, Lisa. 2013. "Bio-Theoacoustics: Prayer Outdoors and the Reality of the Natural World." *Dialog: A Journal of Theology* 52.4 (Winter 2013, December): 292–302.

Lovat, Terrance. 2006. "Practical Mysticism as Authentic Religiousness: A Bonhoeffer Case Study." In *Australian eJournal of Theology* 6 (February 2006), edited by Gerard Hall. Brisbane: Australian Catholic University.

Lovat, Terry, and Dianne Rayson. 2014. "'Lord of the (warming) world': Bonhoeffer's eco-theological ethic and the Gandhi factor." In *The Bonhoeffer Legacy, Australasian Journal of Bonhoeffer Studies* 2.1, edited by Terrance Lovat, 57–74. Adelaide: ATF Press.

Mandela, Nelson. 1994a. *Long Road to Freedom*. Boston: Little, Brown and Company.

Mandela, Nelson. 1994b. "'The time for the healing of the wounds has come' Inaugural Speech 10 May 1994." University of Pennsylvania – African Studies Center. https://www.africa.upenn.edu/Articles_Gen/Inaugural_Speech_17984.html.

Rasmussen, Larry. 2012. *Earth-Honoring Faith: Religious Ethics in a New Key*. New York: Oxford University Press.

Rayson, Dianne. 2012. *Bonhoeffer and Climate Change: Theology and Ethics for the Anthropocene*. Minneapololis: Fortress.

Rayson, Dianne. 2023a. "Bonhoeffer's Practical Mysticism: Implications for Ecotheology and Ecoethics." In *Education, Religion and Ethics – A Scholarly Collection*, edited by Dianne Rayson, 145–156. Cham: Springer.

Rayson, Dianne. 2023b. "From Pacifism to Tyrannicide: Considering Bonhoeffer's Ethics for the Anthropocene." In *Education, Religion and Ethics – A Scholarly Collection*, edited by Dianne Rayson, 237–252. Cham: Springer.

Spencer, Daniel. 2021. "The Challenge of Mysticism: a Primer from a Christian Perspective." In *Sophia, International Journal of Philosophy and Traditions*, 60.4 (December 2021), edited by P. Bilimoria, S.N. Tagore, 1027–1045. London: Springer.

Wilde, Oscar. 1898. "The Ballad of Reading Gaol." Poetry Foundation. https://www.poetryfoundation.org/poems/45495/the-ballad-of-reading-gaol [accessed: 11.10.2023].

13

Freedom and Responsibility in Bonhoeffer's Ethics

A Challenge for our Troubled Times

Carlos Caldas, PhD
Post-Graduate Department of Religious Studies
at Pontifical Catholic University of Minas,
Belo Horizonte, Brazil
ORCID: 0000-0003-0472-7250

About the Author

Carlos Caldas received his doctorate in Religious Studies from São Paulo Methodist University with a dissertation about the Puerto Rican theologian Orlando Costas. Carlos's research currently has two loci: the relationship between theology and the arts, with emphasis on literature and pop culture (movies and comics) and public theology, with emphasis on the theology of Dietrich Bonhoeffer. He is author of *Dietrich Bonhoeffer e a teologia pública no Brasil* (São Paulo: Garimpo, 2015).

Keywords

Dietrich Bonhoeffer, freedom, ethics of responsibility, christological ethics, *nachfolge*

Abstract

This article presents the understanding of the concepts of freedom and responsibility in the thought of the German Lutheran theologian Dietrich Bonhoeffer (1906–1945). According to him, these two concepts are inseparably intertwined, for he thought about them both from a christological perspective. In Bonhoeffer's theology Christ is the paramount example of what it means to be free and responsible at the same time. Therefore, Bonhoeffer developed a christological ethics in which Jesus Christ, who lived for the other, is the model for a life of responsible freedom. Such freedom is understood, not as freedom for doing only what pleases one, but as freedom for a life of service, especially for those who are suffering, those who are (as Bonhoeffer put it) on the underside of history. In its conclusion, the article presents some practical suggestions of what it means to live the *nachfolge* – the following of Jesus (discipleship) with responsible freedom in our world today.

1. Thinking about our troubled times

There are many aspects that characterize our times as troubled. Jürgen Moltmann in *The Coming of God* (1995) presents three great threats that are concrete and real possibilities of the extermination of humankind. Moltmann calls them "exterminations," and in fact they represent a very serious situation, one the world has never seen before. These threats are: the possibility of nuclear extermination, the possibility of ecological extermination and the possibility of socioeconomic extermination (Moltmann 2002, 233–237). A brief word about each one of these terrible threats:

(1) the possibility of nuclear extermination is a nightmare that haunts humanity since 1945, when the United States dropped two atomic bombs on Hiroshima and Nagasaki in Japan. What if this happens again? What if it happens on a global scale? Science fiction (sci-fi) books and movies show us plenty of examples of such a dystopic situation. We know for sure that sci-fi is a sort of fantastic literature, but this literature is like a secular, non-religious prophet who admonishes us of a real danger[1.]

---

1. For centuries theologians have been involved in a conversation with philosophers. "What has Athens to do with Jerusalem?" – The famous question asked by Tertullian in the second century of the Christian era by and large has been answered in a positive way. But due to the threats presented by Moltmann in his mentioned book perhaps the time has come for theologians to start a conversation with writers of sci-fi and "cli-fi" (climate fiction) novels. For an example of such dialogue see Caldas 2020, 61–76.

(2) the possibility of ecological extermination is no less serious than the threat of a nuclear war on a global scale. For decades ecological activists and serious scientists have been warning about the destruction of the environment everywhere. Global warming is not a fairy tale. In the last few years we have seen the rising of a new literary genre: climate fiction ("cli-fi") literature. But this "cli-fi" literature stuff is by no means the pioneer in alerting the world about the dangers of ecological extermination: years before climate literature classical authors of fantasy literature, like J. R. R. Tolkien[2] and C. S. Lewis,[3] criticized the myth of progress that demands economic growth whatever it costs, and destroys nature to build factories and industries. If we destroy our habitat, our environment, we will commit global suicide. After all, the planet is not in danger – we are.[4]

(3) the possibility of socioeconomic extermination: Jesus said "you will always have the poor among you" (John 12.8), but this situation is getting worse worldwide. The gulf that divides the haves and the have nots is increasing. I will provide just one example: according to the *Forbes* magazine, the number of Brazilian billionaires (in terms of US dollars) increased from forty-five persons in 2020 to sixty-five persons in 2021 (UOL 2021), that is, during the worst of the COVID-19 pandemic. The increasing of the world population will increase also the number of those who live below the poverty line.[5]

Besides these three threats mentioned by Moltmann we need also to mention the terrible situation of the COVID-19 pandemic. Since the beginning of 2020 the entire world has been facing this struggle against the "new coronavirus," a completely unheard-of situation. It is literally a pandemic, and not

---

2. See for instance "The Road to Isengard," the eighth chapter of *The Two Towers*, the second volume of *The Lord of the Rings* trilogy, when Tolkien presents a subtle critique to the myth of progress when he shows Saruman, the wizard who surrendered to the powers of the evil spirit Melkor destroying forests to build factories of weapons.

3. See for instance *That Hideous Strength*, the third volume of Lewis's cosmic trilogy, when he presents a character who is an employee of the NICE Corporation (the "hideous strength" that gives title to the book) defending the elimination of natural trees, that, according to him, should be replaced by plastic trees.

4. For an approach to the issue of climate change from a Bonhoefferian perspective the definitive work is Rayson (2021).

5. According to the *WorldAtlas* (Kiprop 2018) "The poverty line is the minimal amount of money an individual can live on in a specific country over a particular period. A method used by economists to arrive at the poverty line involves calculating the cost of the resources an average human requires each year. The international poverty line or poverty threshold is estimated by the World Bank at $1.90 per day based on what the amount could purchase in the United States, as of 2011. According to the definition, approximately 10 percent of the global population lives below the international poverty line." According to the Worldometers the world population as of November 2022 is practically eight billion people.

an epidemic.[6] Up to 31 December 2021 in Brazil alone there were 606,018 casualties due to the COVID pandemic (Gazeta do Povo 2021).

And we have also the troubling situation of conventional – by which I mean non-nuclear – war. It may not be a nuclear war, but it still is war. The eyes and ears of the world are turned to the problematic situation of the war between Russia and Ukraine, and it is much more difficult to speak about that being so very close to the Ukrainian border. But unfortunately war is raging today not only in Eastern Europe but in at least twenty-seven situations around the world: according to website visualcapitalist.com there are right now on our planet territorial disputes, not only in the Russo-Ukrainian war, but also the Turkish-Kurdish conflict, the Israeli-Palestinian conflict and the Nagorno-Karabakh conflict (between Azerbaijan and Armenia). Besides these there is also civil war in Afghanistan, Yemen, Syria, Libya and South Sudan, political instability in Venezuela, Lebanon, Egypt, Ethiopia and in the Democratic Republic of Congo, transnational terrorism caused by groups like the Boko Haram in Nigeria and alarming high figures of criminal violence in Mexico – this list is not an exhaustive one, but it is enough to show us that we live in a very dangerous world (Koop 2021).

And finishing the first part of my paper allow me please to speak about the highly concerning and difficult situation my country of Brazil is facing right now: our democracy is jeopardized by the current President, who never hid his intentions to shut down the Congress and the Senate and to make a coup d'état in the next few months. If that were to happen, civil and human rights will be violated everywhere and all the time, since the President of the country and his thousands of followers are like Miguel de Cervantes's *Don Quixote*: they see "communists" everywhere, and "damn communists" (as they say) must be mercilessly taken down.

What was presented here is only a brief summary of current situations that are very threatening to all of us in our world. The obvious question that is posed before us is: what can we do?

---

6. According to the Merriam-Webster Dictionary (2023), "A disease can be declared an *epidemic* when it spreads over a wide area and many individuals are taken ill at the same time. If the spread escalates further, an epidemic can become a *pandemic*, which affects an even wider geographical area and a significant portion of the population becomes affected."

2. Living with freedom and responsibility – what can we learn from Bonhoeffer's ethics?

The basic presupposition of this presentation is this: in spite of all the differences between our context today and the context Dietrich Bonhoeffer lived in – and I think it is not an exaggeration to state that our global situation today is by far much worse than the one in Bonhoeffer's day – his theology can be a sound guide for us. Regardless, details of our situation today or Bonhoeffer's in his day, it is wise to remember what he said: "We should have so much love for this contemporary world of ours, for our fellow human beings, that we should declare our solidarity with it in its crisis and hope" (DBWE 10:326). And from that presupposition leads to the topic of this presentation: *freedom and responsibility in Bonhoeffer's ethics*. Bonhoeffer's theology displays a remarkable internal coherence. His theology is like a fine tapestry with many threads interwoven, providing a beautiful picture. Or perhaps it is like a spider's web, with several lines that are internally interconnected. In the very center of this web there is his understanding of the person of Jesus Christ. All the great, well-known themes of Bonhoeffer's theology – Christ existing as community, costly grace, discipleship (*nachfolge*, the following of Jesus), his concept of *stellvertretung* (vicarious representative action), the church that is there for the other, and looking at the world from the perspective of the victims and those on the underside of history and religionless Christianity – all of this has Christ as centre. One can say that his Christology is the sun, and all those themes are satellites circling it. From this we can speak about freedom and responsibility in Bonhoeffer's theology.

In a nutshell, this is my understanding of Bonhoeffer's theological ethics: the Christian person has freedom in Christ. Christian life is a life of liberty. But to live in freedom is to live with responsibility for the world, in obedience to God. In what follows I will try to show it in a more detailed way.

In his *Ethics* Bonhoeffer presents his understanding of the relationship between freedom and responsibility as follows:

Responsibility and freedom are mutually corresponding concepts. Responsibility presupposes freedom substantively – not chronologically – just as freedom can exist only in the exercise of responsibility. Responsibility is human freedom that exists only by being bound to God and neighbour (Bonhoeffer 2010a, 283).

In this crystal clear paragraph Bonhoeffer presents responsibility and freedom as related to each other. For him, these two concepts are inseparable, like conjoined twins. For the Christian person, there is no freedom without responsibility. Commenting on the place of responsibility in Bonhoeffer's ethics Larry Rasmussen (1999, 218) said,

> Understanding responsibility in Bonhoeffer's ethics – the core theme – requires that we understand that for him the relationship with God is both "social," or relational, and completely "this-worldly." The transcendent is not found in some other world but in the ordinary relationships of which we are a part, the relationships that constitute who we are . . . In other words, because Christ exists "as community" and is found "in, with and under all that is" (a Luther's phrase, used by Bonhoeffer) and because our own formation and fulfillment reside in being with and for others, it is amidst these relationships that we experience transcendence, and it is here that we meet God. And the God we meet is "the one for others, the one 'for us' (*pro nobis*)."

Bonhoeffer teaches us that freedom is not synonymous of *a laisser-faire*-like lifestyle. Allow me please to say about my particular Brazilian context: in Brazilian society today there is a strong individualistic spirit that leads many people to say "my life, my rules, my body my rules." There is a famous Brazilian *samba* singer – Zeca Pagodinho – who says in one of his songs: "If I want to smoke, I smoke. If I want to drink, I drink. I spend everything I consume with the sweat of my job." These lines reflects very well the individualistic mentality that put everyone beyond and above everything else. "This is my life, you have nothing to do with it": this is a very common sentence which is often said in conversations everywhere in the country. This song is an example of what Luther called *cor curvum in se*, "the heart turned to itself," that means, pure selfishness. But Christian life is quite the opposite. The life of discipleship, Bonhoeffer teaches us, is a life of freedom not for oneself. Rather, it is a life of responsibility for the world and for the other, for the sake of Christ. As it is always the case in Bonhoeffer's theology, his conception of freedom and responsibility are seen through the lens of Christ:

> Jesus Christ is the human being and God in one. The original and essential encounter with the human being and with God takes place in Jesus Christ. From now on it is no longer possible to conceive and understand humanity other than in Jesus Christ, nor God other than in the human form of Jesus Christ. In Christ we see humanity as a humanity that is accepted, born, loved and reconciled with God. In Christ we see God in the form of the poorest of our brothers and sisters. There is no human being as

such, just as there is no God as such; both are empty abstractions. Human beings are accepted in God's becoming human and are loved, judged, and reconciled in Christ, and God is the God who became human. So there is no relation to other human beings without a relation to God and vice-versa. Again, only the relation to Jesus Christ is the basis for our relation to other human beings and to God. Just as Jesus Christ is our life, so we may now also say – from the vantage point of Jesus Christ! – that other human beings and that God are our life (Bonhoeffer 2010a, 253–254).

In sum: for Bonhoeffer Jesus Christ, the God incarnate, is the hermeneutical key for his understanding of freedom and responsibility. Therefore, Jesus is the paradigm for a life of freedom and responsibility. Jesus, the man for the other, teaches us to live freely and responsibly for the world and for the other. In fact, according to Bonhoeffer, responsibility implies being responsible to the other, the neighbour. Christian ethics is a responsible ethics. In other words, it is an ethics of responsibility, not an ethics of individualistic licentiousness. In Bonhoeffer's thought it has to do with obedience to God and responsibility to the world as well.

I believe it is important to think a little bit more about Bonhoeffer's understanding of God himself. In his very well-known poem *Christians and Heathens* (Bonhoeffer 2010b, 460–461) he shows clearly what he believed about the God who reveals himself to us in the person of Jesus of Nazareth:

1. People go to God when they're in need,
   plead for help, pray for blessing and bread,
   for rescue from their sickness, guilt and death.
   So do they all, all of them, Christians and heathens.

2. People go to God when God's in need,
   find God poor, reviled, without shelter or bread
   see God devoured by sin, weakness and death.
   Christians stand by God in God's own pain.

3. God goes to all people in their need
   fills body and soul with God's own bread
   goes for Christians and heathens to Calvary's death
   and forgives them both.

As we have stated elsewhere,

This poem, especially in its second stanza, presents the conviction of a God who is not only transcendent, the *totaliter aliter* of Karl

Barth's theology, but the God who is here, with the downtrodden of society. The poem could be described as an echo of Matthew 25:31–46. The God of Bonhoeffer is the loving and suffering God, not the Aristotelian impassible God. A God like this is a God who is concerned about human life, human suffering, about *das Wesen des Menschen* as a whole (Caldas 2013, 450).

In order to describe this responsibility to the world we could follow the German Jewish philosopher Hannah Arendt, and call it *amor mundi* – "love to the world" (Arendt 1997). This love implies responsibility. This Arendtian conception of *amor mundi* has to do also with responsibility in history. As a matter of fact, for Bonhoeffer the *amor mundi* and Christian responsibility are two faces of the same coin. According to Heinz Eduard Tödt (2007, 144) "presumably conversations with Karl Barth and other Swiss friends made him (Bonhoeffer) see that the question of the Christian's responsibility in history was a problem of utmost urgency."[7]

Bonhoeffer took seriously the pressing questions of his time. Therefore, he criticized the unjust activities of the National Socialist party in Germany, as those activities included heinous actions like compulsory euthanasia, eugenics, rape and torture (Bonhoeffer 2010a, 189–217).

From this it is possible to analyze the concept of responsibility in Bonhoeffer from the two aforementioned vantage points: responsibility to the other – *amor mundi* – and responsibility to God – Christian obedience. For Bonhoeffer, being a Christian and, consequently, being the church, can be understood and lived only in relational terms. There is no such thing as an isolated Christian, as it were possible to have an isolated soul in a vertical relationship with God. Christian life exists only as *Communio sanctorum* – the "fellowship of the saints." The communion the believer has with Christ demands he/she have communion with his/her fellow brothers and sisters. And the Christian church exists in a relational way with Christ, and this will demand a lifestyle of service to the world, specially to the downtrodden, the "least of these brothers and sisters" (Matt 25:40 NIV). In one of his most well-known (perhaps the most well-known) statement recorded in *Letters and Papers from Prison*, the essence of the Church is presented as "being there for others": *Die Kirche ist nur Kirche, wenn sie für andere da ist* (Bonhoeffer 1998, 560).

In the famous essay *The Church and the Jewish Question* of 1933 one finds Bonhoeffer's understanding of what actions the Christian church

---

7. For Bonhoeffer's ethic of responsibility see Bonhoeffer 2010a, 246–298.

can take vis-à-vis the state: *first* (as we have said), questioning the state as to the legitimate state character of its actions, that is, making the state responsible for what it does. *Second* is service to the victims of the state's actions. The church has an unconditional obligation toward the victims of any societal order, even if they do not belong to the Christian Community. "Let us work for the good of all" (Gal 6:10). These are both ways in which the church, in its freedom, conducts itself in the interest of a free state. In times when the laws are changing, the church may under no circumstances neglect either of these duties. The *third* possibility is not just to bind up the wounds of the victims beneath the wheel but to seize the wheel itself (Bonhoeffer 2009, 365).

Therefore, according to Bonhoeffer, the freedom the church has is, must and should be lived for the sake of the "other," regardless whether this "other" is or is not a member of it. His understanding of what it means to be church and what it means to be a Christian is completely relational. My obedience to Christ will be reflected in how I relate to the "other."

We know the context of *The Church and the Jewish Question*: Bonhoeffer was protesting against racist, xenophobic and anti-Semitic laws the Nazi regime was about to launch and against the infamous *Aryan Paragraph*. Our *Sitz im Leben* today is obviously different from the one Bonhoeffer lived in. However, we can contextualize this Bonhoefferian understanding to our specific life situations. Each one of us is challenged to write his/her version of Bonhoeffer's essay, according to our specific contexts. In other words, what does it mean to live as a Christian in freedom and responsibility in the North American context? Right here, in the Polish context, so close to the Ukrainian-Russian conflict? What does it mean to live as a Christian in freedom and responsibility in my own particular Brazilian life context?

Christian life for Bonhoeffer is the life of *nachfolge* – "discipleship," following Jesus in the world. And following Jesus means to love one's neighbour as oneself. To use once more the Arendtian sentence – *amor mundi*: in the sermon on Revelation 2:4–5, 7, preached on the Reformation Sunday in Berlin (6 November 1932) Bonhoeffer asks us a very serious question: "Do we love God and our neighbour with that first, passionate, burning love that is willing to risk everything except God?" (Bonhoeffer 2009, 445). That question points to Bonhoeffer's understanding of Christian free and responsible life in the world: the Christian life is a life of love, the first love we are called to come back to, and this first love means obedience to Christ, revealed in taking care of the "other," the neighbour. This is at the very core of the Bonhoefferian ethics of Christian responsibility.

Conclusion

The challenges we face are so many, so big and so difficult that it makes us feel absolutely powerless. And the feeling of powerlessness can lead us to discouragement and hopelessness. What can we do? Thinking about situations as difficult as the ones mentioned in the opening of my speech, what comes to my mind is a sermon preached by Bonhoeffer on Judges 6:15–16; 7:2; 8:23 in Berlin in 26 February 1933 (the *Sonntag Estomihi*, "First Sunday in Lent," about Gideon the Judge). This was the first sermon Bonhoeffer preached after Hitler's ascension to power in Germany. In this sermon Bonhoeffer states that faith is demonstrated through obedience. The challenges facing Gideon were immense. What God required of him was to believe and obey. For me Bonhoeffer's word choice in this sermon is highly significant: "There is nothing of Siegfried in Gideon" (Bonhoeffer 2009, 462). In the original German (Bonhoeffer 1997, 449) we read: *Gideon ist kein Siegfried* – "Gideon is not Siegfried." As you remember, Siegfried, the dragon slayer, is a German mythical hero, the main character in the saga of the Nibelungs. But not Gideon. Gideon wasn't a hero. In the biblical story when an unnamed prophet told Gideon the Lord had chosen him to be the liberator of his people, "He responded [to the Lord], 'But Lord, how can I deliver Israel? My clan is the weakest in Manasseh, and I am the least in my family" (Judges 6:15). We know how Gideon's story ended: under Gideon's leadership Israel had a total victory over the Midianites. Commenting this outcome, Bonhoeffer stated

> Gideon conquers, the church conquers, we conquer, because faith alone conquers. But the victory belongs not to Gideon, the church, ourselves, but to God. And God's victory means our defeat, our humiliation (DBWE 12, 647).

The victory of God is an humiliation to human pride. Gideon was an ordinary simple man. The turning point in his life was in his obedience, despite his initial reticence. And just like Gideon, *Wir sind nicht Siegfried* – "We are not Siegfried." In our troubled times we are called to act in obedience to God and love to the world – *amor mundi*. We are the church, the fellowship of believers, the *gestalt* of Jesus in the world, and as such we are called to small acts of justice in freedom and responsibility.

Let us remember the threats to the human race that we mentioned in the beginning of this lecture. They are much bigger than us. What can we do? The only possible thing we can do is to act in our respective life situations as obedient followers of Jesus, who reveals to us the God who is there for the other in need. What can we do?

To begin with, we can protest publicly against situations of injustice and disrespect for human rights. We can give voice to the voiceless, those suffering oppression of any kind. We can raise our prophetic voice against situations in which the church surrenders to the political power and to the glory of this world, rendering to Caesar what is God's (and allow me to say, this is happening just now in Brazil with most of the evangelical church). And we can adjust our lifestyle so that it is less consumerist and more friendly to the environment. Let us remember that famous sentence whose authorship is attributed to the French philosopher Jacques Ellul: "think globally, act locally." We are summoned to use our liberty with responsibility. We were not called to be heroes. We were called to be obedient. This is the main lesson we learn from Dietrich Bonhoeffer.

This is just the beginning, but like Bonhoeffer we must start somewhere. For many of us in Brazil and in other places around our globe, seventy-seven years after his execution in the Nazi concentration camp in Flossenbürg, he remains a valuable guide to our responsible, free action in this world God loved and loves so much.

Bibliography

Arendt, Hannah. *O conceito de amor em Santo Agostinho*. Lisboa: Instituto Piaget, 1997.
Bonhoeffer, Dietrich. 1998. *Widerstand und Ergebung. Briefe und Aufzeichnungen aus der Haft. Dietrich Bonhoeffer Werke Volume 8*, edited by Christian Gremmels, Eberhard Bethge, Renate Bethge, Ilse Tödt. Gütersloh: Gütersloher Verlagshaus.
Bonhoeffer, Dietrich. 2008. *Barcelona, Berlin, New York: 1928–1931. Dietrich Bonhoeffer Works Volume 10*, edited by Clifford J. Green, translated by Douglas W. Stott. Minneapolis: Fortress Press.
Bonhoeffer, Dietrich. 2009. *Berlin 1932–1933. Dietrich Bonhoeffer Works Volume 12*, edited by Larry L. Rasmussen, translated by Isabel Best and David Higgins. Minneapolis: Fortress Press.
Bonhoeffer, Dietrich. 2010a. *Ethics. Dietrich Bonhoeffer Works Volume 6*, edited by Clifford J. Green, translated by Reinhard Krauss, Charles West, and Douglas W. Stott. Minneapolis: Fortress Press.

Bonhoeffer, Dietrich. 2010b. *Letters and Papers from Prison. Dietrich Bonhoeffer Works Voume 8*, edited by John W. de Gruchy, translated by Isabel Best, Lisa E. Dahill, Reinhard Krauss, and Nancy Lukens. Minneapolis: Fortress Press.

Caldas, Carlos. 2014, "Dietrich Bonhoeffer's Ethical Theology as a Theoretical Framework for the Elaboration of a Public Theology in Brazil." In *A Spoke in the Wheel. The Political in the Theology of Dietrich Bonhoeffer*, edited by Nielsen, Kirsten Busch, Wüstenberg, Ralf K., and Jenz Zimmermann. Gütersloh: Gütersloher Verlagshaus.

Caldas, Carlos. 2020. "Mad Max and Dietrich Bonhoeffer: Two Views on the Future of the World." *The Bonhoeffer Legacy* 8 (2020): 61–76.

Gazeta do Povo. 2021. "Números do Coronavírus. Entenda o avanço da Covid-19 no Brasil e no mundo." *Especiais*. https://especiais.gazetadopovo.com.br/coronavirus/numeros.

Kiprop, Joseph. 2018. "What Is The Poverty Line?" *WorldAtlas*. https://www.worldatlas.com/articles/what-is-the-poverty-line.html.

Koop, Avery. 2021. "Mapped: Where are the world's ongoing conflicts today?" *Visual Capitalist*. https://www.visualcapitalist.com/mapped-where-are-the-worlds-ongoing-conflicts-today.

Lewis, C. S. 2003. *That Hideous Strength. Space Trilogy, Volume 3*. New York: Scribner.

Merriam-Webster Dictionary. 2023. "'Pandemic' vs. 'Epidemic' vs. 'Endemic'. How they overlap and where they differ." *Commonly Confused*. https://www.merriam-webster.com/grammar/epidemic-vs-pandemic-difference.

Moltmann, Jürgen. 2002. *A vinda de Deus: escatologia crista*. São João Batista: Editora Unisonos.

Rasmussen, Larry. 1999. "The Ethics of Responsible Action." In *The Cambridge Companion to Dietrich Bonhoeffer*, edited by John W. de Gruchy. Cambridge: Cambridge University Press.

Rayson, Dianne. 2021. *Bonhoeffer and Climate Change: Theology and Ethics for the Anthropocene*. Minneapolis: Fortress Press.

Tödt, Heinz Eduard. 2007. *Authentic Faith. Bonhoeffer's Theological Ethics in Context*. Grand Rapids: Eerdmans.

Tolkien, J. R. R. 2020. *The Two Towers. The Lord of the Rings Volume 2*. New York: Clarion Books.

UOL. 2021. "Lista de bilionários da Forbes ganha 20 brasileiros e tem crescimento recorde na pandemia." *Economy*. https://economia.uol.com.br/noticias/bbc/2021/04/07/lista-bilionarios-forbes-brasileiros-crescimento-recorde-pandemia-covid-19.htm.

Worldometers. "Current World Population." 2022. *World Population*. https://www.worldometers.info/world-population [accessed: 11.12.2022].

14

Bonhoeffer's Concept of Freedom, and the Limits as well as the Promises of his Thought in Building a Democratic Community

András Csepregi, PhD
Associate Professor of John Wesley Theological College, Budapest
Pastor of the Budapest-Fasori Lutheran High School

About the Author

András Csepregi PhD is a Lutheran pastor in Hungary, ordained in 1987. He serves Budapest-Fasori Lutheran High School as a pastor and John Wesley Theological College as an associate professor. He got his PhD at Durham University, 2002, with his thesis on "Two Ways to Freedom: Christianity and Democracy in the Thought of István Bibó and Dietrich Bonhoeffer." Besides Bibó and Bonhoeffer, his research area extends to Luther interpretations, Walter Wink, non-violent Christianity and political theology.

Keywords

Dietrich Bonhoeffer, István Bibó, democracy, Hungary

Abstract

The context of my interpretation of Bonhoeffer is the miserable state of democracy in my country, Hungary. During the past hundred years Hungary has usually suffered authoritarian governments: the semi-feudal one between the two world wars ended up an ally of Hitler, the Communist one-party state that lasted until 1989, and, after twenty years of experimenting with democracy, our present government, considering itself Conservative and Christian, has successfully built up an authoritarian system again. This authoritarian context allows me to see the authoritarian character of Bonhoeffer's theology rather clearly. Likewise, being at the losing end of the fight for democracy, I regard Bonhoeffer as a fellow loser too, with respect to the ecumenical movement, the Confessing Church and the secret resistance as well. My purpose is to learn from the mistakes of Bonhoeffer's theology and his ideas related to it and ask him to help us not to make similar mistakes while trying to find a way out of our difficult situation.

Introduction

Before I say anything about Bonhoeffer, let me first identify myself as the speaker. I am part of a political community that has repeatedly lost parliamentary elections against a political power that consciously and systematically weakens democratic institutions and the conditions of democratic life in my country, Hungary. This political power came into power first in 1998, and during their four years in office they showed both their ambition and their ability to go beyond the limits of democratic governance. When they, quite unexpectedly, lost the elections in 2002, their leader, Viktor Orbán announced the slogan "patriots cannot be in opposition" and launched a nationwide program of community building around his party, the Fidesz. (This party started in 1988, and its name is an abbreviation for the Alliance of Young Democrats.) In other words, a rather resolute policy of "we and the others" started in 2002, we, the patriots, the normal people, and, later, even "we good Christians," facing the others, the strangers, the abnormal, the traitors, the unbelievers, the agents of alien forces, the enemy, etc.

During the next eight years five different leftist governments came into power, showing several signs of a lack of direction as well as the lack of ability of gaining the hearts of the voters. Although the coalition of the Socialist Party and the Liberal Party made a second victory, winning the election again in 2006 and gaining a comfortable majority in the Parliament, the opposing Fidesz was stronger both in the media and on the streets, and finally won a landslide victory in 2010, gaining two thirds of the places in the Parliament. This two-third majority is a crucial proportion in the Hungarian system of parliamentary work: this majority can modify or make any articles of law, or even can change the Constitution without any interference of the members of the Parliament representing the opposition. Since 2010 the governing Fidesz party has been using this opportunity in a consistent way, making every possible change of the law. These changes have enabled them to stay in power, to create enormous wealth for friendly oligarchs, to turn the media into a tool of their own propaganda, and, most importantly, to ostentatious ignore all the voters who don't support them, treating them as if they were invisible and non-existent. Naturally, this policy affects Hungary's participation in the European Union as well, of which we have been a member since 2004. Right up to the present day, Prime Minister Orbán has been successful in forcing his will on the Union, even sometimes blackmailing it, and the leadership of the Union has not found effective means against it yet.

The opposing parties, weak and divided, lacking a clear view of a better political future as well as the voice to speak to the voters behind the walls of the masterly run government propaganda, have suffered the fourth shameful defeat since 2010, the last one just two months ago (on the day of the conference, 31 May 2022). I am part of this political community, one of the losers within a losing community. Having identified myself this way, I see Dietrich Bonhoeffer being a loser too; he was part of communities, either the Confessing Church, or the secret resistance group, that lost against Hitler, and some members of these communities had to pay for this defeat even with their lives. On the one hand, as a loser, I have great sympathy as well as empathy towards Bonhoeffer in me, I feel very close to him. On the other hand, I can recognize mistakes in Bonhoeffer's thought and deeds, which might have contributed to their defeat and sorrowful end. I would like to learn from these mistakes, not to repeat them in our still uncertain fight for democracy in Hungary. In the next few pages, I would like to share with you some of my findings that I have learned from reading Bonhoeffer this way.

Let me first tell you something about the way I have been studying Bonhoeffer. The first strong impression of him came to me through the Hungarian Lutheran pastor Ferenc Lehel, Bonhoeffer's student in Berlin in the academic year of 1932/33. Pastor Lehel is known in the International Bonhoeffer Society as the one whose notes of Bonhoeffer's Hegel seminar survived; thus, the text of the course has been restored and published (Bonhoeffer, Lehel, and Tödt 1988). Pastor Lehel befriended me in the eighties and made me enthusiastic about Bonhoeffer. So, when both my wife, Márta, and I were given the possibility to do a full PhD course at Durham University, England, beginning in 1996, I started to work on Bonhoeffer. My first tutor, Bishop Peter Selby suggested that I should incoporate a Hungarian component into my research, so I decided to do a comparison of Dietrich Bonhoeffer and the Hungarian Christian political thinker, István Bibó (2015).[1]

The comparison seemed to be obvious. Bibó, five years younger than Bonhoeffer, resisted the Nazis and later the Communists, became involved in helping persecuted Jews, took part in the short-lived government of the 1956 revolution, was almost sentenced to death, given a life-sentence instead, and, having been released from prison in 1963, he lived in isolation in Hungary until he died in 1979, soon becoming a leading thinker for the opposition which tried to resist the Communist party state. To my big surprise, however, I have found that the two men, so similar in several respects, have a radically different concept of freedom. While Bibó's concept is a combination of negative and positive freedom, the "freedom from something" and the "freedom for something," Bonhoeffer's concept is a totality of positive freedom, "the freedom for." In other words, Bibó's concept makes the legitimate place for saying no and saying yes, but Bonhoeffer's concept does not allow saying no without saying yes at the same time.

During my studies in Durham, I found that this conceptual difference initiates a significant parting of the ways with respect to political thinking. Bibó's concept is compatible with liberal democracy, in all its traditional forms, that is, liberalism, socialism, or conservative (Christian) democracy. Bonhoeffer's concept, the totality of positive freedom, however, is incompatible with liberal democracy. In liberal democratic praxis it is inevitable to have the natural right of all the voters to say no to policies they don't like, or to the governing body altogether. I have found it interesting that Bibó, in one of his early works written in 1933, pointed at Hegel as a chief representative of the understanding of freedom as exclusively positive, arriving at the conclusion that for Hegel the law and even the state can be the very realization of freedom, freedom itself (see Csepregi 2003, 91). If we consider Bonhoeffer's indebtedness to Hegel, we can probably see one piece of the intellectual roots of his concept of freedom.

The differences in the concept of freedom have a crucial role in interpreting democracy in Hungary. During the time of the Communist party-state, our form of state was called "people's democracy," stressing that it is not the same as the declining Western democracies, and arguing that ours is more adequate

---

1. A recent edition of Bibó's works in English with an Introduction by Iván Zoltán Dénes, with a Foreword by Adam Michnik.

and more effective. In 2015 Prime Minister Orbán declared that Hungary has an "illiberal democracy," thereby stressing once again that Hungarians are privileged to live in a better political framework than people in Western liberal democracies. The common point of both the Communist version and today's authoritarian version is that both adjectives, "people's" and "illiberal" destroy the meaning of the signified word, here "democracy," in so far as they deprive it of its essence. Both limit the possibility of saying no to the government; the Communist version did it by severe administrative means and sometimes by brutal violence, the present authoritarian government does it by depriving the opposition of every effective means of articulating the will of their voters, and even of communicating with them. Bibó opposed the Communist version of the abuse of the meaning of democracy, and would certainly oppose this present version of it. I am afraid, however, Bonhoeffer would not have a clear enough conceptual background to do the same.

Interestingly, the adjective added to democracy has appeared with respect to Bonhoeffer as well. Bonhoeffer scholar John de Gruchy introduced the concepts of "genuine democracy" versus "elitist democracy" in his excellent *Christianity and Democracy: A Theology for a Just World Order*, which was very helpful in my research back in the nineties. The difference between the two versions can be described by different fears: while the genuine democrat fears the rule of an elite, the elitist democrat fears popular rule (de Gruchy 1995, 19). De Gruchy thinks Bonhoeffer would represent a sort of "elitist democracy," and, at first, I found this interpretation helpful. However, as my knowledge and experience of the hardships of democracy has been enriched, my opinion has changed: now I think that an "elitist democracy" is not an alternative to "genuine democracy," just as "people's democracy" or "illiberal democracy" are not alternatives to Western liberal democracy.[2] The fear of the elite that appears in the description of genuine democracy is not without reason, and that is why liberal democracy insists on checks and balances, free elections, a free press and all other means of exerting effective control of the government. On the other hand, popular rule, which what the elitist democrat fears, is the very heart of liberal democracy.[3] Let me just quote Abraham Lincoln here:

---

2. See my paper given at the Prague congress of International Bonhoeffer Society in 2008 (Csepregi 2010, 152–161).

3. With respect to the famous words of Bonhoeffer, "being there for the other," I finish my above mentioned paper this way: "we must never forget that 'being there for the other', even giving one's life for the other, is not identical to promoting democracy. Doing something in place of another person may help them and certainly fills one with a good feeling, raising one's self esteem, but democracy develops when more and more people are able to think, act, and

democracy is "rule of the people, by the people, for the people." Any adjective that wishes to specify the meaning of democracy by moving this simple criterion aside, deprives democracy of its very essence.

I finished my PhD thesis on Bonhoeffer in 2002, concluding that with respect to the challenges of the transition toward democracy in Hungary – and, probably, not only in Hungary – Bonhoeffer's theology, although a valuable legacy in several senses, can offer little help in answering this challenge. One could ask why I keep studying Bonhoeffer, notwithstanding this disappointment? My answer is that I realized that the crisis of democracy which Bonhoeffer faced in Nazi Germany and the crisis of democracy Hungary faces today have some similarities, rooted in a somewhat similar political mentality of Germans between the two wars and Hungarians today. Already in 1944 István Bibó, the Hungarian political thinker to whom I compared Bonhoeffer, described this mentality as "political hysteria," of course pointing to Nazi Germany as a chief example of it. The community of political hysteria is a closed community, having suffered a shock that it cannot recover from. All the reflections of the community are focused on this shock. The hysterical community gradually loses her ability to find the real causes of events, losing sight of reality in and around her, trying to create consistency out of inconsistency, thus building up a false and all-embracing system of reference. I think the Hungarian political community could have gotten rid of political hysteria if her political leaders had proposed and pursued a treatment for it. However, our politicians, and especially those in and around the present government, chose instead to use this hysterical mentality for their own purpose, rather than trying to heal it. Having seen the similarities of Bonhoeffer's situation and ours, Bonhoeffer's failures, as well as the failures of his brothers and sisters in the Confessing Church and those of his associates in the secret resistance, are rather instructive for us: they show us what to avoid if we don't want to be the losers they unfortunately and sadly ended up being.

Before I turn to some well-known sentences of Bonhoeffer, let me mention a book that helped me to believe what I found in my analysis of Bonhoeffer's concept of freedom. This book was published seven years after I finished my dissertation. The author is John A. Moses, of Australia, and the title is: *Reluctant Revolutionary: Dietrich Bonhoeffer's Collision with Prusso-German History.* Moses convinced me by his sophisticated historical analysis that, with respect to a possible transition to democracy, Bonhoeffer was also a part of the

---

decide for themselves. And *leaving the other to be what the other can and wishes to be*, leaving her alone, is probably more difficult a task than being there for her" (Csepregi 2015, 161).

problem. Not only his Confessing Church, whose conservative Lutheranism is pointed out in several interpretations of Bonhoeffer, but also the members of his family, his associates in the secret resistance, and the thinkers gathered in the Freiburg Circle, were rather suspicious of liberal democracy, and planned a German government after Hitler that was "being above," by the ordering of God, like a monarch before the first World War. Moses shows in his detailed analysis, how far Bonhoeffer and the *bildungsbürgertum* around him, that is, the educated Protestant upper-middle class, that Bismarck made the leading force for the Second Reich in 1871, was isolated from the other parts of the German society of the time.[4] It could be disputed in detail, whether Dietrich Bonhoeffer himself was rather a critic of his social class, as, I think, Moses seems to suggest,[5] or rather a part of his class, as I tend to think. For a possible reason for the difference of opinion, I think being an insider of a hysterical community, as Bonhoeffer was a part of and I am as well, one may have a sharper sense of similar dangers.

Let us now see some well-known sentences of Bonhoeffer's (2010, 37–52) essay, written to his associates in the secret resistance, *After Ten Years*. "Without ground under one's feet," begins Bonhoeffer's train of thought, asking, "have there ever been people in history who in their time, like us, had so little ground under their feet . . . ?" (Bonhoeffer 2010, 38). One would answer this question with a big "of course," saying that most of humanity has constantly experienced this uncertainty. This question reveals the view of the *bildungsbürger*, who takes social security for granted and is simply unable to see the world beyond his class. In the next section, "Who stands firm?," Bonhoeffer rules out reason, ethical fanaticism, conscience, duty, freedom, and private virtuousness, for the sake of being "the one who is prepared to sacrifice all of these when, in faith and in relationship to God alone, he is called to obedient and responsible action" (Bonhoeffer 2010, 40). To tell the truth, I don't know what this sentence really means. I am especially perplexed while reading about being in relationship to God alone in a text that was written to three men: Eberhard Bethge, Hans von Dohnanyi and Hans Oster (Bonhoeffer 2010, 37). However, I do find it interesting that among the excluded possibilities Bonhoeffer seems to choose *freedom* at last. His decision to take part in the resistance, that hoped for a way out of the crisis by killing Hitler, can be described by his own words: the man of freedom "values the necessary action more highly than an untarnished

---

4. See Moses 2009, Chapter 1, "The 'Peculiarity' of German Political Culture" and Chapter 2, "Bonhoeffer's Formation."
5. See Moses 2009, Chapter 8, "Bonhoeffer as Critic of his Class in Retrospect."

conscience and reputation . . . is prepared to sacrifice a barren principle to a fruitful compromise or a barren wisdom of mediocrity to fruitful radicalism" (Bonhoeffer 2008, 40). Likewise, the warning he issued here may also be applied to his fate. "Such a one needs to take care that his freedom does not cause him to stumble. He will condone the bad in order to prevent the worse and in so doing no longer discern that the very thing that he seeks to avoid as worse might well be better. This is where the basic material of tragedy is to be found" (Bonhoeffer 2010, 41). Without going into a detailed discussion here, I simply mean that the total failure of the coup and the personal price many people had to pay for it, within and without the circle of the resistance, allow us to see this passage as Bonhoeffer's unintended preview.

The next section about "Civil courage" is, for me, one of Bonhoeffer's most sensitive texts. Here he touches the biggest problem of German political culture, informed by the enormous shadow of Martin Luther. While praising obedience, he points out what is crucially important with respect to democratic culture: "[t]he readiness to follow an order from 'above' rather than one's own discretion arises from and is part of the justified suspicion about one's own heart" (Bonhoeffer 2010, 41). In this section, which ends with his statement that "[c]ivil courage can grow only from the free responsibility of free man," and shows enthusiasm that, finally, Germans are "beginning to discover what free responsibility means" (Bonhoeffer 2008, 41), Bonhoeffer still considers suspicion about one's own heart as justified. People who share this suspicion cannot be agents of a democracy and are unable to resist manipulative powers. As Christians, we may be able to distinguish trust, built by God in us, from hubris. Suspicion about one's own heart, as a general requirement, inherited from Lutheran theology,[6] cannot be part of an anthropological basis of liberal democracy.

Let me comment on three more sections very briefly. In "On success" (Bonhoeffer 2010, 41–42) Bonhoeffer, I think, rather easily gives in to actual positions in history. Here, I think, we can detect yet another shadow of Luther's theology: although we cannot understand what the hidden God, *Deus absconditus* is doing in history, we believe that what is happening reflects God's will in some

---

6. I think it is interesting to consider the decision of the editors of DBWE 8 (Bonhoeffer 2010) about referring to Luther with respect to an earlier sentence of this text (Bonhoeffer 2010, 40). Luther says in his Commentary on Paul's Epistle to the Galatians: "And this is why our theology is certain: it snatches us away from ourselves and places us outside ourselves and experience or works, but depend on that which is outside ourselves, that is, on the promise and truth of God, which cannot deceive." God outside us can easily be replaced by some other power outside us, as happened in Germany and it still keeps happening in many places.

way – that is why we accept all the happenings. A long-term resistance simply cannot work with this perspective of history. Secondly, I totally disagree with the opening sentence of the next section, "On stupidity" (Bonhoeffer 2010, 43–44), because I think that it is not stupidity, but malice and evil are the more dangerous enemies of the good. I think, claiming stupidity to be more dangerous than malice and evil simply reflects the impatience of Bonhoeffer towards the manipulated brothers and sisters, who are not the evil but only the means as well as the products of malice, and may be deadly exhausting as conversation partners, however, we must not give them up. Finally, "The sense of quality" (Bonhoeffer 2010, 47–48) with its penetrating criticism of the "rabble" simply does not consider that in a liberal democracy those whom I regard as part of the "rabble" are voters whose votes will decide the next election. One of the main weaknesses of Hungarian political opposition is that highbrow intellectual leaders are very slow in contacting people whose mentality is rather different from theirs. Our task is not to distance ourselves from those whom we would consider the rabble, as Bonhoeffer suggests, rather to step out of our comfort zone and try to enter into some discussion with them.

"Are we still of any use?" – asks Bonhoeffer at the end of his essay. His honest question can be our question in Hungary, it can be my personal question as well. What is more, I don't have any better answer than that which Bonhoeffer gives: "We will not need geniuses, cynics, people who have contempt for others, or cunning tacticians, but simple, uncomplicated, and honest human beings" (Bonhoeffer 2010, 52). Whether we will fulfil this possibility in Hungary, or not, I cannot tell. However, I am quite positive that it is still useful to study Bonhoeffer, even if we sometimes disagree with him.

Bibliography

Bibó, István. 2015. *The Art of Peacemaking*, translated by Peter Pásztor, edited by Iván Zoltán Dénes. New Haven and London: Yale University Press.
Bonhoeffer, Dietrich, Ferenc Lehel, and Ilse Tödt. 1988. *Dietrich Bonhoeffers Hegel Seminar 1933: nach den Aufzeichnungen von Ferenc Lehel*. Munich: Chr. Kaiser.
Bonhoeffer, Dietrich. 2010. "An Account at the Turn of the Year 1942–1943." In *Letters and Papers from Prison. Dietrich Bonhoeffer Works Volume 8*, edited by John W. de Gruchy, translated by Isabel Best, Lisa E. Dahill, Reinhard Krauss, and Nancy Lukens, 37–54. Minneapolis: Fortress Press.
Csepregi, András. 2003. *Two Ways to Freedom. Christianity and Democracy in the Thought of István Bibó and Dietrich Bonhoeffer*. Budapest: Acta Theologica Lutherana Budapestinensia.

Csepregi, András. 2010. "Genuine or Elitist Democracy? Christianity and Democracy in the Thought of István Bibó and Dietrich Bonhoeffer." In *From Political Theory to Political Theology. Religious Challenges and the Prospects of Democracy*, edited by Losonczi Péter and Akash Singh, 152–161. New York: Continuum.

de Gruchy, John W. 1995. *Christianity and Democracy: A Theology for a Just World Order*. Cambridge: Cambridge University Press.

Moses, John A. 2009. *Reluctant Revolutionary. Dietrich Bonhoeffer's Collision with Prusso-German History*. New York; Oxford: Breghahn Books.

15

Cheap Grace Abounding

The Barmen Declaration, A Declaration on the "Russian World" (*Russkii Mir*) Teaching, and Protestantism Without Reformation

Barry Harvey, PhD
Baylor University, USA
ORCID: 0000-0002-4795-099X

About the Author

Barry Harvey is Professor of Theology in the Honors College at Baylor University, USA. He has two degrees in music, the Master of Divinity degree, and the Doctor of Philosophy degree from Duke University. He is author of six books (*Politics of the Theological, Another City, Can These Bones Live?, Taking Hold of the Real,* and *Baptists and the Catholic Tradition,* and *Madness, Theocracy, and Anarchism: Political and Cultural Reflections on the Church*), a co-author of a sixth (*StormFront*), and is currently working on another volume, tentatively entitled *Musica Dei: Performing the Lord's Song in a Discordant World.* He has published numerous articles in collections and scholarly journals such as *Modern Theology, The Scottish Journal of Theology, The Bonhoeffer Legacy: An International Journal, Pro Ecclesia, Theologica Wratislaviensia,* and *Theology Today.* He is an emeritus member of the Board of the International Bonhoeffer Society, English Language Section, and a founding member of the Ekklesia Project.

Keywords

Barmen, Russian world teaching, Dietrich Bonhoeffer, ethnophyletism

Abstract

Telling the gospel story well requires that Christians narrate it in ways that locate them as participants in specific political, historical, and cultural contexts. Inculturation, understood as both "a calling and a matter of contestation," has been a central feature of the church's witness since Pentecost. But it is also fraught with ambiguity, for if Christians wish to be faithful to the witness of Scripture and the teachings of the mothers and fathers, they must not tell a different story. The most problematic area of theology in this regard, at least our present circumstances, involves the question of the relationship between the church and the various structures – states, markets, cultures, ethnicities – that orchestrate this present age.

Introduction

Two of the most significant confessional declarations of the last century have focused on this thorny issue of how the church community should regard its relationship with the institutions of nations, states, cultural and ethnic identities, global economies, and the like. They do so, moreover, in situations where the line between telling the story differently and telling a different story has come clearly into view. The first of these is the Barmen Declaration (1934), which denounces the claim of the German Christian movement, that God has given a unique law to the German people through Adolf Hitler and the National Socialist State, and that only in the fellowship of blood and soil does Christ meet them. The second has only been issued in the last few months in response on the part of Orthodox Christians to Russia's invasion of Ukraine, a denunciation of the ethnophyletism that informs the so-called Russian World (*Russkii Mir*) Teaching. This teaching claims that there is a transnational Russian sphere or civilization, called Holy Russia or Holy Rus', which includes Russia, Ukraine and Belarus, as well as ethnic Russians and Russian-speaking people throughout the world. It has a common political centre (Moscow), a common spiritual centre (Kyiv), a common language (Russian), a common church (the Russian Orthodox Church, Moscow Patriarchate), a common distinctive spirituality, morality, and culture, and a common patriarch (the Patriarch of Moscow) who works in "symphony" with a common president/national leader (Putin) to govern this Russian world.

The relationship between nation and church in the United States of America develops along a different path. Whereas the heresies of the German Christians and the Russian World teaching are perpetrated by corrupted doctrine, in his essay on Christianity in America, Dietrich Bonhoeffer argues that the American error has to do with the failure on the part of Protestants in the so-called "New World" to continue the struggle for the truth of their confessions. This failure gives rise to a version of cheap grace, in which believers no longer regard their freedom, especially their religious liberty, as the power of the gospel to create space for itself on earth, but as the presupposition of faith bequeathed by the state. Faith is thus free precisely to the extent that it has been domesticated, subordinated to national interests, the state, which acts as the repository and guardian of these national interests.

Both the Orthodox Declaration (2022) and Bonhoeffer emphasize the eschatological character of the church's witness and activity. The Orthodox statement asserts that Christians are migrants and refugees in this world, residing in their respective countries only as sojourners. They take part in everything as citizens and put up with everything as foreigners. Bonhoeffer also contends that the Christian community lives a nomad's existence in the midst of this world, and that though it seeks to serve the world, "At any moment it may receive the signal to move on. Then it will break camp, leaving behind all worldly friends and relatives, and following only the voice of the one who has called it."

> For I believe the crisis in the U.S. church has almost nothing to do with being liberal or conservative; it has everything to do with giving up on the faith and discipline of our Christian baptism and settling for a common, generic U.S. identity that is part patriotism, part consumerism, part violence, and part affluence (Walter Brueggemann, *A Way other than Our Own: Devotions for Lent*, 2016).

There is no "one size fits all" account that can faithfully relate the story of Jesus Christ and his ecclesial body. As we respond to the summons to bear witness to Christ we must engage distinct times and places, testify to different people groups, and address a variety of circumstances. We must narrate the gospel in ways that locate us as participants in specific historical, political, economic, and cultural contexts. This is the practice of inculturation as both "a calling and a matter of contestation," a central feature of the Church's witness since Pentecost (Budde 2022, 49). That said, an inherent tension thus runs through every narration we undertake, because it is both our particular story and a universal tale having to do with "the origin, course and destiny of the world" (Lash 1986, 29).

Though a necessary element of discipleship, inculturation is also fraught with ambiguity, for what Christians may not do, if we endeavor to be faithful to the testimony of Scripture and the teachings of our forebears, is to tell a different story. While there is potential for this error in virtually every area of Christian life and thought, perhaps the most worrisome presently has to do with the question of the relationship between the church and the various institutions – states, markets, cultures, ethnicities – that orchestrate this present age.

To be sure, baptism does not cancel all other relationships and affiliations, particularly those we do not choose: family, nation, language, culture. But as Dietrich Bonhoeffer contends, "there are no natural, historical, or experiential unmediated relationships for [Christ's] disciples." These relations to others are not givens, but must pass through Christ, who stands between parent and child, between spouses, and between the individual and the nation-state (Bonhoeffer 2001, 95). The question for Bonhoeffer is whether and to what extent the goals and priorities of these other patterns of association and filiation are compatible with Christ's call to the church to be A sign, instrument, and foretaste of the city that is to come, a colony of the world to come that has its center in God but no ethnic or racial boundaries, and especially today, no national borders.

Two of the most significant confessional declarations of the last century have focused on this thorny issue of the church-community in its relationships with the institutions of nations, states, cultural and ethnic identities, global economies, and the like. They do so, moreover, in situations where the difference between telling the story differently and telling a different story has come clearly into view. Those acquainted with Bonhoeffer are no doubt familiar with *The Theological Declaration of Barmen*, composed in 1934 in response to the false teaching of the "German Christian" movement within the German Evangelical Church (Barmen 2019). The second, entitled *A Declaration on the "Russian World"* (Russkii Mir) *Teaching* (hereafter the Orthodox Declaration), has only been circulated in the last few months in response to a teaching promulgated by influential members of the hierarchy of the Russian Orthodox Church as justification for the brutal invasion of Ukraine by the military forces of Russia (Declaration 2022).

In what follows I touch on Barmen briefly, and spend a bit more time detailing some of the emphases of the Orthodox Declaration, specifically its condemnation of ethnophyletism. I then turn to Bonhoeffer's critique of Christianity in America, drawing primarily from his essay, "Protestantism without Reformation." His assessment is pertinent for the reason that the Enlightenment principle of the separation of church and state has not made us immune to the kinds of racial and ethnic corruptions that occurred in Germany during the 1930s and 40s, and presently in Russia. I conclude with the Orthodox Declaration and Bonhoeffer's contention that Christians are to live, think, and act freely, that is, from the end of all things, learning what it means to be foreigners and pilgrims, "others," in an unjust and violent world.

Barmen and the Orthodox Declaration

Barmen and the Orthodox Declaration follow a similar pattern. Both documents provide introductory commentary detailing the need for their publication, followed by six theses with affirmations and denunciations buttressed by scriptural quotations. Both condemn efforts to conflate the church and its witness with national and ethnic identities. Barmen denounces the principles of the German Christian movement, which claim that God has given a unique law to the German people in Adolf Hitler and the National Socialist State, and that only in the fellowship of blood and soil, *Blut und Boden*, does Christ meet them (Hofer 1962, 131).

According to the Orthodox Declaration, the heretical teaching currently promulgated by Patriarch Kirill asserts

> that there is a transnational Russian sphere or civilization, called Holy Russia or Holy Rus', which includes Russia, Ukraine and Belarus (and sometimes Moldova and Kazakhstan), as well as ethnic Russians and Russian-speaking people throughout the world. It holds that this "Russian world" has a common political centre (Moscow), a common spiritual centre (Kyiv as the "mother of all Rus'"), a common language (Russian), a common church (the Russian Orthodox Church, Moscow Patriarchate), and a common patriarch (the Patriarch of Moscow), who works in "symphony" with a common president/national leader (Putin) to govern this Russian world, as well as upholding a common distinctive spirituality, morality, and culture (Declaration 2022).

As Barmen asserts that the confessional unity and integrity of the evangelical church in Germany was grievously imperiled by the teachings and actions of the German Christians, the principle of the ethnic makeup of the church, which was condemned at the pan-Eastern Orthodox Council of Constantinople in 1872, similarly threatens the Orthodox Church. Should these false principles be affirmed as valid, "the Orthodox Church ceases to be the Church of the

Gospel of Jesus Christ, the Apostles, the Nicene-Constantinopolitan Creed, the Ecumenical Councils, and the Fathers of the Church" (Declaration 2022). Both declarations also highlight the central role of Christ. Barmen states that Christians cannot and should not acknowledge as the source of its proclamation any other event, power, figure, or truth beyond and besides Jesus Christ, the word of God, "whom we have to hear, and whom we have to trust and obey in life and in death." The Orthodox statement likewise declares that the kingdom of the Lord Jesus Christ is "the sole foundation and authority for Orthodox, indeed for all Christians," and that there

> is no separate source of revelation, no basis for community, society, state, law, personal identity and teaching, for Orthodoxy as the Body of the Living Christ than that which is revealed in, by, and through our Lord Jesus Christ and the Spirit of God (Declaration 2022).

State freedom and Christian freedom

Truth be told, the United States has since its inception nurtured its own heterodox form of *symphonia*, in which Christianity crafted an image of itself, as one influential Baptist leader of the twentieth century put it, as "the religion of the State, although not a State religion" (Mullins 1908, 207). There is, however, an ironic twist to this story. Whereas the heresies of the German Christians and the Russian World teaching have been perpetrated by corrupt doctrine, Bonhoeffer argues that the American error can be traced to the failure on the part of Christians in the so-called "New World" to continue the doctrinal struggle for the truth of their confessions that compelled them to leave their homes on the other side of the Atlantic. I am not only talking about White Christian Nationalism, though that is the most obvious and toxic version. A more foundational form of nationalism, articulated predominantly in political, economic, and cultural terms, has been taking root since Europeans first colonized North America.

In his 1939 essay on the state of Christianity in America, Bonhoeffer notes that many of the Protestant groups that made their way to the colonies did so to flee from persecution. There was no disgrace or apostasy in doing so, he adds, because "God does not call every person into martyrdom." Once in North America the refugees "tackled the struggle of colonizing a country in order to be able to live their faith in freedom without a fight." (I wish that he would have addressed the question of colonizing a continent that was already occupied, but that is a paper for another day.) But when they claimed the right to avoid suffering for their faith, they also renounced standing to grapple with the truth of their confession: "By virtue of using the right of flight, the Christian refugee has forfeited the right to fight (*Kampf*)" (Bonhoeffer 2011, 447). In their efforts to avoid the kind of confessional disputes they had endured in the "old country," Protestants inadvertently deprived themselves of a theological standpoint from which to challenge what was happening in the new nation, conforming instead to terms stipulated by the state, terms that they helped to formulate.

Protestant immigrants to the United States (with but a few exceptions) thus became complicit in the moral contradiction present at the founding of the American republic by Europeans – insisting that all human beings are created equal, while assenting, either by active participation or silence, to the displacement and genocidal slaughter of indigenous peoples, the institutions of chattel slavery, and Jim Crow segregation. These actions were part and parcel of a new type of colonization known as settler colonialism. Unlike previous forms, in which colonizing powers sent a small number of soldiers and administrators to another country in order to extract whatever was deemed of value there, but not to transform or eliminate it, settler colonists came to stay, and in ever increasing numbers. They acquired the land in order to create something "new" in this "New World" of unimaginable abundance, not unlike Eden itself. This new thing entailed clearing the land of its original inhabitants, regularly through violent means, and kidnapping and enslaving women and men from Africa to work it.

The theological rationale for this colonial enterprise was first defined by Puritan divines in England as "improvement," which involved using land "for the profitable production of commodities" (McCarraher 2019, 32). Improvement required forcibly dispossessing the indigenous peoples of the land and the forms of life it supported. John Winthrop Jr., governor of the Connecticut Colony, rationalized this violence when he observed that the "Natives of New England . . . inclose noe Land, nor have they any settled habytation, nor any tame Cattle to improve the land by." The glory that God intends for humans is "in the meane time suffer[ing] a whole Continent as fruitfull & convenient for the use of man to lie waste without any improvement" (Winthrop 1864, 310, 312). This combination of colonization and Protestant Christianity represents a distinctive type of cheap grace.

Cheap grace, as Bonhoeffer states in *Discipleship*, shuns discipleship, shuns the cross, shuns "the living, incarnate Jesus Christ." Costly grace calls us to discipleship, condemns our sin, demands our repentance and teaches us how to live obediently as a church-community under the sign of the cross. Costly grace, cultivated in a church-community whose intellectual and moral habits are informed by proclamation and the sacraments, frees us to seek the peace of a fallen world by our participation in its currents and practices, but it also mandates that we contest all that runs counter to that peace (Bonhoeffer 2001, 43–44). By contrast, the American version of cheap grace that justifies sin and not the sinner, offers forgiveness without repentance, baptizes without the discipline of community, communion without the confession of sin, and absolution without personal confession conflates what is offered by the nation-state and what is due to Christ (Harvey 2022, 267–280).

Bonhoeffer draws an important distinction with respect to the two types of grace between those who fled from persecution in the old country and later generations. Seeking refuge constituted a momentous decision of faith that touched on every aspect of their lives: "the renunciation of the confessional battle was a Christian possibility they had fought for" (Bonhoeffer 2011, 442). They made the choice to leave family, friends, professions, and ethnic ties and found their way to the new republic precisely for the sake of the truth of their respective confessions for which they had struggled, often at great personal cost. The children of these refugees, however, inherited a situation that demanded no such momentous life decision. It is not surprising, says Bonhoeffer, that they misunderstood their situation:

> What for the fathers was a right of their Christian faith, which they acquired at the risk of their lives, will be regarded by the sons as a general Christian rule. The confessional battle for the sake of which the fathers fled has become for the sons something that in itself is not Christian (Bonhoeffer 2011, 448).

What was true for the refugees as a conclusion was false as a supposition for their offspring, who set out to secure, not the rectitude of their Christian convictions, but the colonizing of the new nation; that is where their social identity and sense of belonging were situated. The descendants of those first immigrants came to regard their freedom to worship and serve God as the presupposition of faith bequeathed by the state. Subsequent generations have followed suit, regarding their freedom, especially their religious liberty, as the presupposition of faith bequeathed by the state. This supposition comes at a price, viz., the expectation that they accommodate their beliefs and values to the needs of the nation. Religious faith is free precisely to the extent that it has been domesticated, made subservient to the institution and the goods of the nation. As all other goods and commitments must therefore be subordinated to national interests, the state, acting as the repository and guardian of these national interests, regularly breaches the wall it purportedly establishes separating the temporal and profane from the eternal and sacred.

Bonhoeffer counters that the church's freedom does not reside where other authorities grant it possibilities,

> but only where the gospel is truly effective in its own power to create space for itself on earth, even and especially when there are no such possibilities for the church . . . The praise of freedom as the possibility that the world offers the church of its existence might stem precisely from a bond with the world, entered into by the church, which has thereby given up the genuine freedom of God's word (Bonhoeffer 2011, 446–449).

Cheap grace has led Protestants in general to misconceive national citizenship as a social order that binds them together in a type of *herrenvolk* bond, superseding even family and locality. Nationalism thus shows itself to be "the most powerful religion in the United States," with the trope of whiteness a defining feature (Marvin, Ingle 1996, 767).

Christians in America were caught up yet again in the dream of Christendom, that is, "a Christian culture with the power to steer the ship of state and society toward preferred states of virtue" (Budde 2022, 3). To be sure, the desire to create a society in which right relation with God extends to every corner of life should never be summarily dismissed, for it represents a longing for the beloved community. It is nonetheless a quixotic endeavor, for no matter what noble ends are sought – justice, freedom, security – the church must commandeer the political power and economic influence of the state and global market to ensure compliance and subdue resistance (and there is always resistance). Those who are so ensnared are unable to hear the urgent call of the gospel, as Emmanuel Katongole puts it, to "become the mixed-up people whose allegiance to our national, tribal, ethnic, or racial identities is suspect" (Katongole, Wilson-Hargrove 2009, 169).

The eschatological frame of a mixed-up people

Though Barmen and the Orthodox Declaration are closely correlated in many ways, the latter specifies something about the social and political character of the church that is lacking in the former. Whereas Barmen seeks to assure the German people that the Confessional Synod did not wish to disrupt national unity, the Orthodox Declaration repudiates any attempt to integrate the integrity and independence of the Kingdom of God with an earthly regime, rejecting as un-Orthodox any telling of the story of the gospel which denies

> that Christians are migrants and refugees in this world (Hebrews 13:14), that is, the fact that "our citizenship is in heaven, and it is from there that we are expecting a Savior, the Lord Jesus Christ," (Philippians 3:20) and that Christians "reside in their respective countries, but only as sojourners. They take part in everything as citizens and put up with everything as foreigners. Every foreign land is their home, and every home a foreign land" (*The Epistle to Diognetus*, 5) (Declaration 2022).

The challenge of residing as a citizen in the many countries of the world while retaining our Christian calling and identity as nomads is difficult, both with respect to our vocation to follow Christ and in relation to our standing in the host countries. The desire to belong, to make ourselves at home in whatever patch of earth and community we find ourselves feels in some respects natural, but therein lies the tension mentioned earlier. St. Augustine, echoing *The Epistle to Diognetus*, likens our present mortal lives to that of exiles who live in a foreign land but long to return to their native country, using land vehicles or sea vessels to make their way back to their native country where true enjoyment is to be found. But while in exile they become accustomed to the pleasures offered by their carriages or ships, and no longer look forward to finishing the journey as quickly as possible. When Christians become "captivated by such agreeable experiences," they lose interest in returning to their home country (Augustine 1996, 107–108). Perhaps most significantly in our present circumstances, we lose the doctrinal and moral basis to identify with the otherness of migrants, refugees, and members of marginalized groups.

With respect to our relationship to the countries, kingdoms, empires, republics, states, and markets in which we reside, assuming the status of sojourners, and resisting assimilation into the warp and woof of the dominant regime may be one of the most difficult things to even contemplate, in small part because of a deep desire to belong, to be at home, but more so because regimes of *hoc saeculum* – kingdoms, empires, principalities, nation-states, and global markets – invariably brook no rivals (Bourne 1998, 14). In the United States, for example, during World War II Jehovah's Witnesses were subject to intense abuse. On top of verbal abuse, members were beaten, tarred and feathered, and in once case castrated, and their Kingdom Halls were attacked while law enforcement either looked the other way or arrested and imprisoned them without charges. What was their crime? They refused to salute the American flag, symbolically declaring that they did not believe themselves bound by the state's claim to their allegiance (Marty, Moore 2000, 23–29). (The case of Austrian martyr Franz Jägerstätter during the war is another instance.) The not-so-subtle message in these and countless other cases is that the only good religion is one in which everyone holds their beliefs lightly, leaving their hands free to cling tightly to the national identity.

Not long ago I was conversing with a young scholar who, upon learning that I study and write about the life and thought of Bonhoeffer, confessed that though he admired Bonhoeffer, a passage in *Discipleship* had made him very uneasy. Bonhoeffer there states that the Christian community lives a nomad's existence in the midst of this world, bearing witness that its present form is passing away and its Lord is drawing near. While the members of these communities live as pilgrims they gratefully use the goods of this world that sustain the life of their mortal bodies, and strive to acquire virtues such as justice, gentleness, and chastity that allow them to render service to the earthly city. These communities acknowledge they are subject to the authority and justice of this world's rulers, and pray for them as they offer the best service it can. Bonhoeffer then pivots, declaring that this

> colony of foreigners ... is merely passing through its host country. At any moment it may receive the signal to move on. Then it will break camp, leaving behind all worldly friends and relatives, and following only the voice of the one who has called it (Bonhoeffer 2001, 250–251).

What was it about this passage that troubled the young scholar? Sadly, our conversation was interrupted, so I can only speculate. For much of church history, Christians have wedded their understanding and practice of the faith to the structures and ideals of whatever iteration of the present age they found themselves. It is not surprising, then, that when those institutions and values seemed to be in doubt or in peril Christians often construe their liturgical, theological, and spiritual heritage in ways that they hope might buttress their host countries. For many in America, what presently seems imperiled is democracy, which they regard not merely as an exemplary mode of human sociality, but as in some sense "divine." Bonhoeffer's suggestion that Christians might at some point move on from the struggle for this social reality is disconcerting to those wholly vested in this arrangement.

I can only guess that my young interlocutor heard what Bonhoeffer says about the nomadic nature of discipleship as a summons to withdraw from the suffering and joys of a fallen world into some illusory space of purity and holiness, something Bonhoeffer rejects, beginning with his essay *Thy Kingdom Come!*, where he refers to believers as wanderers making their way to a foreign land, and who on that basis are alone able to love God and Earth together (Bonhoeffer 2009, 286). Far from signaling a retreat from a disintegrating world, only those who know costly grace can live in that world "without losing themselves in it," rendering them "truly free for life in this world" (Bonhoeffer 2001, 55–56).

Living from the end, acting from the end, and proclaiming its message from the end (Bonhoeffer 1997, 21), all the while on pilgrimage in a world of violence, death, and oppression, and doing so without losing ourselves in it, may be the single greatest challenge that disciples can face. The tension between the particular and the universal in our narrations of the gospel story that I mentioned at the outset of this paper comes clearly into view for me as an American, living as I do in the country that Martin Luther King, Jr. called "the greatest purveyor of violence in the world" (King 1991, 233). I am persuaded that as disciples we "have been incorporated into Christ's sacrifice for the world so that the world no longer needs to make sacrifices for tribe or state, or even humanity" (Hauerwas 2011, 68). That said, I also acknowledge and embrace the sense of outrage and conviction that moves my sisters and brothers to see matters otherwise (Budde 2022, 130). I have no resolution of this tension for myself or for you; I only know that I must take hold of the one without letting go the other (Ecclesiastes 7:18).

Bibliography

Augustine. 1996. *Teaching Christianity: De Doctrina Christiana*, translated by Edmund Hill, O.P. Hyde Park: New City.

"The Barmen Declaration," https://www.ekd.de/en/the-barmen-declaration-303.htm.

Bonhoeffer, Dietrich. 1997. *Creation and Fall. Dietrich Bonhoeffer Works Volume 3*, edited by John W. de Gruchy, translated by Stephen Bax. Minneapolis: Fortress Press.

Bonhoeffer, Dietrich. 2001. *Discipleship, Dietrich Bonhoeffer Works Volume 4*, edited by Geffrey B. Kelly and John D. Godsey, translated by Barbara Green and Reinhard Krauss. Minneapolis: Fortress Press.

Bonhoeffer, Dietrich. 2009. *Berlin 1932–1933. Dietrich Bonhoeffer Works Volume 12*, edited by Larry L. Rasmussen, translated by Isabel Best and David Higgins. Minneapolis: Fortress Press.

Bonhoeffer, Dietrich. 2011. *Theological Education Underground: 1937–1940. Dietrich Bonhoeffer Works Volume 15*, edited by Victoria J. Barnett, translated by Claudia D. Bergmann, Peter Frick, and Scott A. Moore. Minneapolis: Fortress Press.

Bourne, Randolph. 1998. *The State*. Tucson: See Sharp Press.
Budde, Michael L. 2022. *Foolishness to Gentiles: Essays on Empire, Nationalism, and Discipleship*. Eugene: Cascade.
"A Declaration on the 'Russian World' (Russkii Mir) Teaching." *Public Orthodoxy*. 13 March 2022. https://publicorthodoxy.org/2022/03/13/a-declaration-on-the-russian-world-russkii-mir-teaching/.
Harvey, Barry. 2022. "Cheap Grace, American Style: Confession, Racism, and the 'Gentler' Medicine of Dietrich Bonhoeffer." *Perspectives in Religious Studies* 48: 267–280.
Hauerwas, Stanley. 2011. *War and the American Difference: Theological Reflections on Violence and National Identity*. Grand Rapids: Baker.
Katongole, Emmanuel, and Jonathan Wilson-Hargrove. 2009. *Mirror to the Church: Resurrecting Faith after Genocide in Rwanda*. Grand Rapids: Zondervan, 2009.
King, Martin Luther, Jr. 1991. "A Time to Break Silence." In *A Testament of Hope: The Essential Writings and Speeches of Martin Luther King, Jr.*, edited by James Melvin Washington, 231–244. New York: HarperCollins.
Lash, Nicholas. 1986. *Theology on the Way to Emmaus*. London: SCM.
Marty, Martin E., and Jonathan Moore. 2000. *Politics, Religion, and the Common Good: Advancing a Distinctly American Conversation about Religion's Role in Our Shared Life*. San Francisco: Jossey Bass.
Marvin, Carolyn, and David W. Ingle. 1996. "To Blood Sacrifice and the Nation: Revisiting Civil Religion." *Journal of the American Academy of Religion* 64: 767–780.
McCarraher, Eugene. 2019. *The Enchantments of Mammon: How Capitalism Became the Religion of Modernity*. Cambridge: Belknap.
Mullins, E. Y. 1908. *The Axioms of Religion: A New Interpretation of the Baptist Faith*. Philadelphia: American Baptist Publication Society.
"Richtlinien der Kirchenbewegung 'Deutsche Christen' in Thüringen (vom 11 Dezember 1933) über die 'Deutsche Christliche Nationalkirche.'" 1962. In *Der Nationalsozialismus: Dokumente 1933–1945*, edited by Walther Hofer, 131. Frankfurt an Main: Fischer.
The Theological Declaration of Barmen. 2019. https://cathedralofhope.org/wp-content/uploads/2019/03/The-Theological-Declaration-of-Barmen.pdf.
Williams, Rowan. 2000. *On Christian Theology*. Malden: Blackwell.
Winthrop, John. 1864. *The Life and Letters of John Winthrop*, edited by Robert C. Winthrop. Boston: Ticknor and Fields.

Langham Literature and its imprints are a ministry of Langham Partnership.

Langham Partnership is a global fellowship working in pursuit of the vision God entrusted to its founder John Stott –

> *to facilitate the growth of the church in maturity and Christ-likeness through raising the standards of biblical preaching and teaching.*

Our vision is to see churches in the Majority World equipped for mission and growing to maturity in Christ through the ministry of pastors and leaders who believe, teach and live by the word of God.

Our mission is to strengthen the ministry of the word of God through:
- nurturing national movements for biblical preaching
- fostering the creation and distribution of evangelical literature
- enhancing evangelical theological education

especially in countries where churches are under-resourced.

Our ministry

Langham Preaching partners with national leaders to nurture indigenous biblical preaching movements for pastors and lay preachers all around the world. With the support of a team of trainers from many countries, a multi-level programme of seminars provides practical training, and is followed by a programme for training local facilitators. Local preachers' groups and national and regional networks ensure continuity and ongoing development, seeking to build vigorous movements committed to Bible exposition.

Langham Literature provides Majority World preachers, scholars and seminary libraries with evangelical books and electronic resources through publishing and distribution, grants and discounts. The programme also fosters the creation of indigenous evangelical books in many languages, through writer's grants, strengthening local evangelical publishing houses, and investment in major regional literature projects, such as one volume Bible commentaries like *The Africa Bible Commentary* and *The South Asia Bible Commentary*.

Langham Scholars provides financial support for evangelical doctoral students from the Majority World so that, when they return home, they may train pastors and other Christian leaders with sound, biblical and theological teaching. This programme equips those who equip others. Langham Scholars also works in partnership with Majority World seminaries in strengthening evangelical theological education. A growing number of Langham Scholars study in high quality doctoral programmes in the Majority World itself. As well as teaching the next generation of pastors, graduated Langham Scholars exercise significant influence through their writing and leadership.

To learn more about Langham Partnership and the work we do visit **langham.org**

www.ingramcontent.com/pod-product-compliance
Lightning Source LLC
Chambersburg PA
CBHW071432150426
43191CB00008B/1108